FAULT LINES

FAULT LINES

The Sixties, the Culture War, and the Return of the Divine Feminine

GUS diZEREGA

QUEST
BOOKS

Theosophical Publishing House
Wheaton, Illinois * Chennai, India

Quest Books
Theosophical Publishing House
PO Box 270
Wheaton, IL 60187

www.questbooks.net

Cover design by Drew Stevens
Typesetting by DataPage International, Ltd.

Library of Congress Cataloging-in-Publication Data

diZerega, Gus.
Fault Lines: the sixties, the culture war, and the return of the divine feminine / Gus diZerega.
    pages   cm
Includes bibliographical references and index.
    ISBN 978-0-8356-0918-0
1. Feminism—United States—History—20th century.   2. Women's rights—United States—History—20th century.   3. Nihilism (Philosophy).   4. Culture.   I. Title.
HQ1410.D5894 2013
305.4209730904—dc23   2013014194

5   4   3   2   1   *   13   14   15   16   17   18

Printed in the United States of America

To
Thomas diZerega,
Johanna diZerega,
Lucas Fischer,
Emma Taylor,
and
Adelyn Taylor,
who will inherit the world we leave them.

For each age is a dream that is dying,
Or one that is coming to birth.

—Arthur O'Shaughnessy, "Ode"

CONTENTS

ACKNOWLEDGMENTS

Every book reflects more than the talents of its author. This is particularly the case with *Fault Lines*. The basic idea came together when I was asked to give a presentation on Wicca and Feminism at St. Lawrence University some years ago. The talk that emerged made a rough equivalent of some of the arguments that follow. Many who were present encouraged me to turn the talk into a book.

As I did, I found myself exploring areas of history and knowledge about which I knew relatively little. While I did my best to do justice to these additional fields, in a work of this scope I imagine there will be many areas where experts will find places to quibble. If the quibbles are small and the clear errors few it will be due to the aid of many friends and colleagues who contributed to my efforts at various times along the way.

Whether their feedback concerned gaps in my knowledge, difficulties in following my argument, or insights enriching it, their input was vital. Errors and misunderstandings were caught and exposition was clarified. However, I do not mean to suggest that everyone agreed with everything I say.

Lumping all these good people alphabetically, I thank David Emanuel Andersson, John Berthrong, Bryan Cooper, Alan Draper, Don Frew, Janie Frigault, David Hardwick, Michael Heathman, Nancy Graham Holm, Hummingbear, Baylor Johnson, Georgia Kelly, Richard Smoley, Don Snow, Greg Stafford, Fred Turner, Glenn Turner, and Jim Wilson. All enriched my efforts with their criticisms as well as their encouragement. I want to pick out Nancy Graham Holm for special appreciation. She carefully went through the entire manuscript, giving it the informed and critical reading any writer dreams of getting *before* his or her effort sees print. I also want to acknowledge and thank Will Marsh, my editor, for a wonderful and congenial job reducing this manuscript to less formidable length without losing meaning.

I am also eternally grateful to Peter Barnes and Cornelia Durant of the Mesa Refuge in Pt. Reyes Station, California, for making their space available to me during a time of terrible trauma. Their generosity enabled me to begin giving this argument the depth and strength it needs, which otherwise would have been impossible.

INTRODUCTION

Fault Lines explores the spiritual, social, and political currents that have brought the United States to its greatest internal crisis since the Civil War. To frame these causes I have adopted a metaphor from geology. Perhaps I do so because I live in California, where our rolling hills, peaceful valleys, and tranquil bays are manifestations of continent-shaking geological turbulence, the external signs of giant faults that, when they shift, can create enormous devastation and, in time, new landscapes.

In 1960 the American political landscape seemed as peaceful as those hills, valleys, and bays. Since then the country's deepest fractures have begun to shift. Our land has entered a time of growing upheaval in every dimension of our common life, be it political, economic, social, or religious.

This book argues that three basic faults are causing this disruption. The first is easy to see and is associated with the sixties and their aftermath. Another, more deeply hidden, rises out of modernity's roots in the Enlightenment and the religious wars that preceded it. The third extends to the roots of what constitutes civilization itself. If the first is analogous to California's San Andreas Fault, the second is akin to plate subduction, and the third moves continents.

More concretely, the first is a renewal of conflict between the Founders' American ideal and the first counterculture to arise in this country. This counterculture was originally birthed in the antebellum South, when the principles of our Revolution were explicitly abandoned by a generation of secular and religious Southern leaders. It has continued to today, with the turmoil of the sixties sharpening its conflict with our founding ideals.

The second reflects the dissolution of the moral heritage that supported the rise of Enlightenment modernity. As it dissolves, modernity's defining institutions are ever more deeply distorted by the rise of a society-wide nihilism, politically, economically, and religiously. This nihilism manifests as the elevation of power and domination as ultimate secular and spiritual values.

The third, and most fundamental, is also most hopeful to us today. The same modernity that dissolved its own rootedness in ways of life thousands of years old has opened up the promise of a new society based on different premises. A shift of this magnitude happened only once before in human history, when cultures of hunter-gatherers took up agriculture, initiating a transformation of their spiritual, social, and political practices. Agricultural society with its inherited institutions rooted in secular and spiritual hierarchies and the struggle of farmers with the natural world gave birth to the modern urban and industrial world. Our cultural, political, and spiritual agricultural inheritance is being displaced by modern institutions and practices more deeply compatible with equality, secular and sacred feminine values, and spiritual immanence. Whether this transformation will take place or be aborted by the forces of oligarchy, empire, and reaction is the greatest unanswered question of our time.

Future historians will have much to study and ponder about our times. This book attempts to enable those of us now living through them to understand the powerful forces that shape our lives and call upon us for a response. Due to the complexity of the issues involved a full discussion of every dimension would result in an unwieldy volume. I have made appendices available online (referenced in parentheses in the text by title and URL) that continue the discussion.

SECULAR MODERNITY AND THE HISTORICAL ROOTS OF OUR CRISIS

A s the 1960s opened many academics agreed that two broad cultural and political patterns promised to extend indefinitely into America's future. The first was a wide bipartisan agreement about the shape of American democracy. A new consensus had arisen out of Franklin Roosevelt's New Deal, the unifying impact of World War II, and the subsequent Cold War. Under Eisenhower the Republicans had not tried to roll back Roosevelt's innovations. Traditional ideological battles had apparently ceased to matter.[1] A kind of technocratic pragmatism promised to become the basic rule for the American political game.

Second, Western modernity seemed to have entered a process of increasing secularization. Except for cultural backwaters, mostly within the former Confederacy, religion sought peace with science on science's terms, becoming a purely personal affair and providing social cohesion. Responding to concerns that his Catholicism would compete with his loyalty to America's founding principles, John Kennedy said, "I hope that no American . . . will waste his franchise and throw away his vote by voting either for me or against me solely on account of my religious affiliation. It is not relevant."[2] His critics worried about his sincerity, not his sentiments.

America's future appeared to be one of increasing middle-class affluence within a capitalist economy whose sharpest edges had been blunted by technocratic government and corporate management. A few clouds appeared on the horizon, most importantly the threat of nuclear war with the Soviet Union and the long history of America's brutal treatment of Blacks. But on balance America seemed the very model of a successful liberal democracy, with a solid middle class and its old political and religious divisions mere shadows of what they once had been.

So much for extrapolating the future from the present.

Today the American middle class is shrinking, political partisanship is at its highest level since the Civil War, and religious divisions dominate the country. Profound shifts in the cultural and spiritual strata underlying what seemed a stable American political landscape have shattered the optimistic expectations of those times. This crisis has economic and cultural dimensions, but the cultural dimensions cut deepest. Economic issues involve money, and money facilitates compromises because dollars can be divided many ways. Cultural issues are not so easily compromised. Worse, economic interests can manipulate them to strengthen their own positions.

Contemporary American discussions of our crisis are usually framed in terms of a "right" versus a "left." The right has a religious component, characterized by politicized Baptists, Pentecostals, conservative Catholics, and Mormons, and a secular component dominated by neoconservatives, libertarians, and their allies. On the left we have secular New Deal liberals and progressives that arose to oppose that same New Deal establishment, as well as spiritual communities usually identifying with liberal Christianity or with what are often termed "new religious movements." America's right and left are remarkably diverse, but virtually all, particularly on the right, share a preoccupation with gender.

Our culture war's major protagonists can be distinguished by the contrasting roles played by masculine and feminine values in their self-images. "Culture warriors" use strongly gendered language claiming to exemplify a manly competitive warrior ethos while "liberals" are effeminate men and masculine women. The right's religious movements emphasize a purely masculine image of sacred transcendence.

Secular American liberals see themselves as defending women's rights. Religious groups on the left give greater emphasis to divine immanence and a focus on both masculine and feminine images of the sacred. However, few of these groups see themselves as primarily feminine, more often describing themselves as "balanced."

This cultural and spiritual distinction is not all we need to understand America's contemporary crisis. There is also the increasing consolidation of wealth into a new plutocratic aristocracy and America's overwhelming military power after the Cold War ended. But America's reaction to these phenomena is powerfully influenced by the culture war. A large majority of Americans want higher taxes on the super wealthy rather than cutbacks on basic social services, yet they have not come together on that issue. Both progressives and rank-and-file Tea Partyers worry about excessive corporate dominance, yet they do not cooperate, seeing themselves as separated by more basic cultural issues. We will return to these more traditional political and economic concerns but, important as they are, oligarchy, aristocracy, and empire are familiar patterns in history. The culture war is something else again.

I begin exploring America's shifting cultural geology by examining secularization, which played a pivotal role in modernity's rise.

The modern world is characterized by liberal democracy, science, and previously unimagined physical health and material prosperity. Central to its animating vision is the belief that human action can make life better for all through the use of reason. Progress is real. This modern view is largely the result of the European Renaissance and the Enlightenment. It has born some very sweet fruits indeed.

The issue is different regarding modernity's vision of the meaning of life. The religious and secular right as well as the secular and spiritual left grew out of successive waves of secularization that transformed seventeenth- and eighteenth-century Europe and the new United States. All are modern phenomena. None are truly traditional. Nearly all are responses to the collapse of the traditional moral world and the failure of a new moral order to take its place.

History is a complex tapestry. Many story threads are unfolding at any one time. But for Americans today, this thread is among the most important. To understand the inner tensions within modernity and the secular and spiritual reactions to them, we need to understand secular modernity in the context from which it emerged.

THE SECULARIZATION OF POLITICS AND THE BLESSINGS OF DIVERSITY

Secularization refers to the gradual pushing of religious belief out of our political and social institutions and, for some, out of our lives. Secularization therefore exists in three dimensions: the political, the social, and the personal. The secularization of politics removes religion as a goal of public policy and attempts to remove religious doctrines from political debate. The secularization of society removes religion as a basic social organizing force though it can still have personal importance and be a strong force in community solidarity. The secularization of ourselves removes religion and spirituality as significant forces in our personal lives. The first two are compatible with strong personal spiritual and community religious beliefs; the third rejects them all.

Political secularization is the most visible, least contested, and easiest to understand. Visiting the United States in the 1840s, Alexis de Tocqueville, himself a religious man, remarked on the unusually peaceful relations between different religions, in contrast to Europe. He found that clergymen "differed upon matters of detail alone; and that they mainly attributed the peaceful dominion of religion in their country, to the separation of Church and State."[3]

People's religious beliefs will always influence their political actions, and few if any of our Founders desired it to be otherwise. But when the two are legally separate, no political decision can deliberately encourage or discourage any particular religion or religion in general. The First Amendment states: "Congress shall make no law respecting an establishment of religion, or prohibiting the free exercise thereof."

George Washington wrote a treaty with Muslim Tripolitania, later unanimously adopted by the Senate, and signed by John Adams, our second president. It stated: "The Government of the United States of America is not, in any sense, founded on the Christian religion." In signing it Adams wrote, "I . . . accept, ratify, and confirm the same, and every clause and article thereof."[4]

But the Founders were not hostile to religion. They wanted religion to motivate people but not itself enter into political contention. My religious beliefs may give me the inner strength and confidence to take a stand, but the *reasons* I give my fellow citizens for why they should agree with me need to be framed more inclusively. People have to make their case in terms convincing to people who do not share their religious beliefs. They have to argue as inclusively as possible, as citizens not sectarians, thereby educating society as a whole by emphasizing a common moral framework. From abolishing slavery to civil rights and wilderness preservation, many of America's best moments exemplify this process. When carried out through persuasion and seeking common ground, this kind of religious influence has consistently enriched our society, as was intended.[5]

Today culture warriors attack the separation of church and state, buttressing their claims with quotes by our Founders taken out of context and often falsified.[6] Consequently we need to remind ourselves *why* even very religious Americans supported political secularization. Separation of church and state arose because of horrendous events that took place when there had been no such separation.

Religious wars, ending a little over one hundred years before our founding, had devastated Europe. Lutherans, Catholics, Calvinists, and many smaller groups confidently interpreted the Bible's message as universal and binding, but in mutually exclusive ways. Absolute confidence in their understanding combined with condemnations of different readings led to war, which ended with the Treaty of Augsburg in 1555 decreeing that people had to follow their ruler's religion. In time the Catholic Church sought to install Catholic rulers in place of Lutheran ones to force their Protestant subjects to become Catholics again. In 1618 an even larger and bloodier war broke out.

During the Thirty Years' War millions died as Christian killed Christian for not being the right kind of Christian. Thirty to forty percent of some countries' populations died.[7] So great was the carnage that parts of Europe took one hundred years to rebuild their populations to prewar levels. In terms of the percentage of people killed, the Thirty Years' War probably ranks as Europe's worst.

The Treaty of Westphalia in 1648 sought to remove religious reasons for warring against neighboring countries. Calvinists as well as Lutherans and Catholics were allowed to practice their worship, even if the prince followed a different denomination. Catholic Spain recognized the independence of Calvinist Holland, acknowledging that Protestantism was here to stay. Catholics in Protestant lands and Protestants in Catholic lands still suffered frequent and harsh discrimination, but the treaty marked a major step toward recognizing the legitimacy of religious diversity.

Smaller denominations such as Anabaptists, Pietists, and Quakers continued to be outlawed virtually everywhere because no princes followed these faiths. However, given the opportunity, even some of these denominations proved they could also oppress others.[8] Many within these smaller sects ultimately emigrated, first to the Netherlands and later to North America, seeking to practice their religion as they wished. However, except for the Quakers, once they had the power to do so, they always denied religious freedom to others.

Virtually no Christians anywhere believed they should tolerate alternative views when they possessed the power to suppress "error." If correctly following their religion was necessary for salvation, different groups felt obligated to wage war on other points of view.

The Treaty of Westphalia's success in establishing international tolerance raised hopes among many that genuine tolerance might also ultimately succeed *within* countries. Initially only the Netherlands pursued this path, permitting religious dissenters and even Jews to live together amicably with the official state Calvinist Church, although Catholics were still discriminated against. It created an oasis of religious peace surrounded by a desert of intolerance. During this time, and not coincidentally, the Netherlands became Europe's economic, scientific, and cultural center. It also profoundly influenced America.[9]

From 1683 to 1689 John Locke lived in exile in Holland to avoid execution in England. Locke's political writing established liberalism and ultimately made him the philosophical father of America's Declaration of Independence. But making the case for political freedom was not his only service. Based on his experiences in the Netherlands, in 1689 Locke published "A Letter Concerning Toleration," advocating religious toleration even for pagans and Muslims.[10]

Locke argued that a person need only be a good citizen to merit religious toleration. So long as that condition held, a person's private beliefs should not matter. God could handle it. Locke's argument for toleration was rooted in our being able to separate our duties to our society from our duties to our religion. If we could do this, toleration was possible.[11]

The Founders' Views

Locke's argument persuaded many of our Founders. In 1776 Thomas Jefferson cosponsored a bill in Virginia's legislature to allow Catholics, Jews, and other non-Protestants to become citizens. In making his case, Jefferson repeated Locke's argument that "neither Pagan nor Mahamedan nor Jew ought to be excluded from the civil rights of the Commonwealth because of his religion."[12] Under James Madison's leadership the bill became law in 1786.

In 1790 George Washington expressed identical sentiments, writing to the Hebrew Congregation of Newport, Rhode Island: "All possess alike liberty of conscience, and immunities of citizenship. . . . Happily the Government of the United States, which gives bigotry no sanction, to persecution no assistance, requires only that they who live under its protection should demean themselves as good citizens, in giving it on all occasions their effectual support."[13]

During the Constitutional Convention the question arose whether a religious test should be required of anyone holding national office. Religious tests had long been employed in England and many of the colonies. The idea was rejected. Future Supreme Court justice James Iredell of North Carolina explained why:

> It is objected that the people of America may, perhaps, choose representatives who have no religion at all, and that pagans and Mahometans may be admitted into offices. But how is it possible to exclude any set of men, without taking away that principle of religious freedom which we ourselves so warmly

contend for? This is the foundation on which persecution has been raised in every part of the world. The people in power were always right, and every body else wrong. If you admit the least difference, the door to persecution is opened. . . . It would be happy for mankind if religion was permitted to take its own course, and maintain itself by the excellence of its own doctrines.[14]

James Madison is frequently described as the "Father of the Constitution." His writings in *The Federalist* are widely considered the most powerful arguments for the proposed constitution, and his notes taken during the Constitutional Convention are our chief resource for knowing what happened during those epochal sessions. The Constitution was the work of many minds and much artful compromise, and no one's initial plans prevailed. But historians would probably agree that if any single person had a definitive view about its meaning, it was James Madison. In addition, Madison was responsible for introducing the first ten amendments, the Bill of Rights, and getting them through Congress. He was not just any Founder.

Madison argued that the way to curb political violence was to incorporate many divisions deliberately rather than vainly seeking to create an impossible uniformity of outlook. Better, Madison argued, to follow the Dutch example that had proved so successful within a religious context: "In a free government, the security for civil rights must be the same as that for religious rights. It consists in the one case in the multiplicity of interests, and in the other, the multiplicity of sects."[15] Diversity could prevent any powerful single interest from riding roughshod over the interests of others because no faction on its own could constitute a majority.

In an 1822 letter to Edward Livingston, Madison summed up what he regarded as the defining principle for preserving political freedom and religious liberty:

The danger [of "alliance or coalition between Government and religion"] cannot be too carefully guarded agst. . . . Every new & successful example therefore of a perfect separation between ecclesiastical and civil matters is of importance. And I have no doubt that every new example will succeed, as every past one has done, in shewing that religion & Gov will both exist in greater purity, the less they are mixed together.... We are teaching the world the great truth that Govts. do better without Kings & Nobles than with them. The merit will be doubled by the other lesson that Religion flourishes in greater purity, without than with the aid of Govt.

Madison took this principle so seriously that he opposed Congress appointing a chaplain at taxpayers' expense.[16]

Madison, Jefferson, and other Founders had considerable *religious* support for their efforts. For example, America's Baptists supported Jefferson and Madison's successful efforts to establish the separation of church and state in Virginia. Sadly, today's Southern Baptist leadership repudiates their own history while remaining conspicuously silent on the reasons for their ancestors' actions.

Our Founders' effort to create a space for religious expression free from political privileges was largely successful. Religion provided the moral energy to empower many of the finest reform movements in American history, including the abolition of slavery, the ban on child labor, women's suffrage, and the civil rights movement. Of course religiously inspired reforms were not all wise or successful. The folly of Prohibition comes to mind, as well as the contemporary battle over a woman's control over her body. Religious motivations do not prevent error, but having to put their arguments in broadly secular terms weakens sectarianism's poisonous influence while preserving the strength of spiritual motivations for change.

This kind of influence was what the Founders hoped would happen. It demonstrated that separation of church and state was compatible with strong religious commitments. Culture warriors who argue that a wall between religion and government is antireligious or not really a part of our Founders' thinking are profoundly ignorant.

THE SECULARIZATION OF SOCIETY

We now broaden our view, better to understand what else was happening during those pivotal times of the Renaissance and the Protestant

Reformation. Between them they shaped the Enlightenment that followed, and the Enlightenment shaped us.

Around the beginning of the fourteenth century a new sensibility had begun to emerge in northern Italian city-states, later spreading to the growing cities of northern Europe. This sensibility ultimately transformed the mind and culture inherited from the Middle Ages.

Inspiration from newly available classical texts, particularly Hermetic Neoplatonism, stimulated European intellectual life in ways not seen since the fall of Rome. Aided by the invention of printing around 1440, the rapid dissemination of these texts across Europe enriched the understanding of many Western thinkers. Growing commercial and entrepreneurial innovation was also flourishing in the cities benefitting most from the rediscovery of classical literature, creating economic as well as cultural powerhouses. The European discovery of America demonstrated there was still much to learn that the ancients had not known.

The resulting Renaissance initiated a civilization-wide rethinking of humanity's role in the world.[17] Initially in the arts and humanities and spilling later into the emerging natural sciences, a new optimism and confidence in the power of the human mind arose. Compared to writers during the Middle Ages, writers of this period, like Montaigne and Shakespeare, read like kindred spirits.[18]

For most Renaissance thinkers humanity was the most appropriate subject of study because the world and God were considered too complex for our limited abilities. Leonardo da Vinci (1452–1519), who was interested in almost everything, was not interested in theological speculations. As he put it, why be concerned with phenomena that "the human mind is incapable of comprehending and that cannot be demonstrated by any natural instance?" It is best to focus on what we can know because "truth is of such excellence that if it praises the meanest thing they become ennobled."[19] The humanist skeptics of the time, Stephen Toulmin observed, "no more wished to *deny* general philosophical theses than to *assert* them. . . . Faced with abstract, universal, timeless theoretical propositions, they saw no sufficient basis in experience, either for asserting, or for denying them."[20]

A more tolerant spiritual sensibility began growing among religious writers. For example, the Hermeticist theologian and physician Agrippa (1486–1525) argued that "the rites and Ceremonies of religion . . . are diverse. Every Religion hath something of good, because it is dedicated to God. . . . There is no religion so erroneous which hath not something of wisdom in it."[21] Had this ecumenical spirit continued it would have transformed Europe in directions only approached centuries later. But it was not to be.

The Reformation began in 1517 when Martin Luther nailed his famous theses to the door of the Wittenberg Castle church. It ended in 1648 with much of Europe in ruins. The Reformation's renewed claims to theological certainty and demands for conformity suppressed the tolerant spirit of the Renaissance. Feuding religious leaders and their followers argued for the absolute truth of their various positions, pushing people into taking sides. One was either for or against God, depending on whether one agreed with a particular interpretation or not. In 1560 the humanist Etienne Pasquier criticized the increasing name-calling between Catholics and Protestants, which he foresaw, quite correctly, as leading to catastrophe.[22]

As religious schisms deepened, theological debates grew increasingly rigid. Catholics and Protestants alike demanded adherence to their particular orthodoxies. Inquiry was violently suppressed. Galileo Galelei was put under house arrest for the last nine years of his life, and Giordano Bruno was burned at the stake. Both were punished for expressing views that would not have brought suppression a hundred years earlier.[23]

The Catholic Church had successfully suppressed earlier heretical movements, but this time was different. It suffered its greatest defeat since the final split between Western Catholic and Eastern Orthodox Christianity in 1204. Protestant leaders successfully founded new churches based on competing biblical interpretations, fracturing the unity of Western Christendom for good.

The invention of printing was a key reason. The printed word allowed divergent views and the arguments behind them to disseminate widely throughout Europe. Combined with political protection from princes seeking greater freedom from Rome's demands, printing technology gave religious rebels greater reach than had been the case when the church had successfully slaughtered the Albigensians and Hussites.

The result was a cultural revolution.

The Dissolution of the Integral World

The medieval West was an *integral* society. Like premodern societies in general, people lived in an intrinsically meaningful world where the true, the good, and the beautiful were different dimensions of a commonly acknowledged greater reality. The great tapestry of life was woven according to a universal pattern, and in general terms that pattern could be known. Each individual thread had its place. Within integral societies human events gained their deepest meaning in terms of how they participated within this all-embracing pattern, whose reality and significance was explained by myths. The world was interpreted symbolically, as a kind of text. In such a world everyone had a place, and although that place was usually one of poverty and low status, life was meaningful.

In the West most people had never read the Bible. They were illiterate, and besides it was available only in Latin, which few understood. To know what the Bible taught, people relied on interpretations by priests, and the priests were under the discipline of the Catholic Church.

With increased access to pagan Greek and Roman texts, the Renaissance began injecting a classically derived tolerant skepticism into this medieval framework. It also contributed an enhanced confidence in the power of reason and human effort to shape our lives for the better. But the Renaissance did not challenge the ancient integral vision of the world. In this sense and in this sense alone the Renaissance looked backward, taking inspiration from pagan philosophies such as Neoplatonism, Epicureanism, and Stoicism.

Renaissance interpretations of these philosophies were developing in ways friendly to both scientific experimentation and religion, but unfriendly to the rigid dogmatic attitudes that ultimately brought Christianity into conflict with science. Had this nondogmatic spirit lasted, the modern world would almost certainly have developed more humanely than it did.

But humanity often takes the wiser road only after coming to grief along more foolish pathways, and there was plenty of foolishness ahead. Societies characterized by the Abrahamic religions differed from other integral societies because they emphasized the correct understanding of a sacred book. When disagreements arose all sides turned to scripture to make their case.

In practice the Bible turned out to be a spiritual-fragmentation device once people read it for themselves. Its pages contained a variety of views and accounts that had never been convincingly harmonized. When Martin Luther translated the Bible into vernacular German in 1534, he assumed that others would interpret it as he did. But Luther was only occasionally right. Possessing a Bible they could read strengthened the hold religion had on many people, but it did not provide them with a common understanding. A diversity of interpretations blossomed.

For centuries these divisions had been kept under control through imperial Roman power.[24] Most people could not read Latin, while the church enforced orthodoxy on those who could. But now the lid was off the box. As Alfred North Whitehead observed, "When Augustine died at Hippo in the year 430, [Christianity] was in its main outlines settled. All its capacities for variant forms were already inherent in it. The Papal Church, the Eastern Church, Wycliffe and Huss, Luther and Calvin, Archbishop Cranmer, Jonathan Edwards and John Wesley, Erasmus, Ignatius Loyola, the Socinians, George Fox, and the Vatican Council could with equal right appeal to history. The conclusion to be drawn from the appeal entirely depends upon the value-judgments guiding your selection, and upon the metaphysical presuppositions dictating your notions of a coherent theology."[25]

Each church and sect believed it knew divine truth. But with the best will in the world, sincere people could not agree on what it was. Few readers remembered and fewer heeded Paul's warning that we see through a glass, darkly (1 Cor 13:12). The Dutch humanist Erasmus asked in 1524, "What am I to do when many persons allege different interpretations, each one of whom swears to have the Spirit?"[26] While Renaissance thinkers tended to emphasize the limits of our theological capacities, the dogmatic sensibilities more typical of the Reformation argued that we should know and serve divine truth.

A religion that once guaranteed unity no longer could do so. Historian of religion James Bryne observes that these arguments "continued down to the Enlightenment one of the main intellectual results of the Reformation, namely that Christian belief was not a fixed body of doctrine, clear and unambivalent for all to see and believe."[27]

Intractable religious conflict tore the old integral European world apart. No compromise was appropriate because that might amount to a deal with the devil. As Toulmin observed, "The more brutal the warfare became, the more firmly convinced the proponents of each religious system were that their doctrines *must be* proved correct, and that their opponents were stupid, malicious, or both."[28]

The postwar environment of more militant religion and a brutalized Europe prevented any return to the tolerant skepticism of the Renaissance. Religious war was not new, but, beneath the suffering and militancy, peace established something new. "What was new," Peter Gay wrote, "was the apparent deadlock of hostile religious sects and the complete bankruptcy of traditional institutions and shibboleths."[29] Thoughtful people were desperate for new approaches to understanding that could bring about order so that such horrors would never happen again. What the seventeenth-century philosophers sought were new grounds for certainty.

In an environment coarsened and brutalized by decades of religious war, the return of human inquiry encountered more treacherous conditions than had formerly been the case. Whereas the Renaissance opened the whole world of human experience to investigation, the seventeenth-century Enlightenment narrowed the scope of inquiry.

Logic and mathematics appeared safe. René Descartes (1596–1650) made his most famous arguments through abstract logic alone, rejecting all sense data.[30] Tools like logic and mathematics could help humans discover God's laws governing matter. On these issues everyone might be able to agree, and religious authorities would refrain from intervention. As Voltaire (1694–1778) later observed, "There are no sects in geometry."[31]

Beginning with Descartes, modernity had a rebirth, one we call the Enlightenment.[32] It differed from the Renaissance in several ways that led to a profound change in what it meant to know something and to a different view of faith.

In their ethical studies, Renaissance humanists had focused on cases and specific problems. This kind of reasoning survives today in English Common Law. But during the Enlightenment *general principles were in, particular cases were out*. Truth was increasingly seen as exemplified by universal principles rather than in the messy variety of daily experience. Printed words increasingly took on a reality of their own. "Red" or "justice" or "freedom" existed independently of specific instances of red, justice, or freedom. The idea was that general principles explained what diversity obscured. Left to itself, diversity led to confusion, strife, and worse. Consequently, *"Abstract axioms were in, concrete diversity was out."*[33]

Monopolistic transcendental monotheism shaped the Enlightenment to its core.[34] The people who gave us the Enlightenment were not atheists. Isaac Newton, Robert Boyle, Gottfried Leibniz, and others were devoutly religious. Some were unorthodox and had to keep their personal views quiet, some were theologically intolerant, but virtually all were believers.

Reading Toulmin's account of how the Enlightenment was shaped by the Reformation and the wars it provoked, I was struck by the gradual exclusion of the most human dimensions of experience from what counted as truth. Humanists had focused primarily on the human world. The Enlightenment did not. In the Renaissance, law was the model for a rational enterprise. During the seventeenth century it was increasingly replaced by physical science.[35]

The literalist mentality in biblical interpretation shifted to nontheological issues. The objectivity supposedly existing in a printed text regarded as sacred also ruled over the diversity arising from human experience. Logic had the power to *compel* agreement as did a divine commandment, and we could agree about the compelling force of logic regardless of our religions. One abstract truth applied to the entire world.

Hans Jonas noted, "It is true that the Renaissance philosophy of nature—the most 'pagan' interlude in Western thought—attempted to combine the new vista of the universe with a pantheistic animism in the true classical style: but the seventeenth century . . . reverted to the rigors of Judaeo-Christian transcendentalism, to extract from it the idea of a nature not spontaneous but strictly subject to law."[36]

It was no accident that the Church of England believed the new discoveries being made by scientists would strengthen its legitimacy and power. Even the most rebellious Enlightenment thinkers remained more wedded than they knew to theological styles of thought they intended to reject. But free inquiry anywhere opens the door to the unexpected, and what ultimately emerged was quite unexpected.

Institutionalizing Heresy

Religious toleration was instituted because peace was better than perpetual war. But in accepting even limited toleration traditional Christian ways of thinking about religion were turned upside down.

Religious toleration *institutionalized heresy.* The word *heresy* means "making choices," choices the church's early fathers believed individuals were unsuited to make. Humanity's fallen nature rendered them unfit to evaluate and debate theology, and the inevitable differences that would arise threatened the unity of the church. Irenaeus argued that lay Christians must "*obey the priests who are in the church.*"[37] Augustine called for the violent suppression of heretics.[38] Salvation depended on following the one right way, not the myriad false ways that offered themselves seductively.

For over one thousand years the Christian church backed up by political authority enforced the view that spiritual truth was unitary and scripture's message clear. Now the coercive supports enforcing this totalitarian outlook were dissolving.

Legitimating heresy changed *every* believer's relationship to whatever faith he or she followed. No matter what their faith, people were aware they could have pursued alternatives, because others around them were doing so. Religious faith became a matter of choice. Religion as it had been traditionally conceived no longer played as secure a role in how many people identified with their place in the world. Even people who adhered to old ways knew about new options. As Peter Berger put it, "*Modern conscious-ness entails a movement from fate to choice*"—which is as true for religion as for our choice of clothes, friends, partners, and homes.[39]

As people interacted increasingly independently of their different reli-gious beliefs, the ancient integral order human beings had long lived within began breaking down. Science could give us truths everyone could agree on but had nothing to say about goodness or beauty. Religion promised knowledge of goodness, but the religious could not agree on what it was. And increasingly what counted as beauty was considered a personal choice.

A secular society emerged, but as with political secularization, a secular society is not antireligious. It is compatible with strong personal belief so long as that belief respects others' right to different beliefs. But that single requirement challenged the presuppositions most Christian theologians had shared for over fifteen hundred years.

SECULARIZING THE SELF: THE RISE OF SCIENCE AND DEATH OF THE WORLD

Medieval and early Renaissance Europeans experienced nature as alive, with no clear distinction between the animate and inanimate world. In this respect Christian Europe maintained a strong continuity with views pervasive in pre-Christian Europe, which are often explicitly stated in the Bible itself.[40] Some medieval Christians even identified Nature as a goddess, although she was ultimately under God's authority.[41] The world was more a Thou than an It. Being alive, the world was most appropriately approached with respect.

The Renaissance initially accepted this integral view. For example, Leonardo da Vinci wrote, "The virtues of grasses, stones, and trees do not exist because humans know them. . . . Grasses are noble in themselves with-out the aid of human languages or letters."[42] He also observed, "Great love is born of great knowledge of the objects one loves. If you do not understand them you can only admire them lamely or not at all—and if you only love

19

them on account of the good you expect from them, and not because of the sum of their qualities, then you are as the dog that wags his tail to the person who gives him a bone. Love is the daughter of knowledge, and love is deep in the same degree as the knowledge is sure."[43] In Leonardo's integral outlook the good, true, and beautiful existed in mutual harmony.

Other prominent Renaissance philosophers adopted a more ethically ambiguous view. Granting nature was in some sense alive, she might still best be controlled to serve the investigator's wishes.[44] As this alternative position developed, knowledge was redefined as power under human control, with profound implications for the future. The idea of knowledge as power will be a recurring issue throughout this book.

Sir Francis Bacon (1561–1626) epitomized this view, arguing that mechanical explanations based on experiment would open the door to understanding the physical world and thereby expanding the power of humans. Knowledge should not be sought "either for pleasure of the mind, or for contention, or for superiority to others . . . but for the benefit and use of life, and that they [humans] perfect and govern it in charity. . . . For the matter in hand is no mere felicity of speculation, but the real business and fortunes of the human race, and all power of operation. . . . And so those twin objects, *human knowledge* and *human power*, do really meet in one."[45] In contrast to da Vinci's view, knowledge existed *only* to serve human needs.

Bacon viewed nature as existing in three possible states: liberty, error, and bondage. As he put it, nature "is either free and follows her ordinary course of development as in the heavens, in the animal and vegetable creation, and in the general array of the universe; or she is driven out of her ordinary course by the perverseness, insolence, and forwardness of matter and violence of impediments, as in the case of monsters; or lastly, she is put in constraint, molded, and made as it were new by art and the hand of man, as in things artificial."[46] Of the three, Bacon preferred nature in bondage to our service.

A possibility unmentioned by Bacon is encompassed by the term *cultivation*. We employ this word with respect to people and other living beings, cultivating relationships that facilitate cooperation. Da Vinci had such an outlook. He had long been involved in hydraulic engineering projects but wrote, "Rivers, to be diverted from one place to another, should be coaxed and not coerced with violence."[47] Power was mediated by an ethical relationship to that over which power was exercised. In da Vinci's terms, Bacon was a dog after a bone.

Other early scientists argued that nature was completely inert, with all change and motion arising from a transcendent deity. Galileo and later Descartes were this view's best-known advocates. Historian Carolyn Merchant observed, "Mechanism took over from the magical [Hermetic] tradition the concept of the manipulation of matter but divested it of life and vital action."[48] Whereas in the earlier integral organismic perspective, order arose from each part's function within a greater whole, the mechanists redefined order to mean the predictable behavior of each part according to a basic system of laws.[49]

The astronomer Johannes Kepler (1571–1630) may have been the first to employ a metaphor Newton was to make famous, writing, "My aim is to show that the celestial machine is to be likened not to a divine organism but to a clockwork."[50] The material world consisted of inanimate stuff obeying invariant principles determining the behavior of its most basic units. Galileo elaborated Kepler's view, using it to interpret his astronomical observations. His success convinced many that mechanism accurately described reality, creating what Stuart Kauffman called the "Galilean spell" that has dominated science for over 350 years.[51]

Mechanism offered a guiding metaphor free from the problems plaguing the old organismic one. Three considerations in particular gave it credence. First was the breakdown of traditional sources of certainty within European society during the later Renaissance as religious violence spread. Many people were searching for new foundations for establishing order.[52] To the degree that the universe was mechanical it was stable and predictable and provided evidence that ultimately all was well in heaven.

Second, the earlier organismic model had assumed an unchanging heaven, rooted in a classical view that change was a sign of imperfection. While hardly required from an organismic perspective, this emphasis on stability was the dominant view Europeans had inherited from their classical ancestors.[53] But even before Galileo unveiled his telescope, a new star and comet had been observed. Hitherto thought to be pristine and unchanging, the heavens were increasingly known to be otherwise.

Third, the most important scientific discoveries appeared to sustain the mechanistic viewpoint. In particular, advances in physics by Sir Isaac Newton (1643–1727) strengthened mechanism's persuasiveness for understanding the world. The metaphor of nature as a great clock captured scientists' imaginations.[54]

A machine worked because of the qualities of its parts, and it could be reduced to them plus its design. The parts derived their qualities because of what they were made from. And so it went, all the way down. Because of the many practical successes flowing from this view, by the twentieth century most scientists assumed that in time all of science could be reduced to physics, supplying a "theory of everything," ultimately even absent a designer.

From a mechanistic perspective, reality lacked subjective qualities, a view reflecting Protestant theology particularly well but equally present in the writings of the Catholic Descartes. God was transcendent and stood in relation to the world as a potter to the pot, a potter who also made the clay. Consciousness came from the outside, from God. It was insubstantial, did not interact with matter, and so could not be studied scientifically. Mere matter, however, was amenable to rigorous investigation through measurement, experiment, and prediction.

Today it is clear that the Renaissance Hermeticists sometimes came closer to what we now believe about the world than did the mechanists. For example, Paracelsus emphasized the relationship between mind and body as essential in facilitating healing, a view only recently accepted by mainstream Western medicine. Unlike Descartes and the mechanists who followed, Paracelsus never had a "mind-body problem" to confound his theories. Giordano Bruno was the first to grasp that matter in the heavens was the same as here, that the sun was merely one star among many, that the universe was vast beyond imagining, and that neither the sun nor the earth was its center, for it had no center.[55] Further, the Hermeticists never separated human beings from the world in which we live, providing a foundation not just for a wiser approach to healing, but also for understanding ecology.[56] The latest discoveries in genetics demonstrate that we are far more integrated into our environment than had been assumed in traditional genetics.[57] Finally, today interest in "emergent" phenomena is growing. New qualities appear at more complex levels undetectable by our knowledge of parts.[58]

Mechanists and Hermeticists offered different metaphors to guide future scientific research, and initially the mechanists' outlook prevailed, at least in part because the low-hanging fruit most accessible to modern scientists lent itself to mechanistic interpretations.

Mechanism's successes in physics meant that the study of life declined in prestige, for it seemed to offer little in the way of comparable discoveries. Perhaps life itself would someday be reduced to physics, the living reduced to the nonliving, without remainder. The power science unleashed impressed Europeans with the promise that this new way of knowing would expand human well-being. When I was a graduate student in political science, the ideal for many professors was still to make all the social sciences more like physics, so that someday they could make up a seamless edifice of knowledge from atoms to nations.

Viewing matter as mechanical and inert meant it could be studied effectively through experiment, prediction, measurement, and mathematical explanation *alone*. There was no Thou there, no "ghost in the machine," nothing to love in the way da Vinci had urged. Europeans had found a common ground for shared knowledge, one that could give us reliable knowledge bridging the chasms dividing people of faith. Bacon's prediction that science would transform human life by enslaving the natural world to humankind's service seemed to be coming true.

The Triumph of Mechanism

Mechanistic science easily meshed with a transcendental monotheistic worldview while offering a detailed understanding of that same reality in purely physical terms. The mechanists' metaphor of cosmic laws fit easily into the view that there must be a cosmic Lawmaker, as order was imposed by God from above. After the world's initial miraculous creation, God influenced affairs through occasional outside interventions. The rest of the time the material world ran along just fine on the basis of divinely ordained laws amenable to human discovery.

Initially these discoveries appeared to prove God existed. When Newton first presented his findings, his cosmic clock needed occasional divine intervention. The Clockmaker occasionally needed to rewind his clock.

Mechanism also buttressed traditional political authorities. Machines were constructed. God constructed natural machines that then responded obediently to God's plans. The mechanistic model seemed to suggest the importance of top-down influences on otherwise passive particles, offering a useful metaphor to legitimate monarchical and aristocratic rule.

Increasingly European governments no longer claimed legitimacy because of the divine right of kings. The best rulers, such as Catherine the Great, claimed to be enlightened despots using reason, religious toleration, education, and powerful bureaucracies to shape and mold their societies. In England Thomas Hobbes (1588–1679) developed a mechanistic theory of absolute government in his *Leviathan*: the people gave up their independence to an all-powerful sovereign in return for safety and order. Enlightened despots added claims of rational direction to Hobbesian protection.

The first political liberals also found the mechanistic metaphor helpful. John Locke thought he could deduce natural law in a way analogous to his friend Newton's physics and planned such a work, though he never wrote it. Locke did succeed in giving the new philosophy of liberalism a foundation based on the equality of individual human beings, each possessing a God-given worth no one could legitimately violate. Each unit was equal, and society was the sum of all the units' actions. Government was a kind of machine created by social contract. The people rather than the ruler were sovereign.

Mechanistic individualism laid the most important ethical foundations for the American Revolution. Later our own constitution was defended in mechanistic terms, as in Madison's emphasis on checks and balances to preserve the proper relation of powers between the different branches of government.[59] Whether used from a traditional or a liberal perspective, mechanism had become the dominant ordering metaphor for understanding the world.[60]

The God of Shrinking Gaps

Freya Matthews observed that after the upheavals of the seventeenth century in Britain "the Church [of England] needed to re-establish its authority on appeal to some broad principles on which all 'reasonable and sober' men could agree, regardless of their sectarian affiliations."[61] The Church of England deliberately propagated Newtonian insights as the foundation of a "natural religion." Scientists argued that they could freely explore the "book of nature," which everyone agreed was authored by God. By doing so they could shed further light on his divine plan without trespassing on the Bible, which was essentially a book of history and revelation. The two could coexist.[62]

This apparently simple division of labor between scientific knowledge and religious revelation turned out to be less stable than anyone imagined.

Newton's initial conception of the universe had required God's occasional intervention to rewind its mechanism. That problem was soon solved, and God was not needed to rewind anything at all. But there were plenty of other mysteries needing his intervention. Anything not understood was potential evidence of God's continued worldly involvement.

In scientific terms, God was becoming a "God of the gaps." His interventions accounted for whatever science could not. The world reflected his plan, and miracles were his rare interventions injecting revelations into an otherwise orderly world. Because they came as revelations from without, miracles could not be deduced from science and were a superior source for truth.

For religion the problem with this arrangement was that scientists proved successful beyond their wildest expectations. The frontiers of scientific research extended ever further and in every direction. The gaps where God needed to intervene kept getting smaller. Once created, the world apparently could get along without Him. Deism, a philosophy depicting a largely passive Creator, became popular among philosophers of the seventeenth and eighteenth centuries such as Voltaire, Hobbes, Diderot, and Rousseau, as well as with many of our Founders.

For other people the religious consequences were ultimately more unsettling. Over time the assumption that matter was inert and deity separate from it imperceptibly shifted from an attitude supporting a particular kind of religious faith to one potentially replacing religion with faith in science alone as the road to truth. Modern science's early successes reinforced a monotheistically derived cultural belief that there is one ultimate hierarchical source of truth, but the nature of that truth began to change.

Science's extraordinary success in those areas amenable to scientific study encouraged many people to believe there were no ultimate limits to the knowledge its methods could uncover. This growing confidence in science generated what Karl Popper called a "promissory materialism: the view that science will in time be able to explain mental phenomena as well as it explains traditional physical phenomena."[63]

These changing perspectives meshed with an ongoing problem that had long plagued monotheists: how could evil exist along with an omnipotent and good God? It was a thorny-enough issue that analyzing the problem even had a specialized term: *theodicy*. The case for the Christian God had always been challenged by the seemingly capricious nature of misfortune, the abundant evidence that bad people often flourished, the frequent atrocities committed in the name of religion, and the manifest suffering of millions of innocent people. For many people science's spectacular successes undermined an already weakened confidence in divine Providence.[64] The corruption of churches in lands where the state supported them reinforced this judgment.

For increasing numbers the true was defined by the methods of science and was far removed from the good and the beautiful, both of which were consigned to the inferior realm of the merely subjective. When this belief was added to a caring awareness that human suffering was ubiquitous, with the bad frequently triumphing over the good, God became a hypothesis in which "serious minds" could no longer believe. Science began to take religion's place, and with it came the secularization of the self.

The society that grew from increasing secularization transformed the world, creating previously unimaginable material wealth, good health, and freedom for most. Yet today it is under attack in the country long pointed to as its greatest success. To understand why, I need to step back a bit and explore how modernity changed what it meant to know something, and why that was important.

MYTHOS, LOGOS, AND THE RISE OF SPIRITUAL NIHILISM

We are embedded in a myth expressing itself through matter.

—Jeffrey Kirpal

The modern West differs from earlier cultures in its dramatic narrowing of what counts as knowledge, a narrowing expressed by *mythos* and *logos*, two visions of what it is to know something. Mythos refers to story, which the classical Greeks contrasted to logos, referring to doctrine, theory, and what we today usually call rationality.[1] During the modern era logos has become nearly universally recognized as leading to genuine knowledge, whereas mythos has become associated with falsehoods, primitive science, and naïveté. This narrowing elicited a high cost, but it took time for the bill to come due.

Logos treats facts as things and illuminates the logical relationships between them. It answers the question *how*. Mythos points to meanings that exist independently of our attitudes toward them. It addresses the question *why*. Logos deals with facts as they exist when viewed from their outside. Mythos explores the meaning of facts seen as symbols for insights best communicated through story and poetry.

Removed from mythos, the *subjective* realm of personal feelings and tastes makes no claim to broader truth. My liking for chocolate ice cream is ontologically identical with my feelings of love for another or for the beauty of a sunset. Unlike the mass of a rock, none of these are "really" real.

Before the Reformation, views of spirituality differed sharply from those of modern conservative Christianity, particularly its Protestant form. Myth was primary then because it provided a way to understand the spiritual meaning embedded within the world and within life itself. Before the Renaissance human experience took place within a world saturated with meaning.[2] What we call subjectivity today was not encased in isolated brains; it was present throughout the universe. In such a world, Richard Tarnas observes, "the human psyche is embedded within a world psyche in which it complexly participates and by which it is continuously defined. . . . Because the world is understood as speaking a symbolic language, direct communication of meaning and purpose from world to human can occur."[3] Normally these symbols are also part of day-to-day logocentric reality: coyotes or storms or wine or the earth can be encountered in either dimension. Logos is compatible with secular views of the world whereas mythos is not.

Because mythos sees meaning as communicated through symbols, it views what logos treats as facts from a different perspective. Donald Sandner writes, "By means of origin myths and cosmogonic myths, a picture is built up of what the world is, how it came to be, and how it may be expected to function in the future. It makes no difference whether the facts on which this world view are founded are true or not. The myth makes do with what 'facts' it has, and goes about its business of creating an intuitive emotional interpretation of them."[4]

In myth "facts" are symbols illuminating a meaning behind the symbols that is articulated through them. The Roman pagan Sallustius observed, "A myth has never happened, yet it happens every day."[5] The world is a text, and mythos interprets the text, translating it into human terms. William Irwin Thompson observed that myth "is a translation of experiences from other dimensions into the imagery of this world."[6] To do so, mythos teaches us through story.

Like a story, a myth has no single interpretation. Different readers bring different interpretative skills and contexts to the material. But this is not to say that a myth can mean anything its interpreter claims. Some interpretations are good, some are competent, and some are incompetent.

From Sallustius's perspective, myth properly understood reveals the deepest truths that can be revealed. Myth concerns itself with the truth *within* life, making claims for meaning that go beyond the purely personal and the purely human. As he put it, "One may call the world a myth, in which bodies and things are visible, but souls and minds hidden; the outer shell veils the inner realities."[7] Nearly two thousand years later Thompson made the same point: "Specialized, scientific knowledge is about pieces, but mythology is about the whole, the beginning and ending of things."[8] From a mythic perspective, logos explores the outer shells; mythos plumbs the inner realities.

Imagine our world as an open book, about which we know nothing. We can analyze its size, shape, and particular markings. We can explore whether they appear in certain combinations and look for underlying patterns enabling us to predict their recurrence. But using such methods would never enable us to read the book. *We would not even be aware that the markings were symbols or that the object we were exploring was a book.*

A mythos-based approach would be to try to read the book. Whether it is a paperback, hardcover, or handwritten on parchment is not important. The meaning the symbols point to matters more than their physical characteristics.

Modern science asserts there is no inner meaning to the object, but if there were meaning, its methods are incapable of finding it. Finding meaning requires understanding the text. Mythos seeks to comprehend and communicate the text of the world.

Story is central to mythos. Stories need not be literally true, as must be the case with a handbook describing setting up a music system. A good handbook requires a close correspondence between nouns and verbs and the objects and what needs to be done to manipulate them. By contrast, myth uses words to guide us to a meaning that, literally speaking, the words do not embody.

Myth employs culturally and historically specific symbols to explicate inner meaning. In different Native American cultures Coyote, Raven, and Rabbit are symbols for the trickster dimension of the universe. But they are living symbols. In classical mythology the relations between Aphrodite and Ares, the Greek gods of sexuality and war, can be read as salacious accounts of amoral deities or, as Sallustius argues, can engender deep explorations of the relationship between love and violence, sex and slaughter.

MYTHOS AND CULTURE

Human beings seek to find meaning everywhere and draw upon their culture and environment in trying to understand it. We always live within a particular time and culture, and our myths integrate our local perspectives into their stories, even as they address universal themes such as the meaning of life and death, sexuality, or the seasons.

Even secular cultures such as our own have myths. Ideologies are a secular logocentric replacement of myth, claiming to show the meaning of our world but doing so in literal terms. These secular myths are often themselves derived from myths in the strong sense; secular accounts of meaning are ultimately rooted in a greater-than-human perspective.

If, as Patrick Harpur observes, "the cosmos which every culture inhabits is a self-portrait of its soul," then the cosmos of the secular West is composed of solitary strivers contending against great odds to build their dreams of the future.[9] Prometheus and Faust are central mythic figures in our Western self-understanding. They do not have enviable fates, but that does not detract from the power, nobility, and beauty of their deeds. What matters is their striving. They exemplify a dominant ideal within our culture: solitary will and creativity going beyond the limits set by gods who would hold us back. This Western mythos is heroic, noble, and bittersweet.

Science is an integral player in this mythos, for scientists often see themselves as fearlessly exploring a universe they regard as vast beyond imagination, one that will long outlast us unless sometime in the future we can achieve a so-far-unimaginable immortality. In a way, traditional science fiction is this mythology's sacred literature, with the stars as our destiny. The American Dream is another secular incarnation of that myth. In America with sufficient hard work and brains people can supposedly make their dreams real or live nobly in the attempt.

In a world where the pressures of the mundane and the impact of meeting our needs can narrow our vision to what immediately confronts us, myth enables us to view our lives in a larger context. In a mythic context, faith is confidence in the deeper truths the myth illuminates, not belief in literal truth.

Integral cultures integrated logos and mythos. Charlene Spretnak describes how this integration influenced the day-to-day routines of Native American life: "The Pima and O'odhdam peoples . . . consider their acts of basket making, including the gathering of grasses and vegetable dyes and the weaving itself, to be a ritual recapitulation of the total process of creation. The completed basket is the universe in an image."[10]

Mythos does not deny the value of logos but does deny that logos alone suffices for accessing knowledge. It is too narrow and partial a vision to see things *deeply*. William Blake described this difference: "'When the Sun rises, do you not see a round Disk of fire somewhat like a Guinea?' O no, no, I see an Innumerable company of the Heavenly host crying 'Holy, Holy, Holy is the Lord God Almighty.' I question not my Corporeal or Vegetative Eye any more than I would Question a Window concerning a Sight. I look thro' it and not with it."[11]

Blake's observation alerts us to the close relationship between myth and poetry. Poet Robert Bringhurst writes that poetry is perhaps the purest form of knowing because it is "knowing freed from the agenda of possession and control—knowing in the sense of stepping in tune with being, hearing and echoing the music and heartbeat of being. . . . Poetry is the knowing of which music and painting are the known. But music and painting are equally names for the knowing, and poetry a name for what they know. Why use the same name for an attribute of reality and for the knowledge we hope to have of it, or the condition of awareness we aspire to maintain? Perhaps for the same reason that we say, 'I am in love with you, my love.'"[12] This conception of knowledge is harmonious with Leonardo's but not with Bacon's.

Bringhurst uses dance as an example: "Moving to the tune is knowing; trying to move to the tune is thinking."[13] When we learn a dance we focus on getting the steps right. Once we have made them our own, we no longer focus on the steps but move through them into the feel of the rhythm. The rhythm flows through us, the steps take care of themselves, and we dance.

The knowledge we have when we know the dance is what scientist-philosopher Michael Polanyi called "tacit," or skillful, knowledge. When we have it we no longer focus on getting the skill right but on what we can do with and through it. Polanyi argued that underlying all explicit knowledge was a tacit substrate that depended on its not being explicit in order to be useful. To ride a bicycle well, we do not, must not, think about riding. But when we are learning to ride we have to think about it all the time. Our knowledge and awareness of the world arises out of a tacit background of taken-for-granted capacities that, in principle, can become known explicitly, but if they are to be useful to us as skills they *must* remain tacit.[14] We *live* it.

When deeply experienced, poetry, music, and art become tacit lenses through which we pour ourselves into experiencing the meanings for which they are symbols. A poem's ability to achieve this transparency enables it to carry us to a place beyond the words we hear or read on a page. Bringhurst describes this place as "the resonant silence you hear, and the resonant silence you make in return, when you get the poem and the poem gets you. When you really *see what it means*, what you see is nothing, and the nothing sings a song."[15]

Myth seeks to reveal the *universal* aspects of this poetic dimension. We discover a meaning quite different from the distanced knowledge we get from logocentric thinking, and to describe this experience to others we use mythic terminology.

This way of perceiving is important in science, even if little discussed. When scientists do discuss it, they find themselves moving beyond the terminology of logos to poetic terminology and terms of relationship. In describing her research on chromosomes, Nobel Laureate Barbara McClintock said, "When I was really working with them I wasn't outside, I was down there. I was part of the system. I was right down there with them and everything got big. I was even able to see the internal parts of the chromosomes—actually everything was there. It surprised me because I actually felt as if

33

I was right down there and these were my friends. . . . As you look at these things, they become part of you. And you forget yourself."[16] McClintock was a highly skilled scientist whose empathetic connection with what she studied enabled her to perceive meanings not immediately present in objective data, giving her a deeper insight than logocentric scientific knowledge.

Here is a more personal example. Think of a person you know well, someone for whom you have deep affection. Now think of the most detailed police-blotter-style description of that person: height, weight, dress, all the external details. Include a photograph. Does it capture what you know about that individual? It is not even close. It is not wrong. But such a description does not give us knowledge of the person's interior, of what makes him or her important in your eyes. To describe that dimension you need to tell a story, and if it is successful the story will take listeners beyond the literal facts, connecting with a larger context enabling them to know that person to some degree. This knowing, Leonardo's knowing, leads to love.

In Bringhurst's words, "Myths are stories that investigate the nature of the world *from the standpoint of the world.* . . . Mythtellers often say they listen to the world and *see* the world unfold. The patterns and connections that emerge in the telling of the myth are reflections of an order that is sensed, not an order that is built by humans."[17]

MYTHOS, STORY, AND LITERALISM

Myth originated in oral cultures, and that is partly why myth takes story form. But there is a more fundamental reason. Oral societies lived in a world experienced as alive, with which people could and should enter into relationship.[18] Myths, as Bringhurst observes, "are really about *the nature of nature.*" In myths, "nearly everything—rocks, trees, clouds—is animate enough to speak, to think, to make choices and to pass through transformations."[19] The most fundamental fact about nature is that it is aware.

This anthropomorphic quality in myths may seem a serious weakness, for we know that the earth existed long before human beings. But as Freya

Matthews observes, "We are the only model of subjectivity available to ourselves."[20] Our mythic stories reflect this subjectivity, just as our logocentric thinking is ultimately rooted in bodily metaphor.[21] We *cannot* get the *anthro* out of our thinking.

Anthropomorphism furnishes a metaphor helping us grasp dimensions of subjectivity other than the human. Matthews writes that personification "makes it easy for us to relate to the world around us as communicative and responsive. . . . Personification of those phenomena serves not to explain them, but to enable them to be appropriately encountered."[22]

Iain McGilchrist explains: "The point of metaphor is to bring together the whole of one thing with the whole of another, so that each is looked at in a different light."[23] When the universe was seen as a clockwork, both clocks and the universe were viewed from a new perspective illuminating some features and obscuring others. And in the bringing together we learn about ourselves; as Bruno Snell observed, "Man must listen to an echo of himself before he may hear or know himself."[24] Metaphors that succeed open our awareness in both directions.

Myth as story has another strength. The end of a story is always provisional, for a story can be embedded within other stories, and an event in one story can figure in many others. A story is fuzzy around its edges, and all the way through threads lead beyond it into the larger, multidimensional fabric of reality. At any point new dimensions of a character or an event might emerge, without disrupting the previous flow. Or its meaning may be transformed by changing the context.[25] Stories are open-ended in a way that a discursive argument tries hard not to be.

A powerful argument tries to contain what is relevant and all its details in tight service toward making a specific point, constraining our imagination within its confines. A good logocentric argument provides all the connections in a chain, beginning with premises and proceeding toward an inexorable conclusion. It tries to complete the conversation and have the last word.

In a sense myth is like science. Both are human attempts to make sense of mystery, either the mystery of how things work, which science addresses, or the mystery of why things are as they are, the realm of myth. In both cases we are exploring.

A myth is situated within a context of other myths that together describe the fabric of life's meaning by connecting to a world vaster than the merely human. Every culture has central stories that give it a sense of its identity. America has a number of stories that fit within the West's Promethean and Faustian framework: the myth of American Innocence, the myth of the Hero, the myth of New Beginnings. In Barry Spector's words, these myths "transform history into sacred legends that describe reality to us." He emphasizes that as this happens "myth trumps fact."[26]

Our sense of the literal meant little in mythic cultures, where myth was never intended to be taken literally. They experienced themselves as immersed in a world of meaningful relationships rather than objects. David Abram writes, "Literal truth is a very recent invention, brought into being by alphabetic literacy. The word 'literal,' after all, derives from the Latin word for letter. To understand something *literally* originally meant to understand that it happened exactly *as written in scripture*. . . . Neither actively literal nor entirely metaphoric, the world that articulated itself through our oral stories was rather, at every point, *metamorphic*. The land was alive: each place had its pulse, each palpable presence seemed crouched in readiness to become something else."[27]

In Jeffrey Kripal's words, "The real possesses two faces: a public face involving cause and matter and an esoteric face involving meaning and mind."[28] To be understood, myth has to be approached esoterically.

The Hebrew scriptures originated in mythic cultures, and while many Israelites differed from surrounding peoples in adopting a scripturally based monotheism incorporating an allegedly historical narrative, they also shared much in common with their pagan neighbors. For example, in Genesis God eats and converses with Abraham as a friend (18) and walks in the Garden of Eden in the cool of the day (3:8).

Compare these anthropomorphic conceptions of deity to Moses's words: "When Yahweh spoke to you out of the fire on Sinai you saw no form" (Deut.4:12). Later in the New Testament John writes: "No man hath seen

Elohim at any time" (1:18, also 5:37, 6:46). God does not walk or eat or converse as with a friend. The Garden of Eden account gives a mythic depiction of God that if taken literally would be considered idolatrous by Moses and contradicted by John.

For about fifteen hundred years Christians considered the Bible partly mythic and partly literal. While there was plenty of disagreement on where to draw the line, few argued for only a logocentric understanding of scripture. Referring again to Genesis, Origen, one of the church's early fathers, pointed out that the "seven-days" creation of the earth was not literally possible since much of it happened before the sun and moon were created, making days possible.[29] For Origen Genesis's account was mythic.

In his *Confessions*, St. Augustine described his encounter with St. Ambrose: "I was delighted to hear Ambrose in his sermons to the people saying, as if he were most carefully enunciating a principle of exegesis: 'The letter kills, the spirit gives life.' Those texts which, taken literally, seemed to contain perverse teaching he would expound spiritually, removing the mystical veil."[30]

Sallustius would disagree with Augustine's claims to Christianity's spiritual exclusivity, but on this point they would agree: "Why are adultery, robbery, disrespect for parents, and other unworthy actions celebrated in myths? Is it not possible that this is intentional? Surely it is intended that the obvious absurdity and contradictions will alert the individual's soul that the words are veils, mere cloaks wrapped around an inner mystery."[31]

Literalists look intently at the pointing finger and not where it points. The finger is the myth, the lens that when looked through reveals a deeper meaning. The finger is the merely human, and what it points to exceeds the power of any mind to encompass or express. Looking only at the finger creates an idol. As Joseph Campbell put it, those taking myths literally are "like diners going into a restaurant and eating the menu."[32]

A mythic approach no more guarantees knowledge of inner truth than a logos-centered one guarantees accurate knowledge of physical reality. As Bringhurst describes it, mythtelling "lifts a statement out of the realm of history or experience and drops it into one of the two realms (the timeless and true, the persistent and false) we now call myth."[33] Truth or falsity depends on insight into the internal meanings mythos seeks to illuminate and the discernment of those encountering the myth.

The truths mythos teaches are truths of mutual relation. As we know from our experience with other people, getting relations right can be difficult. What seems straightforward can mislead us. Seen with a discerning understanding, what appears contradictory may not be. What appears harmonious may be otherwise. As a way of knowing, mythos depends on the world having an interiority that we can to some degree understand. If so, we encounter some of the problems we encounter when dealing with other people's interiority: sometimes we get it right, sometimes we don't.

When logos expels mythos as a way of knowing, the door opens to pure secularism because meaning has been expelled from within the world. Meaning might continue to exist at the level of a purely transcendent creator deity or to be encased briefly within the human mind, but the world itself is without value. When belief in such a God is abandoned with no more satisfactory conception to take its place, within a logocentric perspective the world is without meaning.

Mythic time is full of meaning. But modern time, Charles Taylor writes, is empty and, being empty, homogeneous. "Both space and time come to be seen as 'containers' which things and events contingently fill, rather than as constituted by what fills them." This "step to emptiness is part of the objectification of time that has been so important a part of the modern subject of instrumental reason."[34] Compare the Catholic Eucharist with that of Protestantism. For Catholics experiencing the Eucharist mythically, the wafer and wine are Christ's body and blood. For Protestants they are a historical remembrance of Jesus"s Last Supper. (See "Mythos and Time," http://dizerega.com/faultlines/appendices/.)

SPEECH AND TEXT: THE SUBTLE LIMITS OF LITERACY

While critical of many myths of his day, Plato had to use myth to make some of his most important points. His myth of the cave in *Republic* enables us to some degree to *feel* the point he is making and *dwell* in it, first as one chained to see only shadows, then as one blinded by the sun, and finally as one returning to try to describe the true source of light to those unaware they do not know.

Jeffrey Kripal writes that images such as Plato's cave are more accurate than logocentric descriptions, "*not* because the former are literally true (they are not) or because the latter are false (they no doubt capture something important), but because the theological, mystical, and literary metaphors deliver far more imaginative impact. They are closer to the lived experience of things."[35] It is this lived experience that logocentric knowledge cannot grasp.

Far from being static, mythic oral traditions were often more adaptable and flexible than the written traditions that followed.[36] In oral cultures myths can grow and diversify as they are applied to new audiences and new situations. Those found insightful are retold. Others fade. The Navajo's mythic stories changed as their ancestors traveled from the far north to the Southwest's canyon and mesa country.[37] Maize became integrated into the oral traditions of African villages once it arrived there from the New World.[38] But the deepest lessons these stories taught did not vary nearly so much. Oral myths are constant living intermediaries between the sacred and those who hear them.

Peter Gay, a secular historian, considers mythos inferior to logos, writing that mythical "categories are unsettled, alive. They shift under the potent pressures of immediate experience or become rigid under the equally overwhelming weight of tradition."[39] These characteristics are bad for logocentric understanding. But given the work mythos does, this shifting can be an advantage.

Some scholars suggest that the life drained from Greek myths when they were written down, because they no longer could take the specifics of their audience and the place of its telling into account. Describing what happened when Homer's words were transcribed, David Abram writes, "The art of the rhapsodes began to lose its preservative and instructive function. The knowledge embedded in the epic stories and myths was now captured for the first time in a visible and fixed form, which could be returned to, examined, and even questioned."[40] Writing a story down strengthens the hold of tradition and rigidity as the story is removed from contact with the performative world of an audience participating with the teller in mythic time. The rigidity Gay describes seems a result of writing myths down and removing them from their natural environment.

Frozen in words, a myth becomes a kind of skeleton once the living metabolism of the oral tradition that gave it life and place has been removed. Genuine mythic insights always distinguish between the words and the spirit underneath them toward which they point.

In ancient times as today, some people seemed tied to a literal understanding. In *Euthyphro* Plato describes an Athenian resembling today's Fundamentalists in terms of his literalism, and the logical knots arising from such an attitude. Euthyphro had come to court to prosecute his own father for unintentionally killing a murderous hired hand, using a literal interpretation of a myth to justify doing so. Socrates demonstrated that he did not understand the myth at all.

The relation of mythos with logos in written spiritual traditions is a source of tension because writing encourages a different kind of thinking. In the case of writing, Abram observes, "the scribe or author, could now begin to dialogue with his own visible inscriptions."[41] In a conversation with Joseph Campbell, Bill Moyers captured this point: "Religion begins with a sense of wonder and awe and the attempt to tell stories that will connect us to God. Then it becomes a set of theological works in which everything is reduced to a code, to a creed." Campbell responded, "That's the reduction of mythology to theology. Mythology is very fluid. Most of the myths are self-contradictory. You may even find four or five myths in a given culture, all giving different versions of the same mystery. Then theology comes along and says it has to be just this way. Mythology is poetry, and the poetic language is very flexible. Religion turns poetry into prose."[42]

That the sacred could apparently be reduced to teachings in a text encouraged some to think all truth could be recorded in words on a page. Wiser readers knew differently. For millennia sacred texts have been studied through long meditation and deep immersion, using the printed text to discover deeper meanings pointed to by the written words. But such an approach is neither obvious nor easy.

Literal-minded readers are deceived by the text's apparent objectivity. The problem is that when the material at hand is questioned the text, unlike a speaker, simply repeats itself. For some early critics of writing, this weakness was a fatal shortcoming. Plato related how the Egyptian God Theuth once offered the Egyptian king Thamus the gift of writing. Theuth explained that it would "make the Egyptians wiser and improve their memory. . . . Thamus replied, '. . . your invention will produce forgetfulness in souls of those who have learned it, through lack of practice at using their memory, as through reliance on writing they are reminded from outside by alien marks, not from within, themselves by themselves. So you have discovered an elixir not of memory but of reminding. To your students you give an appearance of wisdom, not the reality of it."[43]

Thamus turned him down. Plato said he never wrote down his own most important teachings. They remained oral and now unknown.

THE DEATH OF MYTHOS

Paul Shepard observed of Hebrew scripture, "Its most revolutionary aspect was its repudiation of the cyclic pattern of events, its insistence on the truly linear flow of time, and its pursuit of its own abstract self-confirming truth as opposed to indicators and signs in the concrete world."[44] One of the difficulties in interpreting the Old Testament has been distinguishing history from myth.

Interpreting apparent facts as myths and symbols pointing beyond themselves is often difficult. As Mary Midgley writes, "It can take a great deal of complex metaphysical thinking to explain a symbol which did not seem to need much explaining when it was simply accepted as a fact."[45] King Thamus was right. I suspect this difficulty explains why the Ten Commandments are so popular with many Fundamentalists. They seem like a grocery list. Over time history trumped myth.

Translating and printing scripture during the Reformation so all could read it sparked an enormous growth in the power of logos to shape people's understanding of the sacred. For millions, spiritual experience through Christian mythos-centered ritual, celebration, and encounter was abandoned, replaced by reading claims about *other people's* spiritual experiences long ago. There was no means for knowing what was literal and what was myth.

During the sixteenth and seventeenth centuries both Protestants and Catholics used logocentric strategies in criticizing the mythic elements within the opposing side's interpretations. Both sides strengthened logos and weakened mythos as tools for understanding scripture, although this process went furthest among Protestants. Augustine's praise of Ambrose was ignored.

Early modern science's successes further strengthened this logos-centered cultural inclination. Mathematics required logocentric proofs. Experiment, measurement, and prediction did the same. More and more people looked to logocentric reason alone as their source of authority. Biblical literalism increasingly appealed to modern minds retaining a religious commitment. But taking this position also meant that Biblical meaning could be shattered by new knowledge.

Religion enters spiritually suicidal territory when it makes universal claims applying equally to all, bases its claims on a text supposedly comprehensible to all, and argues that correct interpretation of doctrine matters crucially. As James Bryne put it, both Protestants and Catholics were now "stuck with Biblical literalism and doctrinal integralism in which the truth of Christianity as a whole stood or fell with each of its parts." Consequently, "the Christian churches were for the most part incapable of responding creatively to scientific advances which conflicted with their own orthodoxy."[46] The Navajo could integrate the Colorado Plateau into their mythic traditions, and African farmers could do the same with maize, but written texts were not so adaptable.

When so many Christians accepted logocentric reasoning for interpreting scripture, future conflict between science and religion was guaranteed. Religion focuses on the inner meaning of ultimate contexts but now sought to lay its foundation on the surface characteristics of lesser contexts, and it became hostage to them. Religion left its primary means of spiritual communication behind to try to speak an alien tongue. If we make our claim to truth based on reason and objective evidence, we are logically committed to abiding by the standards of reason and objective evidence, wherever they may lead us. This strategy led many to viewing the sacred as dispensable.

But what about people for whom the sacred was *not* dispensable?

THE RISE OF THE IRRATIONAL WILL

Today's religious culture warriors condemn modern irreligious secularism yet *accept* the secular definition of what counts as knowledge. For all their criticism of the modern world, *they themselves are moderns.* They accept the Enlightenment ideal that truth is universal, impersonal, and objective. They accept the truths of logos, which the modern world has mastered as never before, while rejecting the truths of mythos, to which they have become largely blind.

To the extent that logos replaced mythos the character of faith changed from faith in the meaning *within* the world to faith in reports *about* the world. When those reports no longer fit independently acquired evidence, this faith lost its foundation.

Christian believers were faced with a fateful choice. In *Jesus Interrupted* biblical scholar Bart Ehrman explains how mainstream historical scholarship demolished his belief in the Bible as literally true.[47] The contradictions are too numerous and profound. Initially a devout Fundamentalist, Ehrman faced a powerful spiritual crisis. In time he gave up Fundamentalism, yet remained a believing Christian.[48]

In Ehrman's words, "I came to think of the Christian message about God, Christ, and the salvation he brings as a kind of religious 'myth,' or group of myths—a set of stories, views, and perspectives that are both unproven and unprovable, but also un-disprovable—that could, and should, inform my life and thinking."[49]

But another strategy was available. Protestant sociologist Peter Berger writes that many Christian theologians abandoned both mythos and logos: "The truth of Christianity cannot be established from any of its characteristics, cannot, that is, be made credible by any 'method' of rational or empirical assessment. Rather, the truth of Christianity is accessible only through the self-revelation of the work of God as grasped in faith." The decision to believe is "a heroic act of will, and in . . . much of Protestant Christianity in general, will was elevated over reason in any form."[50] A committed position is taken in the *absence* of evidence.

Faith based on evidence is open to evidence against it. Jesus said, "By their fruits ye shall know them" (Matt. 7:16). Commitment is different. Truth for the believer is what he or she *chooses* to believe as an act of will, and so it is impervious to evaluation by evidence or reason. What is acceptable rationally or by evidence must first be in harmony with the commitment. When the text is contradicted by reason or evidence, the *will to believe* salvages it.[51] So much for logos. To the degree mythos survived, it was relegated to a purely abstract role such as "God has a plan," removed from any concrete story. Neither mythos nor logos can trump the will to believe.

Berger observes that this move opens religion not simply to the irrational, which is dangerous enough; it opens it to the apotheosis of the human will and, ironically for the neo-orthodox Christian position, of the *fallen* human will.[52]

Fundamentalists upped mainstream Protestantism's ante by demanding commitment to the literal truth of the Bible. If Christianity is true by an act of will, it follows that the biblical source for what Christians believe must also be true, again by an act of will. It does not matter how incoherent such a commitment becomes. Having freed themselves from both mythical and logocentric traditions for evaluating knowledge, literalists embrace irrationality because they reject the necessity for reasons and evidence. They justify this by arguing that the world is so fallen nothing within it can be trusted. God is utterly transcendent and alien to the world. In my terminology this position amounts to *spiritual nihilism*.

Mythos remains, but with little substance, while logos is respected only when it supports what is known by commitment alone to be true. What is left is worship of the power of commitment. The trap is not total, for the human heart can and sometimes does rebel at such a harsh conception of religion and of the God it worships, but mythic and logocentric understanding alike are exiled.

When we deny that intrinsic meaning exists we do not abolish it; we blind ourselves to it. A story with a deeper meaning can still be told about us, but it will be a tragedy, a story of the blind who are unaware they are blind. Much of our modern predicament could be captured in a myth of a civilization that became so enraptured with its own image that it forgot its connections to others. It would also be a story of the disaster we brought upon ourselves. Ayn Rand's popularity is symptomatic of such a narcissistic culture.

This blindness came on slowly in the West, and as it did our ability to find our way through the intricacies of the world increasingly shifted to relying on our power to force our way. At first we often seemed to see better than before, but that was because we had inherited important habits from the past, unappreciated and unnoticed habits that would fade. The trap of modernity has snapped shut on logos-centered religion. (See "Roots of Religious Nihilism," http://dizerega.com/faultlines/appendices/.)

CHAPTER THREE

FEMININE AND MASCULINE

Male and female . . . are perpetually passing into one another. Fluid hardens to solid, solid rushes to fluid. There is no wholly masculine man, no purely feminine woman.

—Margaret Fuller

Like mythos and logos, feminine and masculine play a central role in my argument. As I use them, these terms refer to coherent sets of values for experiencing and relating to the world, others, and oneself. While clearly associated with women, feminine refers to more than one side of the basic biological distinction within humanity, as does masculine. This chapter focuses on the feminine and masculine in their secular contexts. I discuss their spiritual dimensions later.

How feminine and masculine values relate to one another among human beings is one of the most important political and cultural issues facing us today. Two broad possibilities present themselves. From one perspective these words identify fundamental dualities in hierarchical relation to one another. According to this view, men ideally incorporate and manifest purely masculine values, and women do likewise with purely feminine ones. Outside the domestic sphere and sometimes inside it as well, masculine values should trump feminine ones, and men should exercise authority over women.

An alternative view conceives these values as falling along a continuum. Women and men possess both qualities, and a balanced individual harmonizes them within and in relationships with others. Emphasizing either end of the continuum, particularly when accompanied with denigration of the other, leads a person into psychological imbalance or worse.

The same observation holds for a society. Societies can also have these values in harmony or imbalance.

In some cultures feminine and masculine qualities are subsumed into even more inclusive categories, as with the Chinese terms *yin* and *yang*, the feminine being considered part of the yin and the masculine included within the yang. Exploring the qualities associated with the feminine/yin and masculine/yang, Edward Whitmont and Robert Ornstein developed complementary lists drawn from differing intellectual traditions in the East and West,[1] to which I have added:

Masculine/Yang	Feminine/Yin
Assertive	Ambivalent
Focused	Receptive
Abstractive	Intuitive
Divisive	Connective
Day	Night
Time, History	Eternity, Timelessness
Intellectual	Sensuous, intuitive
Explicit	Tacit
Analytic	Gestalt
Lineal	Nonlineal
Sequential	Simultaneous
Focal	Diffuse
Causal	Synchronistic
Argument	Experience

Pure yin or pure yang does not exist. The famous Daoist yin-yang symbol illustrates this insight, inserting a small light or dark dot where the other color is at its most dominant, a reminder that we deal with continuums and not genuine dualities.

This value pattern is probably universal, although its symbolic expression is culturally molded. In *The Fragility of Goodness* Martha Nussbaum explored how the classical Greeks twenty-five hundred years ago understood human life could be most appropriately lived.[2] They often conceived the good life in terms of masculine virtue, ideally manifested as a hunter, a person who acts on the world, whose soul is hard and impenetrable, and who places his confidence in what is stable and immutable. From this perspective the good life could appropriately be lived in solitude.

For Aristotle solitary contemplation was the highest human activity, one shading into the divine. In the ideal case contemplatives are self-sufficient or nearly so. Significantly, for Aristotle, women do not engage in contemplation.

Women's status was usually so low that the Greeks did not describe a feminine model for a human ideal. However, they did develop a concept of the good life that could be lived by either men or women. Here, Nussbaum explains, agents were conceived as children, plants, women, or both men and women. These lives were active, but they were also receptive. The soul appropriate to them was soft and porous, although possessing its own structure. The unstable was to be trusted along with the stable, and intellect itself was conceived as flowing water.[3] In this conception the good life was lived in the company of friends and loved ones, immersed within one's community.

The masculine Greek ideal emerging from Nussbaum's discussion is similar to traditional Chinese yang qualities. When the feminine is included in a virtuous existence, it exerts a softening, opening, even liquefying influence. Today the qualities present in this second Greek model but absent in its purely masculine ideal are usually associated with the feminine: children, plants, receptiveness, softness, porosity, and instability. It is yin's entry into the Greeks' masculine hardness, clearness, and solidity.

The connection between particular qualities and gender is not unvarying, for their identification refers to their relationships with one another, not to their intrinsic characteristics. For example, in Greece the unchanging was considered superior to the changing, as were the apparently constant stars to the mutable earth. This attitude was reflected in the alleged superiority of Aristotle's purely masculine contemplation.

Modern Western culture honors the man of action rather than the contemplative. But at a deeper level similar qualities appear. The man of action acts independently of others, either in opposition to them or by leading them. Consider the popular heroes Superman, Batman, the Lone Ranger, James Bond, and the Terminator, to name a few. They are self-sufficient as others are not.

BOUNDARIES

I think at their core the yin/feminine and yang/masculine columns describe different approaches to *boundaries*. Boundary issues shed light on the basic distinction between masculine and feminine qualities.[4] Masculine traits focus on the recognition, maintenance, strengthening, and expansion of boundaries. They exemplify autonomy. The feminine emphasizes that boundaries are open, incomplete, and transitory, seeking interconnectedness by crossing or dissolving them and letting others in.

Consider Aristotle's praise of contemplation and the modern Western man of action. Greek boundaries are self-sufficient and well defined. In the West they expand as the hero imposes his will on others or on his environment. But *neither lets the other in*, in one case because there is no need, in the second because the other must be subdued, kept at a distance, or led. The essence of masculine values is maintaining, defending, and strengthening boundaries; the essence of feminine values is opening and dissolving them.

What makes a symbol feminine or masculine depends on what dimensions of its *relationships* with other phenomena are emphasized. As with the yin/yang symbol, each implies the other. They do not exist in isolation.

I think this perspective sheds light on what otherwise appear to be arbitrary classifications of natural forces as either masculine or feminine. The ocean is usually described as feminine. However, for some Hindus Shiva is the ocean and Parvati, his wife, is the seashore. The seashore is where boundaries are fluid and open. It is both wet and dry, the proportions of each in continuous flux.

In most cultures the sun is masculine and the moon feminine, but for the Inuit the moon is masculine and the sun feminine. In the Arctic the moon provides the only light in winter, a distant light that gives no warmth. With the return of the sun and its boundary-penetrating warmth, life returns. In the far North the moon is cold and distant while the sun is the sensuously warm nurturer of life.

Most interesting for my purposes, Francis Bacon defined the human mind as feminine when it was receptive and able to be "impregnated" by masculine God. After impregnation, the mind becomes, as Elizabeth Fox Keller described in writing about Bacon's views, "potent and capable of generating virile offspring in its union with [feminine] Nature."[5] For Bacon, the mind is feminine when penetrated by God, masculine when penetrating nature.

There is a boundary paradox fundamental to us all. From one perspective the individual is a self-consistent physical and biological unity. From another the individual manifests as the focus of multiple relationships. As individuals, we are defined by our bodily boundaries and are simultaneously expressions of our relations with everything around us. The character of our society, the religions we take for granted, the structure of our families, and virtually every other aspect of the social environment we encounter while growing up shape us, and their collective impact is enormous. These social constructs initially appear to us as real as trees and rocks, and as children we orient ourselves based on these perceptions. We create our societies and our societies create us.

This paradox of our being both discrete individuals and nodes of integrated awareness arising out of multiple relationships is no more a contradiction than is the fact that photons manifest as particles when subjected to some experiments and as waves when subjected to others. Neither the model of a particle nor that of a wave can do justice to a photon. We should not be surprised that similarly simple dichotomies do not adequately describe human beings. Applied to people, the individual/particle view with its distinct boundaries is masculine; the relational view with no clear boundaries is feminine.

If we are to survive and flourish, creating and maintaining our boundaries is necessary, but so also is opening them to allow in air, nutrition, information, and love. For human beings, the dance of feminine and masculine, yin and yang, extends to our very core.

BALANCE

Let us return to those yang qualities that can most plausibly be called masculine: assertion, focus, abstraction, division, intellect, explicitness, analyticity, and argumentativeness. Being assertive need not mean being aggressively domineering. It can also mean standing up for oneself and one's responsibilities or following one's own path, even when the going gets tough. In sports, assertion is often far removed from domination, for ideally athletes compete with relative equals and anyone could win.

Being focused and explicit need not mean narrowing one's attention. It also can mean becoming better able to accomplish a task even in the face of distractions. In the absence of focus, we drift.

Being intellectual and thinking abstractly need not simply mean distancing oneself from the concrete and particular. It can also refer to perceiving what is most central to a complex issue or phenomenon and identifying the broader patterns hidden behind and within the many details. Science could not exist without people who strongly exemplify this quality. Through it insights arrived at intuitively are examined, clarified, and made accessible.

Being divisive need not mean promoting discord. The ability to differentiate is vital in distinguishing what is important from what is unimportant. Nor is willingness to argue necessarily negative. Arguments lead to learning when people with different perspectives listen to one another and honestly compare alternative views. Science depends on thousands upon thousands of such arguments.

Each of these masculine characteristics possesses positive and negative qualities, depending on the context and the frame of mind of the person exhibiting them. In this regard they are no different from feminine qualities. Our task is not to become purely masculine or purely feminine, or to seek perfect equality between them, whatever that might look like. It is to balance them in a way that works for us and those around us.[6]

Too much masculine concern with maintaining boundaries means all that is different becomes a threat, including the feminine. To people who overemphasize the masculine, any change can appear to be a kind of death or disloyalty to a previous commitment. They transform masculine values of loyalty, steadfastness, and firmness into the vice of rigidity. We have repeatedly witnessed this behavior within the contemporary conservative right, where disagreement is considered disloyalty rather than a different view to be evaluated on its merits.

Context determines when virtue becomes vice. Sometimes change *is* death or disloyalty, but not always. Few changes are more drastic than a caterpillar becoming a butterfly, but we would pity the caterpillar that so feared temporary dissolution that it refused to create its chrysalis.

Ultimately, feminine and masculine values are complementary. The feminine is more accepting of relationship, the masculine more concerned with individuating itself with respect to the other. A psychologically healthy man or woman has a strong sense of self *and* the ability to enter into good relationships.

There is no shortage of healthy predominately masculine ways of living: the provider, explorer, protector, mentor, and builder are examples. All rely on assertion, focus, a strong distinction between the person acting and what is being acted on, and analytical thinking. However, to be at their most impressive they must be complemented by feminine qualities. For example, an excellent mentor must be able to empathize with and care about his or her student. The successful explorer in any field must be open to clues missed by those trapped by preconceptions.

The most creative scientists bring together the intuition that generates hypotheses with the critical intellect that tests and refines them. The artist does the same with a vision of the possible and the perseverance and skill to bring it into existence. At their best, both science and art rely on balancing masculine and feminine qualities. Dealing appropriately with other people does so as well. In more general terms, manifesting the good, the true, and the beautiful in one's character depends on integrating masculine and feminine qualities.

Where boundary definition and maintenance are strong priorities, relationships often become hierarchical. Where boundaries are relatively open or unimportant, relationships have a corresponding tendency to become egalitarian. Neither hierarchical inequality nor egalitarian equality is always good or bad. Good parents' relationship to their child is necessarily hierarchical, while that between two friends is necessarily egalitarian. In the first, respect for the other remains; in the second, recognition of differences in abilities or resources is not denied.

Nurturance is *both* active care for others *and* respect for the boundaries that make them separate beings. It is a virtue that requires a balance of feminine and masculine qualities. If parents err in nurturing their children, it seems men will generally do so by being too distant and women by being too involved. But both genders are equally able to nurture because doing so requires a rough balance of masculine and feminine qualities. A good farmer nurtures crops; a good teacher nurtures students. Being a farmer or teacher does not make a man feminine. Describing nurturance as only feminine impoverishes the term and diminishes our understanding of male and female excellence. (See "Science and the Feminine," http://dizerega. com/faultlines/appendices/.)

SCIENCE ON LINEAR REASON

Logocentric understanding is masculine. Its ideal is a logical chain of reasoning, each link entailing the next. Intuition is associated with the feminine. It is preverbal and not easily made explicit. In *A Whole New Mind* Daniel

Pink describes recent research by cognitive neuroscientists involving brain imaging of people experiencing insights, perceptions of new and unexpected relationships: "'Aha' moments are accompanied by a large burst of neural activity in the brain's right hemisphere." However, when people apply a logocentric analysis to a problem, "This 'eureka center' remains quiet."[7] Different areas of the brain are involved in these two ways of thinking.[8]

Recent research suggests that our decisions often come from thinking that is not even conscious. The reason, neuroscientist Chris Frith suggests, is that "the unconscious brain is very good at taking many things into account at the same time." Conscious reasoning by contrast is much more limited in what it can take into deliberate consideration. Frith argues that conscious reasoning "is an attempt to justify the choice after it has been made. And it is, after all, the only way we have to try and explain to other people why we made a particular decision."[9] Intuitive awareness and tacit knowledge is primary; explicit awareness is derivative. We find a fascinating parallel in the relationship between intuition and scientific method and the one between mythos and logos.

What gives science its power to advance our knowledge is *having to explain to others* in rationally constructed logocentric steps how to get from point A to point B. But our initial arrival at point B likely did not happen that way. It often occurs in a flash of insight and intuitive perception, which the prepared and disciplined mind then uses as a guide in explaining to others how the world appears to work. Einstein, for example, wrote, "The words or the language, as they are written or spoken, do not seem to play any role in the mechanism of my thought."[10] Were science merely looking at and measuring data we would likely still believe the sun orbits the earth. *Science at its best is both masculine and feminine. Like nurturance, it is balanced rationality.*[11]

In his studies of the creative process in human beings, Mihaly Csikszentmihalyi concluded, "When tests of masculinity/femininity are given to young people, over and over one finds that creative and talented girls are more dominant and tough than other girls, and creative boys are more sensitive and less aggressive than their male peers." The result, he argues, is a gain for both. "A psychologically androgynous person in effect doubles his or her repertoire of responses and can interact with the world in terms of a much richer and varied spectrum of opportunities."[12] Creative men and women are better balanced than their more one-sidedly masculine or feminine contemporaries.

Rooted in the Earth

As a culture we fantasize that mind and reason can be considered separate from the body and the world. Some scientists think the time may come when we can download our minds into machines, becoming potentially immortal.[13] It would be the ultimate Faustian cheating of death, but perhaps at the cost of giving up our humanity.

This cultural ideal of the disembodied intellect able one day to inhabit a machine is being challenged as never before. Much recent philosophy and science alike is reuniting us with our bodies and our bodies with the earth, bringing together what years of transcendental monotheism split asunder. George Lakoff and Mark Johnson have shown that our conscious thinking is metaphorical, with our most basic orienting metaphors rooted in our bodily experience. Mind cannot exist in an abstract realm removed from our physicality. Awareness can, mind cannot. If a disembodied intellect could exist, it would not be human.[14]

In *Descartes' Error*, Antonio Damasio demonstrated how rational thought *depends* on our bodily emotions and feelings.[15] He underlined David Hume's often-cited but rarely absorbed insight that "reason is and ought to be, only the slave of the passions."[16] The Western fantasy of a disembodied pure intellect is a Faustian fantasy.

What is more, the brain is not the center for all our bodily mental coordination. The heart has what neurocardiologist Andrew Armour called a "little brain" that enables it to operate independently from the larger brain in the head. When the nerves are severed during a transplant, the heart continues to beat without connection to the brain. Additional studies suggest that the heart also processes information differently than does the brain, and influence between them goes in *both* directions.[17]

THE FALSE DICHOTOMY OF NATURE VS. NURTURE

Hormones play a major role in differentiating between males and females, even while in the womb, and exert significant influence throughout life. In men the *relative* stability of our hormonal states supports the common illusion that our mind is somehow independent from our body, or that it should be. Our sexual urges often create a contradiction between bodily desire and good sense, but when they are absent or low and we are healthy the body does not seem to matter much for our thinking. Thinking can seem to be impersonal and has often been so depicted in popular television characters such as Mr. Spock and Data in the *Star Trek* genre. But this vision of a disembodied mind is a masculine fantasy.[18]

The relationship between bodily states and perception is more complex among women, who have far more complex hormonal cycles. The tension between sexual desire and good sense is universal in both genders, but it is not the only way healthy women frequently experience their body and mind as powerfully intertwined. They are aware of the complex and shifting relationships between the two in a way men are not.

In many cultures a girl becomes a woman with her first menstruation, which is often formally recognized and honored, as it should be. But the pain and discomfort involved in becoming a woman is internal and a natural part of her growing up. That transformation is her initiation, her shedding of her previous life and entry into a new one.

The same does not happen for boys becoming men. No clear biological line separates a boy from a man. In traditional societies attaining manly status usually requires going through a serious initiation or triumphing over an external challenge. In some cultures newly circumcised boys are compared to menstruating women, but their symbolically similar ordeal is imposed from without.[19] Even in societies like ours with hazy transitions between childhood and becoming an adult, boys treat overcoming obstacles and confronting challenges as the surest signs of showing they are "a man." For many men, joining the military "makes a man" out of them. I doubt any woman who joined the Army would say it "made a woman" out of her. Men must be made in a way women are not.

Competence in dealing with the world and its challenges has traditionally been considered a sign of adulthood in boys but is less emphasized in girls. I think this reflects more than sexist cultural attitudes, present as they are. It is normal for a young man to focus on defining himself through external achievement in ways that for many young women are less personally compelling. Our cultures reflect, reinforce, and often exaggerate our biology.

Because male adulthood must be achieved, a man can lose adult male status in his own eyes and those of others by failing to assert or expand his boundaries. For example, Stephen Ducat observed that classical "Greek men experienced gender as a terrifyingly mutable trait. All that was required for an adult male citizen soldier . . . to be reduced to the social equivalent of a woman (or a slave) was to be seen as servile."[20]

These threats take a different form in our society. Unemployment, even when voluntary, threatens a man's sense of himself more radically than it does for women, attacking his sense of competence and preventing him from providing for those who depend on him. Recent research indicates that men who retire early have significantly higher death rates than do women who retire at the same age or even men who retire at a normal age.[21]

Neurological Dimensions

After observing differences in the behavior of little girls and little boys, Carol Gilligan modified Jean Piaget's boy-centered work on children's moral development, concluding, "Women not only define themselves in a context of human relationships but also judge themselves in terms of their ability to care. Women's place in man's life cycle has been that of nurturer, caretaker, and helpmate, the weaver of those networks of relationships on which she in turn relies."[22]

Today Gilligan's work appears supported by neuroscience. In *The Female Brain* and *The Male Brain*, neuropsychologist Louann Brizendine provides an entertaining account of recent gender-related research in neuroscience.[23] In its earliest weeks of existence, the fetus has a unisex brain, one that absent other intervention will ultimately develop into a female brain. However, around the eighth week of pregnancy future boys receive massive infusions of testosterone that actually shrink some parts of the brain while enlarging other parts. In particular, areas associated with communication and emotional memory are pruned, and those associated with sex and aggression grow. (I winced when I read this.) During the remaining months of pregnancy, testosterone and MIS, another hormone, defeminized the fetus's brain and body.

On average, female brains have 11 percent more neurons in brain centers for language and hearing than do men's. According to Brizendine these characteristics lead to "a person whose reality dictated that communication, connection, emotional sensitivity, and responsiveness were the primary values." Female infants less than twenty-four-hours old demonstrated this capacity to a significantly greater degree than did male babies of a similar age when responding to distressed cries of other infants.[24]

This process is not entirely biological. Arguing in favor of the nurture side of the nature/nurture dichotomy, Stephen Ducat observes, "Changes in testosterone levels are often preceded by certain social experiences. But once hormone levels are changed, they in turn affect the likelihood that particular behaviors will be expressed. Those behaviors will then lead to experiences that can further alter hormone levels and so on."[25] Culture also matters.

Whatever the ultimate causal findings may be, those parts of the brain oriented toward relationships with others are most strongly developed within women. Brain imaging research shows that "the mere act of observing or imagining another person in a particular emotional state can automatically activate similar brain patterns in the observer—and females are especially good at this kind of emotional mirroring." In fact, Brizendine notes, "Because of her ability to observe and feel emotional cues, a girl actually incorporates her mother's nervous system into her own."[26] Boundaries do not get much more open than that.

Every parent I have asked replied that girls and boys play together in different ways. Brizendine notes that little girls' "pretend play" normally focuses on "nurturing or caregiving relationships," whereas little boys' play concerns the game itself as well as "social rank, power, defense of territory, and physical strength."[27] Victory is so essential with small boys that they often cheat, and have to be taught to be good losers.

Very importantly, the male's greater orientation toward social rank is not the same as seeking domination. Studies of social leaders among boys found their leader status correlated less with their physical size than with their refusing "to back down during a conflict."[28] Aggression chiefly emerged during challenges to boundaries, not in picking on weaker boys.

Boys' and girls' behavioral patterns continue into adulthood. Manhood must be earned, and the bravery to overcome challenges is central to it. Many men have become friends with other men by fighting them physically. The conflict was not about dominance but about demonstrating strength in defending boundaries. This behavior is incomprehensible to every woman I have asked about it. I have never met a man who found it inexplicable. (See "A Bar Fight," http://dizerega.com/faultlines/appendices/.)

This difference also makes evolutionary sense. Individually, males are more expendable for a society than are women. Men therefore can better serve as its chief protectors during times of danger. To do this job well, men must be steadfast in threatening circumstances.

In contrast to women, Brizendine found that with men emotions are less likely to trigger gut sensations and more likely to trigger *subsequent* rational thought. When I am deeply bothered I often need considerable time to figure out how I genuinely feel. Women friends sometimes pick up that I am troubled before I can put it into words, leaving me to wonder, "How does she know?" Adult women, by contrast, are usually more adept than men at mirroring in interacting with others. There is good evolutionary logic for women developing this capacity better than men. It enables them better to anticipate the needs of preverbal infants.[29]

Nurture matters. But nurture does not paint on a blank canvas as postulated in the Lockean ideal of the human mind as a *tabula rasa*. It sculpts its patterns into an organism possessing predilections to experience and perceive its world in certain ways shaped in part by its gender and in part by its environment. The image of a sculptor bringing out a form intuited within a stone is a better image for this process than painting a blank canvas. As Brizendine puts it, "The brain's first organizing principle is clearly genes plus hormones, but we can't ignore the further sculpting that results from our interactions with other people and with the environment."[30]

In *Becoming Animal*, David Abram asks, "Once we acknowledge that our awareness is inseparable—even, in some sense, indistinguishable—from our own material physiology, can we really continue to maintain that mind remains alien to the rest of material nature?"[31] Abram's answer is no. Let us consider an example.

Chimpanzees living on the edge of forestland spend much of their time in a savannah environment thought to be similar to the one where humans first diverged from apes. These chimpanzees were discovered acting in unexpected ways. Unlike others living deep within forests, they live in caves, relax in waterholes on hot days, and make spears to hunt other mammals. Some even sharpen their spears with their teeth. Making tools to hunt other mammals is something only humans had previously been known to do.[32]

Apparently it took the savannah to bring about this change in chimpanzee behavior. As Abram put it, "Sentience is not an attribute of a body in isolation: it emerges from the ongoing encounter between our flesh and the forest of rhythms in which it finds itself."[33] Just as we are products of our society, so our society and we ourselves are expressions of our relationships with the earth.

It appears that nature and nurture intricately interpenetrate. Perception can alter hormone levels, and hormone levels can alter perception. The interrelationship between biology and culture probably extends to the earliest instances of organisms learning.[34] Human beings *cannot* be deeply understood separately from their environment, but by *environment* we must include the entire history of organism/environment interaction for millions of years or longer.

Describing these differences as arising from nature or nurture subtly perpetuates the modern conceit that somehow human beings are distinct from nature. The distinction we are discussing here is better described in terms of biology contrasted with nurture, *both being a part of nature.* We are describing codevelopment, with biology *and* nurture ultimately inextricable in nature.

The Pathological Feminine and the Pathological Masculine

There is a difference between a psychological development one-sidedly weighted in favor of the masculine or feminine and its pathological development. When the masculine focus on defining, maintaining, and extending boundaries denigrates the feminine or the feminine focus on weakening, opening, and dissolving denigrates the masculine, it become pathological because it rejects a central dimension of what it is to be human. Today the pathological masculine is *by far* our society's major personal and social problem, but an analogous pathology can exist with the feminine.

The pathological feminine controls through manipulation, blurring boundaries the better to mold another's actions to serve the manipulator's desire. Feminine manipulation takes forms such as, "If you *really* loved me/cared for me/respected me/are a good person, you would X." Sometimes this terminology is well taken. It is *because* this terminology is sometimes justified that it can *also* be used manipulatively in cases where it is *not* well taken. Manipulation is a tactic for those who believe themselves otherwise powerless in getting what they want and at least to some degree lack respect for the person manipulated. Manipulation is how the apparently mastered can sometimes dominate the master.

Masculine qualities become pathological when they actively reject the feminine and define themselves against it. Assertiveness twists into the desire to dominate. Focus easily becomes fanaticism and inability to appreciate the importance of context. Abstraction devalues the concrete, reducing it to what is useful, threatening, or irrelevant. When wedded to one-sided assertion, division leads to thinking in dichotomies and so to conflict. Staying purely analytical fosters a one-sided intellect. Divorced from intuitive and sensuous perception, the intellect becomes a mental mobius strip turning back upon itself, unable to perceive larger contexts of meaning and mystery. Emphasizing differences and disparaging similarities destroys empathy, facilitating fear of other people and the desire to dominate them in self-defense. Argument can become a tool for domination rather than for exploration and discovery.

Many feminists make the error of conflating masculine one-sidedness with pathological masculinity. They argue that the perfectly androgynous individual is the best human ideal. I think their image artificially simplifies human character and relations. Worse, it does so in ways ultimately *supporting* pathological masculinity.[35]

The currently favored term for societies rooted in pathological masculinity is *patriarchy*. This choice of words makes it too easy to equate biological gender with particular qualities, making it difficult to describe any strong sense of healthy masculinity. Masculinity is not simply the opposite of femininity. There is and must be a tension between the two because *they pull in opposite directions along a continuum where there is no one right balance.* This distinction is rooted in when, where, and how much boundaries matter. Each set of qualities helps define and deepen the other, and different contexts favor different balances. But tension need not mean antagonism, and those who manage this tension well are hardly in equilibrium.

Patriarchy also blurs two different expressions of masculinity, enabling pathological masculinity to appear as simply a strong variant of, to use Harvey Mansfield's terminology, "manliness," rather than the perversion of male human potentials that it is.[36] (See "Neoconservative 'Manliness,'" http://dizerega.com/faultlines/appendices.)

Patriarchy reads into one-sidedly masculine development a taste for domination that need not be there. Many one-sidedly masculine men sacrifice their lives for those they love, whether on battlefields or in long hours spent in unrewarding and often demeaning work. Finally, the term leaves any sense of strong masculinity open to appropriation by advocates of its pathological variant, which is exactly what today's culture warriors have done. Men and women alike are the poorer for it.

For all these reasons I prefer terms such as Val Plumwood's "master model" with its focus on domination for describing the problems classified as patriarchal.[37] In Plumwood's sense, the master model arises out of a strongly dualistic mentality; as Evelyn Fox Keller put it, "Domination guarantees the indissolubility of differences by construing all difference as inequality."[38] This attitude has a masculine focus on maintaining and strengthening boundaries, but within a context of hierarchy, distrust, and fear. Plumwood's master model spotlights problems usually labeled patriarchical, but describes them in terms of qualities rather than identifying them with gender.

In societies rooted in mastery, Plumwood states, "power construes and constricts difference in terms of an inferior and alien realm."[39] One side of a dualism justifies its domination over the other by arguing that differences imply inferiority. She argues that reliance on dualisms of this sort is key to understanding Western thinkers as different as Plato, Aristotle, Descartes, Rousseau, Hegel, and Marx.[40] As her examples attest, Western society has long had a strong dualistic tendency that evaluates differences as sometimes exotic and interesting but always as seen through relations of inferiority or superiority.

This important point distinguishes pathological masculinity from the more frequently encountered one-sided development of masculine values because a man feels constrained to "be a man" without necessarily desiring to dominate. Such men often seek women to provide the feminine values they know they need in their own lives. That does not mean they seek to dominate them.

Domination always implies a lack of respect for the other. Normal people are uncomfortable dominating an equal; however discomfort falls away if they believe the other is inferior, leaving both themselves and the other susceptible to manipulation by those seeking to dominate both. Authoritarian and totalitarian movements present their targets as personally defective, as well as wrong, to neutralize many people's opposition to their crimes. The Nazis did it to the Jews; the Communists did it to the bourgeoisie. Today the American right wing uses the same logic against liberals and increasingly Hispanics and Muslims as well. Extreme degradation can eliminate any feeling of responsibility to actually deal with peoples' arguments, hopes, or expectations of fair treatment while making it easy to employ violence against them, initially verbally but ultimately physically.[41]

All societies engage in these practices when they are at war. It is hard to kill a person one identifies with, but slaughtering a Gook, raghead, Commie, sand nigger, running dog, class enemy, jihadist, or bourgeois pig is another matter.[42] In this respect totalitarianism is the application of the logic of war internally instead of externally. That culture warriors employ this kind of dehumanization against people *within their own society* is disturbing evidence that when they use the language of war, *they mean it*. Violence against others is prevented not by respect or recognition of common norms, but by the belief they cannot (yet) get away with it. A similar process happens among Muslim extremists, the authoritarian left, or any similar group. But in today's America the problem is overwhelmingly associated with culture warriors.

POWER, MASTERY, AND HIERARCHY

We all need power to act effectively, and we all encounter times where our power to act is insufficient. Power is fundamental to life. In human relationships power manifests in complex and often subtle ways. There is the power that comes from persuading others and the power that comes from commanding or manipulating them, or both. Power makes getting what we want easier. In seeking power we can shift from wanting it because we need it to wanting it because it seems to simplify our lives. Problems exist because of inadequate power, so getting more power will solve all our problems.

But like fire, power is a useful servant and a dangerous master. There is a high hidden price, described by Maildoma Some: "When power comes out of its hiddenness, it shrinks the person who brought it into the open and turns that person into a servant. The only way that overt power can remain visible is by being fed, and he who knows how to make power visible ends up trapped into keeping that power visible."[43]

If we feel we need to rely on power as a source of attraction, we are open only to relationships available on terms that preclude relations with who we actually are. Others relate only with the image of power we project. That keeps us "safe" but at the price of never opening our hearts enough really to connect with another. When we desire more power than another person has before we feel able to relate to that person, we never encounter a Thou, only an It. And a person attracted to another because of his or her power also relates to an It. But possessing or dominating Its is ultimately not fulfilling because what we really need are relationships with Thous.

Significantly, in societies deeply rooted in mastery as their defining relationship, *friendship* was often distrusted. In classical China Confucius was wary of but not quite condemnatory toward friendship, the one relationship between people of his time that was not hierarchical. Later Neo-Confucians, writing after China had become far more despotic, found friendship among equals to be undesirable.[44] The same attitude existed in Europe. Writing from within a deeply hierarchical European society, Francis Bacon observed, "There is little friendship in the world and least between equals."[45] In such cultures "masterless men" were considered a social and political threat.[46]

The person of power becomes an intermediary, an It, between domination and the dominated. Relationships with Its are instrumental on all sides. I relate with you because you are useful to me. If I could gain more by breaking it off, I would drop you in favor of more profitable relationships. You reciprocate on both counts. But for you to be able effectively to affirm my inner value rather than just my power, I must see you as possessing value yourself. Because this value is internal, manifested through the other's being, I can experience it only by opening myself to you, and letting you in while simultaneously respecting and valuing you for yourself. As I do, the world of instrumental relations is transformed into something quite different.

In mastery societies human relations are hierarchical, reflecting and usually emphasizing differences in power. Such societies usually recognize a common humanity among their members but emphasize differences as more important than similarities. These differences form a hierarchy and justify the rule of some over others. If necessary they justify employing violence against those lower in the hierarchy.

The dominator's boundaries matter but those of the dominated do not. We see this as America's government becomes increasingly independent of its citizens and its corporations increasingly independent of their customers. In the United States those who rule increasingly employ secrecy toward the public. These same people also claim that "mere" citizens have no inviolable sphere of privacy themselves.

The same pattern appears in the corporate world. Substances that spill over into others' property and bodies are said to be "proprietary." Fracking substances get in people's drinking water, while corporations say that what they inject into the ground is safe but refuse to divulge what it is. This insanity even extends to the codes used in voting machines. Only private companies know the codes that record the public's votes. Meanwhile, ordinary Americans have a rapidly shrinking sphere of personal privacy.

Formal party affiliation does not matter. Former Democratic Representative Jane Harman of California approved of warrantless wiretaps of plain citizens but was incensed when her conversations were picked up in a completely legal wiretap.[47] It is hard to find a better example of the dominator's mentality, and Harman's example demonstrates that it need not be male or Republican. Harman was no patriarch, but she was a dominator, the values she represented, masculine.

America's Founders intended the opposite relationship between power and people. Government was to be open to the citizens, who ultimately controlled it. The constitutional protection given a free press was to ensure this openness even when those in office tried to hide what they were doing. Meanwhile, citizens were protected from abuses by the powerful through a Bill of Rights. No one ever criticized our Founding Fathers for being insufficiently masculine.

Pathological masculinity is the purest expression of domination as an ethos. All other values are subordinate to it, but domination takes different forms depending on the context within which it manifests. However it may manifest, at its core the reigning principle is domination. The form of the moment is simply its cloak.

Nihilism denies that there are any intrinsic values. Pathological masculinity recognizes no other ultimate value than domination and only when it is the dominator. It is ultimately nihilistic and has more than a passing relationship with the spiritual nihilism I previously described.

As we shall see in the next chapters, the collapse of Enlightenment modernity's moral compass triggered a crisis of nihilism of epidemic proportions, first in Europe and today in the United States. Its clearest contemporary American expressions are among the culture warriors, both secular and religious, who talk the talk of values but at bottom seek only domination.

ROADS TO NIHILISM: THE INTELLECTUAL CRISIS

Tell me how you seek and I will tell you what you are seeking.

—Ludwig Wittgenstein

The secular modern ideal of knowledge derives from logocentric images of reality. Only from this perspective do we encounter "objective truth," which we contrast with subjectivism and fantasy. But by setting mythos aside and focusing on logos alone, modern civilization developed a dangerous one-sidedness. The rejection of mythos as a valid form of knowledge ultimately undermined modernity's ethical foundations, with disastrous consequences for Europe in the twentieth century and potentially for America today.

As chapter 1 explained, modern secular culture can be usefully understood as a complex intertwining of two logocentric traditions: the Baconian view that knowledge is power in service to human ends and the contrasting liberal Lockean argument that while this outlook holds well enough for the nonhuman world, human beings are exempt from it.

Baconian and Lockean perspectives are usually considered compatible, and in many ways they have been. However, they are rooted in different assumptions, and their views ultimately carry different implications. Today the tensions between these two logocentric perspectives compose the central cultural fault line running through the modern West. Many of the twentieth century's defining intellectual, social, and political events as well as the crisis of our own time emerged from these stresses. Many are rooted in the intellectual and moral collapse of liberalism.

In all their many forms, liberals view the individual as society's fundamental moral and ethical unit. In this sense they agree that all individuals are equal. A good society arises out of the cooperative interactions of inter-dependent equals.

While Bacon was no liberal, liberalism's principles created and sustained the institutions that facilitated the discovery of Baconian knowledge. The Baconian and Lockean outlooks were symbiotic in practice, a symbiosis depending on maintaining a sharp distinction between the moral human and amoral natural world. When this distinction broke down, a slow process of cultural disintegration ensued, with liberal and Baconian traditions alike ultimately the losers. This chapter charts one major path to this unfortunate outcome.

Power and Logos

Abandoning mythos narrowed the criteria for truth and meaning to the power of explicit ideas and impersonal evidence for them. Logos focuses on external relations between what appear to be fundamentally distinct entities, an outlook comfortable with a mechanistic view of reality. Because so many of us still experience our physical world in these terms, these assumptions easily carried over into today's post-Newtonian world, even though scientists themselves have moved far from this view.

Measurement, prediction, and especially repeatable experiments consti-tute science's principal means for discovering reliable knowledge. Along the way these methods also advance human control. William Barrett called this approach "man's self-assertion in the face of nature." At its core, "objectivity consists precisely in those quantifiable aspects that fit into our calculation and control. Nature sinks to the level of mere material for exploitation, and man towers as the master over it."[1]

Maximizing the power to manipulate and control some *thing* is the hidden value at the core of the Baconian approach to knowledge. As tradi-tionally conceived, scientific knowledge is confirmed through the predic-tion and, even better, the successful control of a world of objects. Objects are useful or interesting to us, impediments to our projects, or irrelevant.

They have no inner life, no presence in their own right, no interiority we can relate to or respect. We relate to objects in terms of our power to manipulate or understand them. All else being equal, the more power we exercise over objects, the greater their potential utility.

Early in the rise of science René Descartes captured this vision, writing, "Give me matter and motion, and I shall make the world once more."[2] This vision's attractiveness lay in its double promise of power to improve the human condition and knowledge free from the turbulence and controversies into which the Christian West had collapsed. But a high price was exacted for these alluring promises.

Contemporary physicist Steven Weinberg observed, "The more the universe seems comprehensible, the more pointless it seems."[3] Weinberg is not criticizing this outlook. He accepts it. Nor are his views outliers within the scientific community. In such a world, if a broader context of meaning exists it must come from without. It is not intrinsic to matter.

This conclusion is not a scientific discovery. It is an assumption built into the methodologies scientists accept as able to reveal scientific knowledge. Biologist Richard Lewontin observed, "It is not that the methods and institutions of science somehow compel us to accept a material explanation of the phenomenal world, but, on the contrary, that we are forced by our a priori adherence to material causes to create an apparatus of investigation and a set of concepts that produce material explanations, no matter how counter-intuitive, no matter how mystifying to the uninitiated."[4]

Methodologies do not discover the basic nature of the world; they assume it. Scientific methodologies designed to learn all we can about a world of objects cannot discover the degree to which the world's contents are not objects. What does not fit a methodology cannot be illuminated by it. The Western ideal for acquiring knowledge has proven to be an unsurpassed means for manipulating and controlling things. However, if intrinsic meaning or value exists, *it cannot be perceived this way.*

Because it cannot be directly observed, predicted or even clearly defined, consciousness eludes scientific exploration, although with the rise of neuroscience and brain imaging we are able to find many correlations between people's reports of their conscious states and external physically measurable correlates. "Meaning" refers to a mental insight about significance. It cannot be discovered "objectively."

The unsettling implications of accepting a meaningless model of the universe in order to understand it were initially moderated by two factors. First was the exhilarating sense of unbounded possibilities opening up through physical science's world-transforming discoveries. In a world filled with enormous suffering and destitution these real and tangible promises usually counted for more than cautionary warnings by a few theologians and philosophers. And these promises were often kept. The universe appeared to lie open before us to explore, study, and perhaps in time even tame and subject to human ends.

Second, this view arose within a Western Christian world sharing an almost universal belief in a transcendent God and in humankind's special place in his divine plan. The universe might be a great machine, but it was *God's* machine. People didn't worry about whether there was any meaning inherent in a pulley because they knew it reflected its maker's intentions. Both revelation and what we could learn about God's handiwork through science could shed light on his reasoning, but God's reasons remained extrinsic to the world. Meaning was transcendental with no necessary connection to mere matter.

As special subjects created in God's image, human beings were excluded from this view of physical reality. Ultimately we were separate from nature. The world was made for us, and we were commanded by scripture and enabled by science to go forth and subdue it.

From philosophers and scientists to men and women on the street, most people believed we possessed free will, were subject to divine rules we could either accept or reject, and as individuals with souls possessed intrinsic importance in the greater scheme of things. While modernity's logocentric vision removed meaning from the physical world, its cultural context retained it for us. At least it did so until crises during the late nineteenth and early twentieth centuries swept away the comforting veils of human uniqueness.

DISSOLVING THE BOUNDARIES

Early liberal thinkers rooted their arguments for individual freedom and equality, private property, and government by consent within a religious framework that assumed individuals were morally valuable. Everything else was valued to the degree it served us. Here Locke's liberal Protestantism distinguished his political theory fundamentally from Thomas Hobbes's (1588-1679) earlier, more Baconian analysis. When liberalism's theological foundations were secure, so was the moral edifice Locke and others had erected upon them.

The central tension between the Baconian commitment to knowledge as power in service to humanity and the liberal argument that individuals are exempt from this perspective remained relatively harmless so long as the case for human uniqueness remained persuasive. The uniqueness claimed was not just quantitative, which no one questioned, but also qualitative, so that moral categories applied to people but not to the rest of the world. Only such an argument could justify a strong distinction between human moral worth and everything else's status as a tool for our use, impediment to our goals, or irrelevant.

By the late eighteenth and early nineteenth centuries many liberals no longer believed in even a liberal form of the traditional Christian God. They had shifted toward belief in a more distant Deist God, one who after creating the world for all intent and purposes simply watched it. With God not involved in human affairs, the case for human rights needed a new foundation.

One initially promising alternative played an important role in America's founding and in making the case against slavery. Jefferson's and other Founders' argument that rights were self-evident arose from their belief that freedom and responsibility were fundamental dimensions of human nature. We *could not* alienate our moral responsibility, and therefore our freedom of choice was self-evident. In the context of the times this belief depended on maintaining the view that human beings were radically distinct from nature.

More immediately, the Declaration of Independence's assertion of self-evident rights arose from practical arguments drawing on legal principles reflecting the practical experiences of human life. Unlike animals, slaves were held responsible for their actions. If my horse kicked you, I was liable under the law. If my slave kicked you, the slave was liable. Human beings could not alienate responsibility and therefore could not alienate moral agency. Machines were tools for attaining their owners' purposes. Animals were treated as machines. But slaves always had responsibility for their actions.

Genuine ownership of another person was therefore impossible. Efforts to subjugate human beings and make them property violated the universally recognized fact of humans' moral responsibility and therefore their intrinsic freedom. It was a "legal fiction."[5]

The Declaration's argument focused on the moral structure intrinsic to human life. However most people were seeking a philosophical equivalent to God's *commands*. They were looking for *binding* moral principles *outside* human life and sought a stronger foundation for rights than arguments rooted in universal human experience.

Consequently, philosophers attempted to discover new foundations for establishing absolute moral principles able to replace increasingly contested theological ones. The most influential of these attempts were Immanuel Kant's (1724–1804) deontological theory of ethics and the utilitarian moral theories initially developed by Jeremy Bentham (1748–1832) and James Mill (1773–1836). They approached ethics from opposite directions.

Deontological ethics bases right action on following a rule. Think of something like the Ten Commandments but derived from reason rather than from God. Kantian ethics were based on abstract principles that must be universally applied. Kant argued that the determining factor of whether an action is morally right was whether the person acted from duty to a rule that could be universalized. He denied the moral relevance of practical results. If I intended to deceive, even if by so doing I got positive results for myself or for others, my act was morally wrong because no universally coherent duty can be devised requiring me to lie.

By contrast, utilitarians argued that ethics ultimately depended on getting desirable results. Their standard was to act for the greatest good for the greatest number. If I intend to deceive in order to serve a greater good measured by results and succeed, I act appropriately. In utilitarian ethics results trump rules, whereas in Kantian ethics rules trump results.

Many people found Kant's lack of concern for the results to be a fatal shortcoming. Results matter. Utilitarianism dealt more satisfactorily with the issue of results and in one form or another is probably today's dominant secular moral perspective. But utilitarianism has problems of its own.

A classic objection with considerable contemporary relevance asks, if torturing an innocent person increases everyone else's happiness, should we torture? Strict utilitarianism has no argument against going ahead. Decent people cringe at this conclusion. Here many believe a Kantian perspective has the better case.

Recent findings in neuroscience suggest that being at ease with strictly utilitarian thinking can be evidence of brain injury. Stuart Kauffman describes research investigating people who sustained damage to "a small region in the ventromedial frontal cortex." This damage seems to disrupt connections between our emotional and rational capacities. Such people readily agree to sacrifice the innocent for the benefit of all. Kauffman writes, "They have become good utilitarians."[6]

Utilitarianism confronts another problem: *who determines* what counts as results? Who calculates the net amount of happiness? When and where do we draw the line in determining something's effects as being bad or good? Strictly speaking we can never tell because the impact of our actions extend outward in space and time, like ripples in a pond, interacting with others' actions. But for utilitarians a decision must be made. Those benefiting at one point will want the line drawn in their favor, even if it injured others earlier or might injure others in the future. Those worried about being injured will want it drawn in their favor. No objective demarcation principle exists.

Power is the ultimate arbiter underneath all the fine talk about maximizing the good, because we *cannot* know the full results of our actions as they send those ripples off into the future. Those who are weaker are not in a position to determine where the line must be drawn between ripples that matter and those considered too far away to count. By their very nature, future gains and losses will get less consideration because they will have weaker or absent advocates.

But why discount future generations? Many parents make enormous personal sacrifices for their children despite knowing nothing about their future desires or choices in life. Their sacrifices are part of what it is to be a good parent. Yet future children's voices are weakest in utilitarian deliberations. It may be that the good is what benefits the greatest number, but there is no way to calculate it.

Neither Kantian nor utilitarian ethics ultimately proved convincing enough to take the place of weakened theories of natural right. Few investigated the insights that had motivated our Founders. As a fallback, many "practical" liberals simply based their arguments on liberalism's political and economic success. Liberalism works.

Working was usually defined in terms of the power and prosperity unleashed by liberal institutions, subtly shifting the ground under liberalism's moral foundations. Liberalism's opponents strengthened this tendency, for they denied the relevance of its founding ethical arguments. Marxists and some conservative thinkers alike argued there was no major distinction between Lockean liberalism and Hobbes's Baconian perspective. It was all basically Hobbesian, and all ultimately translated into power.[7]

SCIENCE AND LIBERALISM

In important respects modern science helped lay liberalism's foundation. In a world where most human relationships were formally hierarchical, the "republic of letters" out of which modern science grew enabled men and even the occasional woman to meet as relative equals. As Michael Polanyi observed, "In the free cooperation of independent scientists we . . . find a highly simplified model of a free society."[8] Locke was a physician and a member of the Royal Society as well as a philosopher and political thinker and so had extensive personal experience with this kind of free association. I think we do not go too far in saying that among its other qualities Enlightenment science served as a kind of successful trial run for liberal principles in an illiberal world.

Both liberalism and science accept the ideal of formally equal status among members of a community and people's freedom to follow their insights. The scientific ideal is that all those making an argument are subject to common standards when evaluating their work, but they are free to work on whatever questions they choose. They are entrepreneurs of knowledge and free citizens of what Polanyi termed the "Republic of Science." While never perfectly attained, these ideals have been realized closely enough so that reliable knowledge discovered by scientists continues to expand, rather than petrifying into a *ruling* orthodoxy. Scientific orthodoxies abound but do not rule and are often replaced.

The basic ideals scientists practiced within their own community liberals advocated for humankind in general. In both science and liberalism persuasion was supposed to trump power or claims of authority. In a liberal society all people were to be equal in the eyes of the law and enjoy freedom to live their lives by their own lights so long as they respected similar freedom for others. In a genuine sense both science and liberalism sought to define and protect a sphere where people could freely explore opportunities.

As with science, generalizations about liberal equality and freedom conceal many complexities and have never been perfectly realized. Even so, the historically unusual degree to which they have been realized, as well as the widespread illegitimacy of anyone's explicitly denying them, distinguishes liberal modernity from other kinds of civilization. It is symbolically fitting that Isaac Newton and John Locke knew each other. Over a century later Thomas Jefferson, one of America's greatest liberals, wrote Benjamin Rush that Locke, Newton, and Bacon were "my trinity of the three greatest men the world had ever produced."[9] Jefferson even commissioned their portraits, which were hung in his home. Whatever the personal beliefs of individual scientists, the intellectual and moral connection between science and liberalism is profound.

A powerful tension also lay hidden within this relationship. Originally invisible, today it impinges massively on our lives. This tension rests on the nature of humanity's status in the world.

As scientific knowledge grew, the case for excluding people from the kinds of analysis scientists applied to animals increasingly appeared arbitrary. As people learned more and more about the world and God's special creative gaps continued to shrink, it seemed we might ultimately be as much subject to scientists' research as anything else in the world.

Writing well before Locke, Sir Francis Bacon had envisioned an elite of scientific experts toward whom tolerant principles would apply, while all others would be ruled for their own good. In many ways Bacon conceived scientists as a new priesthood exercising benevolent control over its laity.[10] Still rooted in premodern ways of thinking, he had difficulty seeing relationships among human beings, or even among scientists, in terms that were not hierarchical and defined by power, as my reference to his view of friendship in the previous chapter illustrated. He assumed that despite their power scientists somehow could keep their disinterested ideals of service toward a humanity that had become their ward. But for a long time Bacon's vision of wise scientific overseers had not amounted to much.

In large part science had advanced because it did *not* resemble Bacon's utopian ideal and no permanent hierarchy existed to oversee scientific exploration as a whole. As a human activity science is ethically liberal. The history of science is of one group of experts after another being replaced by younger scientists successfully challenging the received knowledge of their time. Entrenched groups would often resist new theories and evidence, but whether they ultimately prevailed was based on how persuasive *others* found their views. They had no power to impose an orthodoxy for long. In contrast to Bacon, there is much truth in Nobel Laureate Richard Feynman's definition of science as "the belief in the ignorance of experts."[11]

The success of liberal principles, particularly their place deep within the scientific community, combined with the firm belief that we were different from animals, kept Bacon's authoritarian ideal largely at bay.

Some intellectuals advocated variants of Bacon's vision, but few listened. Yet it would always remain a potential development because science's methods had evolved in harmony with that vision even if science as a human endeavor had not. Scientific knowledge could always be used in service to power and domination.

Now the case for liberalism's ethical foundation was being dissolved by science itself. God's role was increasingly questioned, while the habits of thought logocentric civilization encouraged undermined philosophers' attempts to replace him in the realm of ethics. We were increasingly suspected of being the products of natural processes ourselves. If we could come to understand these processes we could eventually manage them rather than letting them unfold without human direction. Of course, this ideal meant that some would do the managing and others would be managed.

Social Darwinism and Liberalism's Decline

This issue came to a head when Charles Darwin published his theory of natural selection and the origin of species. Ideas of societies as evolving entities were in the air, and influential work on that subject was being written by liberals such as Herbert Spencer (1820–1903) seeking to integrate the study of human society with principles applying to the natural world. In Spencer's view liberalism's traditional dependence on theological or philosophical moral principles could be replaced with science. As his American colleague William Graham Sumner (1840–1910) put it, "Before the tribunal of nature a man has no more right to life than a rattlesnake; he has no more right to liberty than any wild beast; his right to pursuit of happiness is nothing but a license to maintain the struggle for existence."[12]

But things did not work out the way they imagined.

Charles Darwin (1809–1882) was both a liberal and a deeply humane man. He held the slave societies he observed in contempt and hoped that his argument in *The Origin of Species* would improve our treatment of animals once we realized our common kinship. But things did not work out the way Darwin hoped either.

Darwin had developed an insightful explanation of how morality itself was a natural evolutionary development that, once established, trumped natural selection. He argued that morality arose naturally within the world rather than from divine or human sources external to it, writing in *The Descent of Man*, "The aid which we feel impelled to give to the helpless is mainly an incidental result of the instinct of sympathy, which was originally acquired as part of the social instincts, but subsequently rendered . . . more tender and more widely diffused."[13] Morality was dependent on neither God nor logocentric rules discovered by philosophers.

While later powerfully validated,[14] Darwin's insights about the evolutionary foundations of cooperation and morality were swamped at the time by opposing interpretations and misinterpretations of his work. For most people, the idea that morality might be an emergent property of the world itself seemed inconceivable. Darwin's insights were largely ignored.

Sadly, many of Darwin's supporters did not share his broad moral sense and considered animals to be things rather than subjects, no more intrinsically worthy of respect than a rock. Some argued that if we looked at human beings unblinkingly and without sentimentality, that is also what we were, drawing conclusions Darwin himself opposed. Like da Vinci's ideas about knowledge and love, David Hume's and Adam Smith's analysis of sympathy, and our Founders' views about inalienable rights, Darwin's approach represented a road not taken, one where value is located within the world rather than without it.[15]

The term *social Darwinism* has been used to describe a claimed connection between Darwin's evolutionary ideas and important social theories of the time. The term became well known when applied to Sumner and Spencer, whose ideas did not grow from Darwin's, and omitted others who could as easily be included.[16] But it has taken on a life of its own, and so long as we remember Darwin would not have considered himself a social Darwinist, the term is useful.

Early social Darwinists such as Spencer and Sumner were genuine liberals. They praised the culture of commerce as distinct from and opposed to the world's older militaristic traditions. While their advocacy often put them on the side of businesses, they were critics of companies supporting tariffs, imperialism, or similar political ventures to benefit themselves. They were outspoken anti-imperialists and committed advocates of what Samuel Huntington describes as "business pacifism."[17]

In making their arguments Spencer and Sumner crossed an analytic ridge, entering a new intellectual watershed. They used illiberal reasoning to defend liberal institutions, shifting from the individual as society's fundamental ethical unit toward biological standards for success, from defending liberal principals ethically to the seemingly more secure task of rooting them in science. But their "Darwinian" thinking, as Richard Hofstadter later put it, "was a neutral instrument, capable of supporting opposite ideologies."[18]

How far social Darwinist reasoning departed from traditional liberalism depended on the unit of evolutionary selection. Illiberal social Darwinists picked groups rather than individuals, choosing races, nationalities, or states, and argued for *their* superiority as evolutionary units. For example, in 1906 the prominent Progressive Lester Ward wrote that race conflict was the "sociological homologue of natural selection."[19] If individuals needed to be sacrificed for the flourishing of the race, nationality, or state, that was just how it was.

Sumner and Spencer emphasized competition between individuals but they also emphasized the evolutionary advantages of greater cooperation opened by commercial culture. By choosing groups over individuals, "collectivist" social Darwinists changed the dynamic to conflict between groups. They were powerful advocates for imperialism, racism, and eugenics. In Europe many had no commitment to liberal institutions, but in America many did.

Collectivist social Darwinists who supported liberal institutions abandoned the liberal affirmation of the individual for the different ideal of individuals as contributors to social health and human progress. Unlike Sumner, collectivist social Darwinists were among America's most committed political and economic reformers, constituting a large part of the Progressive movement. Among their motives for promoting reform was a concern for the biological vitality of the United States and individuals' roles in contributing to that vitality. Often these concerns dovetailed with concerns for individual well-being typical of liberalism, but when this well-being was evaluated from a collective perspective individual citizens became resources valued for their utility to the country. Sometimes the results were tragically antiliberal.

Eugenics illustrates this profound shift in perspective, comprising one of the most deservedly embarrassing periods in America's scientific history. Across the political spectrum, but with considerable Progressive leadership, citizens regarded as unfit for biological reasons were sterilized, often unwillingly. In *Mein Kampf* Hitler admiringly cited America's role in eugenics. When the Nazis later vastly increased the rate of sterilization of their own citizens, some prominent American eugenicists admitted they were envious. Ultimately scientific research discredited eugenics, and support for its ideals died in all but the more racist regions of the country. (See "Eugenics," http://dizerega.com/faultlines/appendices/.)

Eugenics died a well-deserved death, but the dilemmas it highlighted remain. What roles do morality and meaning play in a world understandable only by scientific standards? Eugenics was a troubling example of scientific reasoning's inability to supply the moral foundations needed to maintain a free society, even as science itself depends on those principles within its own community. Science was proving no better at protecting human freedom than seventeenth-century Christianity had proved able to accommodate religious toleration.

Bacon had envisioned rule by scientific experts to benefit a largely ignorant population. Scientists were to be a new priesthood exercising benevolent control over its laity. If knowledge's underlying goal is power to improve the human condition, as Bacon had proclaimed, and if people are not really distinct from entities best approached as objects, the clear-eyed pursuit of knowledge should also lead to power over people, for the good of the whole.

Liberal principles and the general belief that human beings were not animals had kept this authoritarian ideal largely at bay. Now these principles were being dissolved by science itself, with liberal complicity. We appeared to be products of natural processes, and if we understood these processes we could manage them ourselves rather than letting them unfold without direction. Of course, some should do the managing and others be managed.

It came to a question, ultimately, of who wielded power in the absence of an encompassing moral framework to limit power and give it direction. Power was becoming the genuine principle underlying reality as Bacon's goal of serving humanity was to be interpreted only by the powerful over everyone else. The German philosopher Friedrich Nietzsche (1844–1900) realized this more clearly than perhaps any other thinker of his time.

THE WILL TO POWER

Nietzsche blasted the cheerful liberal and early social Darwinian assumptions that took Europe's inherited moral world for granted, arguing that society's comfortable moral underpinnings had dissolved, but the implications were not yet widely grasped. What seemed to be an exhilarating opening to freedom from God's arbitrary dictates was in fact a leap into a yawning abyss. In his description of the "death of God" Nietzsche wrote, "*We have killed him*—you and I. All of us are his murderers. But how did we do this? How could we drink up the sea? Who gave us the sponge to wipe away the entire horizon? What were we doing when we unchained this earth from its sun? Whither is it moving now? Whither are we moving? Away from all suns? Are we not plunging continually? Backward, sideward, forward, in all directions? Is there still any up or down? Are we not straying, as through an infinite nothing?"[20]

For all his ability to foresee the collapse of the West's inherited moral traditions, Nietzsche, unlike Darwin, could not see an alternative ethical framework within the world itself. For Nietzsche the result was nihilism. "What does nihilism mean?" he asked. "*The highest values devaluate themselves.* The aim is lacking; 'why' finds no answer."[21] The result for many, he argued, was a general paralysis of the will.[22]

Religions decrying power had been successful efforts by the weak to dominate the strong through the power of guilt. Power had always been the real standard for past action, albeit usually hiding under moralistic frosting. Power should now be embraced openly, to create a new world free from illusion or the envy of the weak.

Value was to be declared by those strong enough to impose a new morality. The "will to power" was the true standard for all action in the world. There is considerable discussion as to what Nietzsche meant by this term, but many of his readers interpreted him as advocating "a Zarathustrian standpoint of 'active nihilism.'"[23]

When this outlook was combined with antiliberal politics the results were catastrophic. Whatever his intentions, Nietzsche strengthened the rise of a power-oriented nihilism in Europe. Mussolini put it clearly: "In truth, we are relativists *par excellence*, and the moment relativism linked up with Nietzsche, and with his Will to Power, was when Italian Fascism became, as it still is, the most magnificent creation of an individual and a national Will to Power."[24]

Nietzsche also helped legitimize what I call pathological masculinity. The pathological masculine is the cold, hard, virile assertion of pure will, the will to power in its "life-affirming" form. Feminine values needed to be rejected.

As for women, Nietzsche wrote in *Thus Spoke Zarathustra*, "Everything about woman is a riddle, and everything about woman has one solution: that is pregnancy. Man is for woman a means: the end is always the child. But what is woman for man? A real man wants two things: danger and play. Therefore he wants woman as the most dangerous plaything. Man should be educated for war, and woman for the recreation of the warrior; all else is folly."[25]

Ayn Rand

Yet it was a woman, Ayn Rand, who was Nietzsche's primary vector into American culture. In 1991 the Library of Congress and Book-of-the-Month Club surveyed the books Americans found most important in their lives.

More Americans reported Rand's *Atlas Shrugged* than any other title except the Bible. Over fifty years after her books appeared, Rand's writings sell in the hundreds of thousands with twelve million of her books in print.[26] Many secular conservatives owe more to Rand than to traditional conservative thinkers. She even dominates the thinking of right-wingers claiming to be religious, such as Paul Ryan.

Ayn Rand wrapped Nietzsche's ideas in the ill-fitting but for Americans culturally comfortable language of rights. Her explicitly Nietzschean terminology largely disappeared, replaced by language closer to Sumner's social Darwinism. But underneath her rhetoric her reasoning was even more illiberal.

Rand celebrated capitalism for enabling the superior to realize their visions, making life better for the inferior along the way so long as the inferior stayed out of the way. But when the existence of the weaker inconvenienced the stronger, the will of the powerful trumped the rights of the weaker. This belief flies in the face of her public persona but not of her real beliefs or the ultimate impact of her writing.

Late in her life Rand gave an address at West Point. A cadet asked what she thought of American aggression against the Indians. She replied: "They had no right to a country merely because they were born here and then acted like savages. . . . You can't claim one should respect the 'rights' of Indians, when they had no concept of rights and no respect for rights. . . . Any European who brought with him an element of civilization had the right to take over this continent, and it's great that some of them did."[27]

Darwin, the social Darwinists, and Nietzsche all denied that human beings were privileged players on the global stage. If Darwin's work on morality and evolution was ignored, as it usually was, this claim gave the edge to Bacon's view of knowledge over the liberal view. What each of us possessed, and some considerably more than others, was will, and will mattered to the degree it was accompanied by power. Even many identifying themselves as liberals accepted this message. But when a moral framework larger than will and power is abandoned, the center of intellectual gravity becomes domination.

The Paradox of Power

When subordinated to a vision, power makes great things, great deeds, and great people possible. However, when sought for its own sake power never keeps its promise to expand those who possesses it. It shrinks them.

The Baconian vision ultimately delivered all that was most vulnerable in the world into human power, but at the cost of ultimate meaning. In a meaningless world what is not subordinated is a source of threatening uncertainty. Power and control must always expand if we are to be safer. This logic is the logic of empire, whether applied to people or to the natural world.

Today the United States is the most economically and militarily powerful country on the planet, its military budget nearly equal to the rest of the world combined. Yet Americans are fearful. It becomes in "our interests" to control fights between tribes in Afghanistan or intervene in Libya or perhaps launch a war on Iran. Along the way Americans sacrifice their schools, roads, and domestic well-being, all of which are increasingly outclassed by their equivalents in many countries.

When the logic of power overrides any sense of limits, power has become the master. Hooked on the drug of domination, the power-craving seek more. Americans' domestic politics are subordinated to the needs of empire. Empire rules America. Only when power is subordinated to a larger context, to values that establish appropriate limits, is power a servant to human beings rather than their master.

The Illusions of Efficiency

The worship of power is hidden behind the seemingly benign term *efficiency*. As our servant, efficiency helps us gain our goals with more resources left over afterward for pursuing other goals. What counts as efficient is determined by the nature of our goals. Sometimes efficiency is important, as when we build a house. But for many human purposes efficiency is not so important. It makes little sense to seek efficiency in being a loving human being, although if I use my time efficiently I may have fewer distractions from loving. Having friends enables me to accomplish things I otherwise could not, but if I choose my friends based on how efficiently they can help me attain my goals, I am no friend.

When power dominates, efficiency becomes independent from human ends and serves power, not people. It does so by diminishing everything's capacity to resist being used as power dictates. When efficiency becomes the standard for good government, powerless subjects result, because powerful citizens can resist government and make it inefficient. When efficiency dominates economics, humans become powerless resources best allocated efficiently by managers.

When efficiency is a good in itself, everyone but the powerful is disempowered. The Faustian vision of knowledge as power to serve humanity ends with humanity as servants to power. In a world ultimately without meaning, domination exists for its own sake. Efficiency is the fig leaf behind which nihilism and the apotheosis of power hide in secular guise.

CONSERVATIVE INSIGHT, CONSERVATIVE BLINDNESS

There are important similarities between my argument regarding logocentric modernity's slide into nihilism and arguments once made by insightful conservatives opposed to liberalism. They argued that societies obtain their moral ballast from their spiritual foundations, and when those foundations weaken they are cast adrift in stormy seas. They also argued that liberal modernity lacked the moral weight to replace the traditional religion it had weakened. Liberal modernity undermined traditional religious authority and would itself gradually slide into nihilism.

I have strong sympathies with these arguments. *But conservatives identify a problem in a way that prevents their effectively addressing it.* Worse, today contemporary conservatism has itself become an expression of nihilism.

First, most conservatives are themselves moderns. They do not have a pre-Enlightenment view of religion as focusing on an all-embracing integral reality. They argue instead for religion's social and political *utility*. When pressed, many admit they do not themselves believe but contend it is vital for social order that most *other* people do.

Serious readers of Leo Strauss (1899–1973), possibly the most influential conservative thinker of our time, cannot agree on whether the man had religious beliefs.[28] Given the importance Strauss attached to religion, if he really believed, this uncertainty is perplexing. All his readers agree that he found religion useful. But defending religion because of its utility through its power to create order in society is ultimately a nihilistic defense.

This dilemma led to the moral collapse at the heart of much serious conservative thought. Dishonestly relating to others "for their own good" leads to hypocrisy. Newt Gingrich, long a major Republican leader and powerful voice among culture warriors, illustrates this problem with rare bluntness. According to Marianne Gingrich, his second wife, when Gingrich returned from speaking about "family values" and his hypocrisy was pointed out, he answered, "It doesn't matter what I do. People need to hear what I have to say. There's no one else who can say what I can say. It doesn't matter what I live."[29] The endless supply of conservative moral scandals demonstrates that Gingrich has plenty of company.

But what about sincere Christian conservatives? Thinkers such as Russell Kirk, Richard Weaver, and Malcolm Muggeridge were believing Christians who sang the praises of "traditional religion" in today's world. *But the religion they praised was the same monopolistic transcendental monotheism that generated the cultural crisis they were trying to resolve.* As chapter 1 explained, traditional religion's fall from cultural dominance was self-inflicted, brought about by the excesses of its own followers and the inability of believers to agree on what scripture actually said. In the absence of theological despotism Christianity proved unable to maintain a traditional society that would not ultimately tear itself apart because of doctrinal differences. The Enlightenment addressed terrible problems that had repeatedly arisen within Christian society. Finding flaws in what replaced traditional Christianity in no way ameliorates its own fatal deficiencies.

In addition, conservatives of both sorts often missed the crucial distinction between Baconian and liberal modernity. Leo Strauss in particular emphasized Locke's similarities to Hobbes that made them both moderns, but de-emphasized Locke's equally important differences from Hobbes. Consequently Strauss could not distinguish clearly between a Hobbesian world where ultimately only power matters and a Lockean world where preexisting society rightfully subordinates political authority to a moral and social order. This blindness prevented conservatives from appreciating liberalism's claim that value is intrinsic. To the degree that contemporary neoconservatives and other conservatives are themselves nihilists they are guiltier than many liberals of the failings for which they attack liberalism.[30]

Ultimately conservatives see order and hierarchy as barriers against an allegedly chaotic alternative. But as a philosophical and political movement they have been unable to provide a convincing foundation for order beyond its utility. Regarding these people one is reminded of the Grand Inquisitor in Fyodor Dostoyevsky's *The Brothers Karamazov*, who told a returned Christ it was necessary to execute him to preserve religion and good order.

In such a movement utility trumps truth, and what counts as utility is ultimately determined by power. Therefore the "wise'" must control the "not-wise." For nonbelievers this control can happen only by enforcing on others what they themselves believe to be false. Order and hierarchy can be maintained against criticisms only by imposing power and domination. This approach worked during the Middle Ages, at least until the printing press and the Renaissance, but back then many in power believed in their doctrine. Today many modern conservatives import nihilism into their attack on nihilism.

In his magisterial *The Conservative Mind* Russell Kirk (1918–1994), whom many regard as America's foremost conservative theorist, wrote that the full expression of the modern state against which conservatism protested would seek to keep the public "constantly in an emotional state resembling that of a people at war" because otherwise "obedience and co-operation wane." Such a state would be dominated by narrow patriotism, cupidity, fear, and hatred.[31] Kirk's description comes remarkably close to the dominating political strategies of the contemporary conservative movement. What Kirk described was not something left or right, but rather the full expression of power as the dominant political value. Since from the standpoint of power everything is a resource to be used, an enemy, or irrelevant, it is happy to package itself as either left or right. Were he alive today Kirk would probably be appalled at what now calls itself conservatism.

Because Western conservatives conceive of religion only in terms of transcendental monotheism, they have been unable to appreciate many strains of both secular and spiritual thought that located morality *within* the world rather than separate from it. In various ways these approaches addressed the problem of nihilism at its source: value was a part of the world itself.

But nihilistic ideas circulating among elites do not bring a culture to ruin. At most they weaken it, opening it to dissolution by other forces. More is needed.

ROADS TO NIHILISM: THE SOCIAL AND POLITICAL CRISIS

[George Bush's adviser] said that guys like me were "in what we call the reality-based community," which he defined as people who "believe that solutions emerge from your judicious study of discernible reality. . . . That's not the way the world really works anymore. . . . We're an empire now, and when we act, we create our own reality. And while you're studying that reality—judiciously, as you will—we'll act again, creating other new realities. . . . We're history's actors."

—Ron Suskind

So long as major crises do not intervene, foundational issues rarely matter to anybody beyond the intellectual community. But major crises do intervene. A society's dominant ideas shape how people perceive alternatives, and as these ideas change, some of what once seemed unlikely becomes likely and some once accepted is abandoned. There were many steps from major thinkers becoming nihilists to these attitudes infecting the bulk of a culture whose members never consciously concerned themselves with these issues. But those steps were taken. The twentieth century proved to be a century of crises and challenges for liberalism in all its forms.

EUROPEAN CATASTROPHE

Shortly before World War I, philosopher George Santayana wrote, "We are not condemned, as most generations have been, to fight and believe without an inkling of the cause. . . . The whole drift of things presents a huge, good-natured comedy to the observer. It stirs not unpleasantly a certain sturdy animality and hearty self-trust which lie at the base of human nature."[1]

No one anticipated the scale, length, or bloodiness of the conflict just ahead. When peace finally returned to Europe 65 million men had been mobilized for battle, 8.5 million of them had been killed, and total casualties for the dead, wounded, POWs, and missing were an astounding 37 million.[2] And for what? Once the fighting ended not one of the grand promises victorious leaders had made to whip up popular support had been realized. Santayana would not have written his comfortable words in 1920.

Arthur Bullard had encouraged President Woodrow Wilson to manipulate and control popular opinion on a scale never before attempted, arguing, "Truth and Falsehood are arbitrary terms. There is nothing in experience to tell us that one is always preferable to the other. . . . The force of an idea lies in its inspirational value. It matters very little whether it is true or false."[3] Actually, it came to mean quite a lot once people began to gain perspective on the noble lies they had been told to justify the slaughter. The war's aftermath bred growing cynicism and disillusionment as people grasped the scale of lies and deceptions by authority figures during the war.

In Europe Christianity and liberalism alike came under renewed and embittered attack. The warring countries had called upon their Christian clergy to bless them in the conflict, and bless them they had. Enthusiastically. In Germany God was pro-German. For the English, he favored their cause. As the horror finally sunk in of what had actually happened behind all those fine phrases, many Europeans lost their faith. For more than a few it never returned.[4]

World War I was the death knell of liberal Christianity. The attempt to harmonize Enlightenment reason and religious belief was widely considered a failure. For those who remained believers, neo-orthodoxy and the irrational theology of commitment increasingly took its place.[5] We arrive at the same insight we reached by a different route earlier when examining Christian theologians: huge numbers of people began abandoning logos after their ancestors had previously abandoned mythos.

The causes of World War I arose out of the least liberal forces in European society, but the victors' dominant ideology was liberal. They waged war in the name of liberal values, yet the peace they imposed seemed to be punitive, dishonest, and cynical. Wilhelmine Germany's aggressive rulers were ousted just before the country's surrender, replaced by liberals, who then sued for peace. At the time many Germans still believed the old government's propaganda that Germany was winning, propaganda that continued until the last weeks of the war. Germany had its own Arthur Bullards. For many Germans victory seemed denied by insufficient domestic support and liberal traitors; they accepted an early version of the "stab-in-the-back" theory that appeals today to many American right-wingers regarding Vietnam.

Pathological Masculinity and the Supremacy of Will

This spiritual and political disillusionment led to a darker style of politics. On the right and left antiliberal movements took advantage of the disillusionment to aggressively seek political power. The horrors of fascism, Nazism, and communism were facilitated and in some cases made possible by liberalism's self-inflicted wounds.

Attacks on liberalism by post-WWI conservatives and the revolutionary right contained many of the themes we encounter with today's culture warriors. Liberals were weak willed and effeminate, liberal feminists were inferior "men-women," and all were disloyal. What was needed to replace them were strong men with a manly clarity of purpose and strength of will. Liberal talk needed to be replaced by decisive action.[6] Will and commitment trumped reason.

The German intellectual Ernst Baeumler emphasized, "Man overcomes his doubts and anxiety, not because he sees himself as absolutely good, but because he knows where he belongs, in what community or unit [*Verband*] fate has placed him."[7] Achim Gercke of the Nazi Interior Ministry made a similar point: "Against everyone who is incapable of saying a total yes or no to anything, we uphold a hard, masculine, relentless and logical consistency."[8] Commitment trumps reason. The German legal theorist Karl

Schmitt emphasized that "since general rules are inherently inadequate for purposes of adjudication, instead of following a norm, we must simply *decide*."[9] For Schmitt and for fascists in general the bourgeoisie knew only how to talk, not to decide.

This style of assertion shares striking similarities with the Protestant theological arguments of Soren Kierkegaard. Liberalism emphasized generalities common to everyone, and for Kierkegaard, "Endless talk of the general is *boring*."[10] The act of faith, an inward act of commitment, is what counted.

Applied internally this attitude insulated its possessors from doubt in their religious path. Applied externally, as did Baeumler, Gercke, and Schmitt, this attitude had more disturbing consequences: all that was needed was the power to make and enforce the needed decision. European nihilism was generating the logic of tyranny. As domination for its own sake became the goal, women and the feminine were further devalued. Pathological masculinity paraded as manliness, as it does again today.

Fascist manliness defined itself in opposition to the feminine. Hitler told women Nazis that "the catchword 'women's emancipation' . . . [was] merely a phrase invented by the Jewish intellect."[11] In Germany and Italy alike women's role as breeders for the *Volk* or nation were exalted, while alternative roles were discouraged and attacked.[12] Abortion and contraception were outlawed (except, in Germany, for non-Aryan women). Women, particularly married women, were gradually deprived of full-time work positions, particularly supervisory ones, because "only a masculine will could provide leadership."[13]

Describing a widely used book in German schools, Claudia Koonz writes: "The author told boys to 'tolerate' girls—because without them there would be no *Volk*. Girls should be patient with boys' 'physical and mental discipline, iron control, which alone can restore our nation.' Both boys and girls were admonished: 'Harden yourselves. Strengthen and empower your bodies. Guard your mind and soul.'"[14]

There is a strong connection between focusing on the power of will against logos and mythos, rejecting the feminine as inferior, and viewing women simply as helpmates for manly men. People of inflexible will must be preoccupied with preserving their boundaries against infection from other ideas or new information.

While strong similarities exist between these views and those of America's culture warriors, the parallels are not exact. The European right had never been liberal and was aggressively collectivist, elevating the nation or the race above individuals. Personal fulfillment was through immersion in and service to the nation or the *Volk*, both serving as secular substitutes for the lost integral order of old Europe. German students were surrounded with posters telling them "You are nothing. Your *Volk* is everything!"[15] As Robert Paxton explains, perhaps fascism's most revolutionary impact was changing "the practice of citizenship from the enjoyment of constitutional rights and duties to participation in mass ceremonies of affirmation and conformity. . . . The individual had no rights outside community interest."[16]

America's involvement in the war had been brief, her casualties relatively light. American culture was also more liberal than Europe's and even its Southern conservative counterculture reflected its liberal and individual-istic origins. (See "America's First Counterculture," http://dizerega.com/faultlines/appendices/.) Collectivism was a defining feature of European fascism and Nazism, but much weaker in America. There was no power-ful collectivist movement on the right, nor a powerful antiliberal left push-ing more centrist groups to make common cause with an antiliberal right. America's equivalent crisis had to wait for a future stage set with different furniture.

The stage was set by the breakup of American liberalism.

THE DISASTROUS TRANSFORMATION OF LIBERALISM

The unanticipated successes of science, democracy, and relatively unfettered markets created challenges that liberalism's seminal thinkers had never anticipated. These challenges ultimately led to the dissolution of any coher-ent sense of a common liberal core to American culture.

In Europe authoritarian Marxists on the left along with authoritarian and theocratic conservatives (and later fascists) on the right continually reminded liberals they were up against powerful political enemies. They could not take their earlier accomplishments for granted. By contrast, in America liberals were free to focus on their growing differences without fear of being displaced by revolutionaries on the left or reactionaries and fascist revolutionaries on the right.

Northern and even many Southern conservatives were powerfully influenced by America's founding values.[17] Most of the country's intellectual, economic, and political elite considered themselves liberal, and the broader population was also liberal or sympathetic to liberalism.[18] In such an environment liberals could take what they shared for granted and focus on where they disagreed. As they did. During this period between the world wars, American liberalism fractured into the increasingly hostile schools of thought that remain today.

Liberalism's founders had developed their arguments during the modern world's formative years. Their analysis of people's rights and relationships had been illustrated by examples taking place on a human scale. Locke established his theory of just ownership by describing a person picking up an acorn or building a fence around unowned land. Possessing land gave owners the security to live as independent farmers, free from economic subjugation and political domination. The major liberal reason for America's initial territorial expansion was to acquire land for future generations of small farmers. Adam Smith published his *Wealth of Nations* and the American Revolution broke out in the largely preindustrial year of 1776.

By the late nineteenth century Locke's and Smith's reasoning and the universal principles enunciated by the American Revolution encountered very different societies. Market exchanges had generated a world of wage laborers, a declining proportion of independent producers and farmers, and ever-larger giant companies. When growing numbers of men were becoming employees, the values of liberal equality and freedom in Locke's sense were challenged. In many people's judgment, the relationships between freedom and the economy needed to be rethought.

Locke had also defended political equality. Institutionalizing it generated modern large-scale democracy. Individual citizens became ever-smaller fragments within a vastly more complex society. Neither Locke nor anyone else had anticipated the rise of mass political parties, growing urbanization, or a mass media. Political issues grew in complexity and often required considerable expertise to comprehend. A growing economy and burgeoning technological innovation knit separate households ever more closely together, no matter how far apart they were physically. These new developments challenged the American ideal of liberal equality.

The rise of mass politics posed another problem. When combined with an illiberal nationalism that ranked the government and "the people" above any individuals or other peoples, mass politics challenged liberal ideals of freedom. The difficulties raised by this issue became more intractable, particularly as liberals came more and more to make their ethical case on utilitarian grounds. How could individual selfishness be allowed to stand against the people or the nation? Jane Addams, a liberal progressive, observed with concern, "Many people had long supposed liberalism to be the freedom to know and say, not what was popular or convenient or even what was patriotic, but what they held to be true."[19] The rise of active government manipulation of public opinion and suppression of alternative perspectives, first widely instituted by Woodrow Wilson, brought this conflict to a head.

Locke had no idea of how much science would grow or the sense of power it increasingly gave people throughout the nineteenth and into the twentieth centuries. Scientific schools arose, consisting of narrowly competent specialists. All too often these experts extrapolated from their tightly bounded expertise to the world at large, assuming they and those like them could manage the country better than laypeople. Knowing only a little, but knowing it deeply, they thought they knew a lot.

With the gap between "experts" and the average person widening, the Baconian abstraction of a vast humanity skillfully managed by a knowledgeable elite came to compete with the ideal of individuals and their rights as society's moral foundation. Eugenics was its nastiest initial expression, public health measures perhaps its most noble. This Baconian ideal cut across political divisions. It was neither uniquely right nor left.

Misunderstandings of Darwin combined with rising nationalism directly challenged liberalism's liberating message to humanity as a whole, while the rise of oligarchic wealth challenged it domestically. Some nations or people were superior to others and should rule them. A hierarchy of domination, whether by experts or classes or races or nationalities, seemed scientifically affirmed. From all these antiliberal perspectives liberalism's universal claims for ideals such as equality and freedom could easily be challenged as obsolete and naive.

CLASSICAL, MANAGERIAL, AND EGALITARIAN LIBERALISM

In different ways late nineteenth- and early twentieth-century liberals sought to meet these challenges. In a complex world, varied responses were inevitable, but with liberalism's unifying moral principles in decline these differences were more divisive than they need have been.[20]

Three broad liberal orientations emerged out of the early decades of these debates: classical liberals, managerial liberals, and egalitarian liberals, distinguished by which defining liberal institution received their greatest confidence in addressing the country's challenges. Classical liberals feared government and relied on the market to solve social problems. Managerial liberals feared ignorance and "irrationality," admired efficient business organization, and believed science plus good political administration could solve social ills. Egalitarian liberals feared the growth in inequalities of wealth and political power and sought to strengthen democracy to solve the dangers they saw arising. These divisions led to intense disagreements, with the competing parties usually more aware of what divided than what united them.

Labels such as mine, created after the fact, fail to do full justice to the complexities people faced at the time. Not every American liberal during those times fits easily into these categories. One of the most prominent,

Henry George (1839–1897), certainly did not. But many did, and as public discussion of liberal proposals developed over time these frameworks took on an independent existence of their own, shaping and channeling the thinking of future generations. I think this trend is why George, who was internationally influential during his life and raised issues still important, is almost unread today. His analysis does not fit easily into any of liberalism's dominant narratives.

Despite their growing differences, egalitarian and managerial liberals were allied against classical liberals because both looked to democratic government to offset rising financial inequality and growing corporate power. Even so they can be distinguished by the kinds of reforms they advocated. Managerial liberals created many of our earliest regulatory agencies and the civil service, while egalitarian liberals triumphed more often at state levels, giving America primaries, the recall, voter initiatives, and the referendum. The first strengthened the power of experts and sought to remove day-to-day decision making from special interests and political pressures, whereas the second weakened government's independent power vis-à-vis popular voting.

Jane Addams would fall into the broad egalitarian liberal orientation whereas Herbert Croly would be an extreme managerial advocate, even though both are commonly called progressives. In her essay "Americanization" Addams wrote of working with immigrants: "We believed that America could be best understood by the immigrants if we ourselves, Americans, made some sort of connection with their past history and experiences. We extolled free association and the discussion of common problems as the basis for self-government and constantly instanced the New England town meeting."[21]

Herbert Croly disagreed: "Increase in centralized power and responsibility, expedient or inexpedient, is injurious to certain aspects of traditional American democracy. But the fault in that case lies with the democratic tradition; and the erroneous and misleading tradition must yield before the march of a constructive national democracy. . . . The average American individual is morally and intellectually inadequate to a serious and consistent conception of his responsibilities as a democrat."[22]

Earlier Croly had argued: "The Promise of American life is to be fulfilled . . . not merely by the abundant satisfaction of individual desires, but by a large measure of individual subordination and self-denial."[23] By contrast, Addams emphasized trusting "the very energy of existence, the craving for enjoyment, the pushing of vital forces, the very right of every citizen to be what he is without pretense or assumption of virtue."[24] But for Croly "Democracy must stand or fall on a platform of possible human perfectability."[25]

These distinctions within America's rapidly fragmenting liberal culture reflected very different views of people and their status vis-à-vis government and markets. To the degree that the original liberal emphasis on the moral status of individuals remained, it did so disproportionately among egalitarian liberals, who resisted the promises of unfettered markets that appealed to many classical liberals and the Baconian visions of a scientifically trained bureaucratic elite that attracted many managerial liberals. Egalitarian liberals distrusted both kinds of power and looked to politics to create more equality.

Liberalism Today

Managerial and egalitarian liberals formed the core of both American progressivism and Franklin D. Roosevelt's later New Deal. Both progressivism and the New Deal focused on using governmental action to address the problems industrial society brought to the original liberal vision. Consequently, both egalitarian and managerial liberals were vigorously opposed by classical liberals, who argued that any strengthening of "the state" inevitably tended toward tyranny and that a democratic state was no better than an undemocratic one.

In their search for political allies against managerial and egalitarian liberals, classical liberals increasingly associated themselves with business interests. Both supported the market ideal over government although from Main Street to Wall Street businesses had always used government to promote their interests whenever they could. Their alliance seemed promising, for business interests were often entrenched within the states and feared losing out to reformers at the national level.

However, after the WWII businesses increasingly dominated nationally as well. Classical liberal antistatism began focusing on government aid to citizens and ignored government aid to business. By this time liberalism's three dimensions had become simplified popularly into "liberalism" versus "conservatism."

Reframing their self-identification as conservatives blurred classical liberals' identification with the liberal tradition, ultimately opening them to allying with genuinely antiliberal supporters of hierarchy in the American South. But initially that development lay far in the future, awaiting the civil rights movement. Southern conservatives still voted for the Democrats, as they had since the Civil War.

Today, when the word has any meaning left at all, Americans calling themselves liberals usually have a managerial liberal bias emphasizing how enlightened administrators can best address our problems so long as they remain subject to democratic processes. Unlike many of their New Deal and progressive forbearers, many also believe corporate management has an important role in this oversight, sometimes to the complete merging of government and corporate elites. Today egalitarian liberals are more often called the left or progressives.

These two liberal variants compose the major division within the Democratic Party, insofar as ideas matter to it at all. The recent Occupy Wall Street demonstration illustrates this division. Egalitarian liberals celebrated its impact; managerial liberals in the White House worked covertly to undermine it.

Despite their different emphases, classical, managerial, and egalitarian liberals share the insight that individuals are society's fundamental moral and ethical unit. None want to replace markets with comprehensive government planning, override political freedom with rule by an expert elite, enforce equality of wealth and possession on everyone, or subordinate science to political or theological dogmas. Compared to genuine antiliberals such as fascists, communists, or contemporary Christian dominionists, their differences remain ones of degree.

THE DEGENERATION OF AMERICAN LIBERALISM

In his effort to determine what we shared in common as moral beings, Locke abstracted people from their history, focusing on equal individuals living in "a state of nature." He attempted to encompass everything politically or morally relevant to people's lives. In his *Second Treatise* Locke also analyzed marriage relations based on equality between men and women and argued that the rights of children had greater ethical weight than the power or convenience of their parents.

Locke's conception of a human being was much richer than the consumer and entrepreneur of classical liberal thought, the layperson, client, and expert of managerial liberals, or the citizens abstracted from every identifying characteristic but economic resources of egalitarians. Locke's individuals generated society in all its complexity. When problems arose, they created a social contract, acting as legislators for their community. Lockean human beings integrated their familial, political, economic, and scientific lives within the larger order of civil society.

From the writings of Locke, Jefferson, and John Stuart Mill to those of Milton Friedman, Robert Dahl, and John Rawls, we observe an increasing narrowness, abstraction, and superficiality in liberal conceptions of what is centrally human. Liberals increasingly praised the abstracted human fragments their particular schools claimed to represent.

Managerial liberals overestimated the ability of hierarchical organizations to serve the public good while pursuing personal well-being. They also overestimated how easily science could be used to achieve public goals, thinking logos alone provided the tools needed to understand society. Managerial liberals also consistently underestimated average citizens' capacities to make their own choices and overestimated their own ability to choose for them.

When managerial liberal optimism about being democratic technocrats faltered in the 1960s and '70s, many embraced other organizations as additional managerial tools, particularly corporations. Contemporary managerial liberals embrace government's alliance with large corporate and financial organizations, although their commitment to science has been narrowed to a commitment to economic reasoning. The Clinton and Obama presidencies are contemporary examples of managerial liberalism, now called neoliberalism.

Classical liberals' opposition to government was vitiated by their refusal to acknowledge that successful people and companies often used their wealth to acquire political privileges for themselves. Classical liberals usually defended corporate supporters for strengthening and centralizing government whenever it could serve them as exemplars of free enterprise. As apologists for a new American oligarchy, classical liberals generally facilitated the rise of American corporatism even while sometimes denouncing corporate influence as insufficiently free market, as with the libertarian Koch brothers.

Egalitarian liberals recognized that new economic and political realities challenged and often undermined traditional legal and political equality, and they often sought some "objective" ideal of equality as a result. They failed to appreciate how individual freedom both generated and relied on inequalities of many sorts. Equality as a value became increasingly separated from its linkage with self-governance to become a good in itself. The ideal of equality had become separated from the full complex of human values and so ended at odds with the desires of real people. Robert Dahl, a prominent egalitarian liberal, observed, "The greatest obstacle to democratization and reducing inequality in the United States is not . . . an elite of wealthy men, or even that military-industrial complex so much referred to, but rather the military–industrial–financial–labor–farming–educational–professional–consumer–over-and-under-thirty–lower-middle-upper-class complex that, for want of a more appropriate name, might be called the American people."[26]

From Active to Passive

Along with reducing the rich tapestry of human character and potentials to one-sided caricatures, all three liberalisms favored remarkably *passive* images of human beings.

At best, classical liberals treat most people as consumers who choose from goods placed before them by entrepreneurs. Consumers sell their labor, putting it under another's control so they can make the money to consume. For most of their lives workers take orders, which for classical liberals is as it should be.

The most widely read proponent of laissez-faire is Ayn Rand. In *Atlas Shrugged*, when a tiny creative minority went "on strike" civilization collapsed, because most people were incompetent. Ludwig von Mises, the most influential proponent of laissez-faire at the time, congratulated Rand: "You have the courage to tell the masses what no politician told them: you are inferior and all the improvements in your conditions which you simply take for granted you owe to the effort of men who are better than you."[27]

Many classical liberals ultimately embraced a corporate form of managerial liberalism: people should be managed by business, not government. People are "human resources," and efficiency, not rights or decency, is the standard to evaluate their use as tools. Almost without exception classical liberals are as blind to coercion of people by business management as they are exquisitely sensitive to the slightest coercion of businesses by politics.

For some classical liberals individuals disappeared entirely, to be replaced by "the market," which allegedly simply reflected individual choices. They argued that the market only reflects what we really want when we are free. The conservative Michael Oakeshott criticized this outlook: "Economics is not an attempt to generalize human desires or human behaviour, but to generalize the phenomena of price."[28]

For their part managerial liberals look on most people as clients who need guidance by experts. In an early version of this view, Walter Lippman wrote that society is "too big, too complex" for citizens to comprehend. Most were "mentally children or barbarians. . . . Self-determination [is] only one of the many interests of a human personality."[29] At best laypeople can choose between experts; otherwise they are best subordinated to those who know better. Robert McNamara represented the spirit of managerial liberalism that dominated the Kennedy and Johnson administrations when he said, "Undermanagement [of society is] the real threat to democracy," and, "Running the Department of Defense is not different from running the Ford Motor Company or the Catholic Church for that matter."[30]

Today the optimism of managing through government characteristic of McNamara's time has been replaced by optimism of managing through an alliance of corporations and government. With the rise of neoliberalism, the passivity of consumers is combined with the incompetence of clients, as people become raw material to support a new corporatist elite that increasingly abandons any pretensions to liberalism.

Chris Hedges provides a good example of why it is impossible to separate corporations from government today: "There are [in 2011] eighteen U.S. intelligence agencies on the military and civilian side, and seventy percent of their combined budget is outsourced to for-profit private corporations who simultaneously work the United States government as well as multinational corporations and foreign governments. . . . Sixty-nine percent of the Pentagon's entire workforce, and I am not talking only about the battlefield, is now privatized." These corporations give enormous amounts to political campaigns in both parties, then lobby them for policies benefitting their bottom lines. Tax money is used to lobby, bribe, and threaten politicians for more tax money. As a result, Hedges observes that "100 percent of people in this country that make $100,000 or less might as well remit everything they owe in taxes to contractors rather than paying the government."[31]

Market logic has almost eliminated any conception of public spirit, to be replaced by economic concepts, particularly efficiency in service to power. Even liberalism's emphasis on political equality, let alone the democratic value of self-governance, is increasingly replaced with being a consumer of government services. I can consume in isolation; I cannot be a citizen that way. The efforts of Republican governors in Michigan and Wisconsin to replace city governments with private managers illustrate this degeneration.

Bacon's vision has triumphed, and in its triumph service to humanity morphed into service to power. By combining the radically instrumental values of the market with the hierarchy and control of managerial liberalism, liberals are increasingly abandoning their own traditions. People are not moral agents, only resources to be deployed efficiently by their betters.

The egalitarian liberals' view of equality also treated real people as passive units on which public policy was to sculpt its ideal pattern of justice. So long as some measure of equality was obtained, it was irrelevant that a great many people opposed bussing their children for reasons other than racism. The goal could be obtained only by making many parents powerless and empowering managers to enforce it. This policy shows the incoherence of focusing only on equality: every step to increase it in one dimension weakens or eliminates it in another.

No ideals inducing more passivity have ever been proposed as the proper model for a philosophy that supposedly values individuals or membership in a free society.

There is a high price to liberals' abandoning people as active and competent citizens for people as subjects of bureaucratic and managerial manipulation and control. Powerless individuals apparently tend to make more irrational decisions than do those who feel capable and effective. Recent research indicates that when people think they are powerless and their world overwhelmingly complex, they increasingly perceive patterns that do not actually exist. Science writer Ed Yong writes about a series of experiments conducted at the University of Texas. Students who experienced lack of control over experimental events were more likely to perceive nonexistent patterns and believe that unhappy outcomes resulted from deliberate malicious or conspiratorial action.[32] A nation characterized by such attitudes is unlikely to maintain the tolerance of different perspectives and openness to debate required for democracy to survive. Today conspiracy theories abound, and tribalism increasingly substitutes for democratic citizenship.

This prolonged devolution of liberal thought is a rapidly rising cost of modernity's privileging logocentric instrumental knowledge over all other forms. One-dimensional "actors" can be understood logocentrically, *but people cannot.* People are meaning-seeking, empathetic beings. Each life constitutes a story, and each story is different. While in most of their analyses liberals have left the full complexity of people far behind, culture warriors speak incessantly of values, family, morality, and marriage. Their reasoning behind these values is contradictory, their commitment to them weak to nonexistent, but they give them lip service.[33]

What was once a vital liberal tradition has abandoned almost all its former principles in order to serve corporate and political power. (See "Corporations, Capitalism, and American Nihilism," http://dizerega.com/faultlines/appendices/.) Consider Larry Summers's words. In 1991, while he was the World Bank's chief economist, Summers argued, "The measurements of the costs of health impairing pollution depends on the foregone earnings from increased morbidity and mortality. From this point of view a given amount of health impairing pollution should be done in the country with the lowest cost, which will be the country with the lowest wages. I think the economic logic behind dumping a load of toxic waste in the lowest wage country is impeccable and we should face up to that. . . . I've always thought that under-populated countries in Africa are vastly UNDER-polluted, their air quality is probably vastly inefficiently low compared to Los Angeles or Mexico City."[34] Summers' logic is a repudiation of liberal morality in any form and illustrates the ultimate moral bankruptcy of utilitarianism.

Jose Lutzenburger, then Brazil's Secretary of the Environment, wrote Summers, "Your reasoning is perfectly logical but totally insane. . . . Your thoughts [provide] a concrete example of the unbelievable alienation, reductionist thinking, social ruthlessness and the arrogant ignorance of many conventional 'economists' concerning the nature of the world we live in."[35]

Lutzenberger lost his job while Summers went from the World Bank to secretary of the treasury under Bill Clinton and then became president of Harvard. Later, after helping destroy our banking system by his role in removing long-established checks on corporate sociopathy, under Barack Obama Summers again served the corporate oligarchy as loyally in government as he had out of it.

With Larry Summers and those like him, neoliberalism has become the ideological justification for oligarchy and the corporate state. People are valued by what the market indicates their labor is worth. The poor have no claim to good treatment because they are human beings. Like rocks, human beings have only instrumental utility. They are worth only the money they make for others.

THE END OF THE ENLIGHTENMENT DREAM

In all its guises modern nihilism is characterized by desire for power for its own sake. Newt Gingrich once said, quoting Mao Zedong, "War is politics with blood; politics is war without blood."[36] He could have as easily quoted Nazi jurist Karl Schmitt: "The hallmark of authentic politics is the moment when the enemy emerges in concrete clarity as the enemy."[37]

With these sentiments the logic of democracy is abandoned. There is no loyal opposition but an enemy to be defeated. The point is not to serve the country or to find common ground, but to win it all. If the well-being of the country is damaged, that is just collateral damage.

Republican brinksmanship over raising the debt ceiling to get budget cuts that the vast majority of Americans oppose or efforts to crash the economy in hopes Obama is blamed are examples of this mentality. We encounter in contemporary form the Nietzschean will to power and the cynical ethics of Arthur Bullard. Appeals to evidence and talk of values are only pretty packaging covering the struggle for domination. If a lie is more effective, it will be employed.

Pervasive dishonesty undermines political debate and the ability to compromise that makes democracy possible. When words like *conservative, liberal, patriot, fascist, racist,* and *communist* are reduced to simple dichotomies, and often to epithets without content, conversation becomes impossible. When people no longer try to tell the truth, genuine communication becomes impossible.

Lying and exaggeration have always disfigured politics. They always will. But something deeper is at work today: an attack on honest communication as such. What we are witnessing is the reduction of politics to Newspeak, the deliberately simplified language in George Orwell's *1984* that allowed people to cheer for their rulers and hate those they opposed but prevented any attempt really to think about things or understand others.

When language is debased we live in greater isolation. Since none of us can tolerate isolation, many reach out to those they see as most like themselves and fear those unlike themselves. Their moral imagination has been short-circuited, their humanity diminished. As Robert Bringhurst puts it, "Those who empty words of their meaning are making themselves (and maybe their neighbors and heirs) inarticulate."[38] No greater attack on a free society is possible.

Where does this end? Hannah Arendt wrote in her study of Nazi death-camp-administrator Adolf Eichmann: "The longer one listened to him, the more obvious it became that his inability to speak was closely associated with an inability to *think* . . . from the standpoint of somebody else."[39]

During the latter half of the twentieth century the West entered what appears to be the final crisis of the Enlightenment project. Its Faustian dream of bringing nature under human control for the benefit of humanity had turned into one of bringing humanity to serve power and arbitrary will. Seeking to ground truth on logos without mythos proved unable to protect logos's own foundation in reasoned argument, because such arguments demanded allegiance to truth over winning. Westerners exist within a moral context they cannot themselves justify. And logos alone had dissolved all values that might be used to subordinate will and power. As Lutzenberger said of Larry Summers, "Your reasoning is perfectly logical but totally insane." Government, industry, finance, and academia are filled today with various versions of Summers.

But powerful healing forces are also alive in the United States, forces able to rebuild the dream of a society of free men and women. They are the offspring of a period now almost universally vilified by both the corporatist Neoliberals and the culture warriors, that period labeled "the sixties." It is to that period in American history that we now turn.

Chapter Six

The Sixties

Maybe it was sentimental, if not actually stupid, to romanticize the sixties as an embryonic golden age. . . . Certainly this fetal age of enlightenment aborted. Nevertheless the sixties were special; not only did they differ from the twenties, the fifties, the seventies, etc., they were superior to them. Like the Arthurian years at Camelot, the sixties constituted a breakthrough, a fleeting moment of glory, a time when a significant little chunk of humanity briefly realized its moral potential and flirted with its neurological destiny, a collective spiritual awakening that flared brilliantly until the barbaric and mediocre impulses of the species drew tight once more the curtains of darkness.

—Tom Robbins

During "the sixties," really more from 1965 to 1975 or so, creative new insights and revitalized values entered American life on an unprecedented scale, providing a rich interaction between new, more feminine values and the one-sidedly masculine traditions preceding them. Combined, they opened the door to resolving the crisis of nihilism that was slowly undermining the country's institutions.

Today's culture war is a pathological masculine response to that period and the cultural alternatives it presented. As a result, America's nihilistic trends emerged into the open and expanded with unprecedented ferocity into America's version of the post–WWI crisis that assaulted Europe.

The culture war was launched by political intellectuals, religious leaders, and unprincipled politicians to split the country and thereby solidify their power. Since its inception in the early 1970s their effort has taken on a life of its own. The political sorcerer's apprentices who launched it ended with a split bigger and nastier than most intended, one extending to modernity's deepest foundations. But to understand what they did we need to look at the period they reject so fervently.

The sixties generation were the children of those postwar families now idealized by culture warriors as close to perfect. If the families of the fifties were as today's culture warriors fantasize, perhaps we should ask why so many of their bravest and most idealistic children chose to act as they did. When we do, we will find their motives deeply rooted in American traditions. In particular, the sixties shared strong affinities with the ferment and creativity that enriched the United States after the War of 1812.

Until then the new country had been preoccupied with survival and establishing basic political institutions. When peace came and the founding generation began to fade into history, Americans' attention turned toward building new lives within the world's first close approximation to a liberal democracy. As the impact of political freedom began to work its magic, Americans responded, some to enrich their bank accounts, some to enrich their lives.

By the war's end, universal white male suffrage existed in many states, and slavery had been abolished in a majority of states. Women's rights, abolition, labor reform, health reform, marriage reform, better treatment of Native Americans, prison reform, abolition of the death penalty, and even free love were familiar themes within the more spiritually innovative communities of this time.[1] Utopian communities were established by secular and religious reformers.

Then, as now, these currents were strongest in the North. The South was beginning its own trajectory into the first genuine counterculture, as the influence of slavery led its leaders to reject explicitly the principle of the Declaration of Independence many years before the outbreak of civil war. (See "America's First Counterculture," http://dizerega.com/faultlines/appendices/.)

Cultural innovation was closely tied to spiritual innovation. Upstate New York was the San Francisco of its time. The Burned-Over District's spiritual energy energized America's second Great Awakening. Sarah Pike describes this period as a time of "communal experiments that rejected traditional marriage arrangements, séances in which spirits spoke through adolescent girls, hypnotic trance healings, cures using water baths, herbal healing, homeopathic medicine, interest in yoga and meditation."[2] God was described as feminine as well as masculine, Mother as well as Father, even by male religious reformers.[3] Popular Christianity emphasized emotion over doctrine in its services and supported the reform movements of the time.

While most religious creativity was broadly Christian, the new openness and optimism led many Americans to learn from other spiritual traditions. The rise of New England Transcendentalism marked the first hesitant influence of non-Abrahamic religions in American cultural life. Mesmerism and the teachings of Immanuel Swedenborg became important influences as well. At its height Spiritualism numbered between 4 and 8 percent of Americans, and Spiritualist practices provided the earliest forms of religious and political leadership for American women. Séances even took place in Lincoln's White House.[4]

This period also generated a powerful peace movement protesting American military aggression. The Mexican-American War triggered citizen protests proportionately larger than those opposing the Vietnam War. Former president John Quincy Adams attacked the war as a Southern ploy to expand territories suitable for slavery, and future president Abraham Lincoln spoke out in opposition on the floor of the House, condemning President Polk as a liar.[5]

Transcendentalists such as Ralph Waldo Emerson and Henry David Thoreau also opposed the Mexican-American War. Thoreau's "On Civil Disobedience" argued that it was everyone's duty to have nothing to do with murderous imperial ambitions. He advocated peaceful civil disobedience intended to push otherwise complacent citizens into confronting the moral implications of governmental murder. Thoreau's argument later inspired Gandhi in his struggle for Indian independence from Britain and reappeared on lunch counters in Greensboro, North Carolina, helping launch the civil rights movement.

Environmentalism also appeared for the first time. Thoreau's *Walden Pond* opened many people's eyes to dimensions of life lost from sight in the rush toward development and material wealth. Once the sixties and its exploration of alternative ways of life arrived, his work received renewed interest. As a pioneering voice for peace, right livelihood, and the natural world, Thoreau could be described as the sixties' patron saint.

Thoreau was hardly alone in his regard for the natural world. Emerson had already challenged the view that nature was nothing more than a pile of resources for our use. As he put it, "We are as much strangers in nature as we are aliens from God."[6] Herman Melville's *Moby Dick* transformed how many Americans viewed whales. Edward Law Olmstead, designer of New York's Central Park, became the "de facto head" of the commission that protected Yosemite Valley and the Mariposa Grove of ancient sequoias.[7]

Despite this period's cultural, political, and spiritual richness, its impact waned after the Civil War. But while it lasted it demonstrated that a creative and openhearted willingness to make the world a better place lay deeply embedded in the character of many Americans.

The sixties were not a strange mutation of the American spirit. They were the most recent upwelling of the vision and values that flower in a free society. But the sixties were more than that. They also opened moral, philosophical, and spiritual doors capable of healing the nation's decline into nihilism.

POST-WAR AMERICAN ONE-SIDED MASCULINITY

Much of the sixties cultural impact can be understood with the masculine/feminine contrast I described in chapter 3. From the midsixties to the midseventies a counterculture arose injecting feminine values into the American masculine ideal. It was badly needed. The early sixties marked the high-water mark of a confident masculine/yang culture in the process of seriously overreaching itself.

Today when "liberal" is assaulted from the right as "unmanly," it is illuminating to read how liberals of this period employed similar terminology against their progressive critics. Arthur Schlesinger, Jr., the dominant New Deal liberal spokesman for this period, argued that a "hard" stand against communism was "masculine." Progressives were "hopelessly and irrevocably feminine," and strong liberals were the only leaders able to guarantee "a secure and restored American masculinity."[8]

The cultural mainstream's image of human virtues mirrored this bipartisan love of power, strength, and technology and dismissal of the feminine as subordinate. Many scientists agreed. Charlene Spretnak describes how, beginning in the 1950s, psychological experiments by Herman Witkin and others convinced many psychologists that men were relatively "field-independent," whereas women were "field-dependent," paying far more attention to contexts, a supposedly inferior kind of cognition. In 1962 Witkin described women's cognitive style as "conforming," "child-like," and "global," resembling the "(supposedly) undifferentiated thought processes found in 'primitive' cultures." Men's style was "self-reliant." Spretnak writes, "Those esteemed psychologists actually categorized the half of humanity who tend to correctly perceive that reality is inherently relational as being slightly sub-standard."[9]

The intellect was separate from the body, and "manly men" gloried in that belief. As Linda Jean Shepherd observed, "While our culture values physical health and intellectual abilities, it largely dismisses the value of emotional and spiritual health."[10] In *Toward a Psychology of Being* Abraham Maslow reported that while there was much in psychology about mental illness, there was no discussion of mental health. In the sixties Maslow became famous for arguing there should be.[11]

The United States had taken the leading role in defeating right-wing aggression during World War II and continued to militarize its society in response to the communist threat afterward. It probably had no choice, but the price was very high. Decades of building the world's most powerful military forces began to transform the country.

After forty years of the Cold War, America's new status quo had become an economy split between competitive businesses serving the market and other businesses dependent upon government contracts for their prosperity, a prosperity made secure by access to political privilege. These interests were particularly involved in military and energy production. America's political institutions had always given the status quo effective tools to preserve its dominance, and this new status quo was no different. Communism lost the Cold War, but future historians may judge that America did not win.

Not that we had not been warned. In his 1960 farewell address as president, Dwight D. Eisenhower, a Republican and commanding general of our forces during World War II, cautioned: "We must guard against the acquisition of unwarranted influence, whether sought or unsought, by the military-industrial complex. . . . We must never let the weight of this combination endanger our liberties or democratic processes."[12]

Ike was ignored. American military spending is now greater than during the Cold War and greater than most of the rest of the world *combined*. We have a huge economic investment in war, and within that realm public and private spheres are becoming indistinguishable. For example, in Afghanistan 68,000 troops are accompanied by 104,000 contractors. The Department of Defense's corporate contractors finance political campaigns and lobby with taxpayer money for policies benefiting their bottom lines.[13] Simultaneously American schools are laying off teachers, paved roads are being converted into gravel because local governments can no longer afford to pave them, and, most ominously, the middle class is shrinking.

Even to speak of the military-industrial complex today is to sound like a leftist, not a victorious general and president of the United States. Pointless wars and open-ended occupations multiply no matter the party in power or popular opinion. The government spends and spends, enriching the burgeoning corporate state, spreading collateral damage across the globe, and impoverishing America in the process. Box cutters and hijacked jets brought down the World Trade Center. Software used to hack into $10 million drones in Afghanistan and Pakistan cost $25.95, off the shelf.[14]

In the sixties, young men and women tried to check these malignant tendencies.

AMERICA IN 1960 AND AFTERWARD

By 1960 the successes of Roosevelt's New Deal and the postwar prosperity that followed appeared to promise a better future for all through enlightened political direction. The 1960 presidential election ushered in a government dominated by managerial liberals filled with boundless confidence in their ability to lead America toward a better future. Economists in the Kennedy administration argued that their technical knowledge enabled them to fine tune the economy, guaranteeing perpetual prosperity. They were also confident that science and enlightened administration could solve other historically intractable public problems, symbolized by the subsequent Johnson administration's War on Poverty. Economists such as John Kenneth Galbraith were willing to go even further, arguing that, unlike the communists, they could plan the economy in a way that preserved, and even improved, democracy.[15] Planning seemed to be here to stay.

Universities were to be factories for producing the technically trained men and women needed to realize these possibilities. Educating citizens was subordinated to training young people in useful skills. Initially this application of industrial production to education appeared to work. In 1956 author William Whyte quoted an economics professor praising his seniors: "These men do not question the system"; instead, "they want to get in there and lubricate and make [it] run better. They will be technicians of the society, not innovators."[16] Adding a stick to its educational carrot, the government used the military draft to "channel" young men into professions bureaucrats deemed nationally essential.

In the early sixties we were still in the midst of a passionate love affair with technology. As in all infatuations, we were blind to any problems. In the public mind pollution chiefly existed as Los Angeles's famous smog; DDT was often used indiscriminately, and industrial waste spilled unregulated into American streams and rivers. Giant dams were being built even as their rationale became increasingly strained. Plans were made to dam the Grand Canyon, and an even bigger dam and lake would supposedly be created on Alaska's Yukon. Other engineers planned to build canals sending "wasted" water from Canada's watered north to the drier American Southwest. In California there were serious proposals to cut the tops off the hills surrounding San Francisco Bay, using them to fill most of it in. The flattened hills and bay-fill would provide for massive subdivisions surrounding an artificial fresh-water lake. The growing use of nuclear power supposedly promised an era of virtually free energy. There were even proposals to explode an atomic bomb under part of Panama to create a second canal. Our earth was a rock on which humanity would carve its dream, and the chief carvers (and interpreters of the dream) would be America's scientific technocrats who were feeling their oats in government and business alike.

The moon landings constituted the high point of this optimistic postwar masculine culture. The astronauts' personal glory and praise for the genius of NASA's engineers and scientists are fully deserved. Landing men on the moon according to schedule and bringing them home alive was a magnificent achievement.[17] It also supported the ideal that science and planning could achieve the all-but-unimaginable.

The only major concern, and it was widespread, was the possibility of nuclear war. There was a pervasive fear that humanity might wipe itself out with a nuclear holocaust. Growing up in Wichita, Kansas, home of major aircraft producers as well as the large McConnell airbase, I remember lying in bed as a child wondering whether the blast from a hydrogen bomb hitting the base would obliterate my house and family, miles away. I was not alone. But if we avoided this grim possibility, the horizon looked rosy indeed.

Since then technology has progressed in unimagined ways, witness the computer on which I write these words. My cell phone has greater computing power than the computers aboard the Apollo moon missions. But the way we think about technology has changed. The sixties initiated this reconsideration.

Beginning in the midsixties, a reaction to the managerial ideal developed with the rise of a populist student left and a young conservative decentralist movement identifying with Senator Barry Goldwater's largely Jeffersonian vision.[18] University students increasingly resisted being treated as massproduced cogs in an industrial machine, products of the "multiversity."

As military technology became increasingly hair-trigger, thoughtful Americans worried we might be on a path to collective suicide. In the early days of long-range radar, the rising moon had once been interpreted as a Soviet missile attack. No one had anticipated that the new radars could pick up the rising moon. Fortunately the error was discovered before we launched a counterattack.[19] But the episode was chastening. Pervasive worries over nuclear war and the safety of nuclear power encouraged second thoughts about the wisdom of the technocratic managerial ideal. There was growing unease that it might not be sustainable.

By the end of the sixties the national outlook had changed dramatically. Managerial liberals of the era questioned their capacity due to their Vietnam debacle. As the seventies progressed, new doubts arose over their ability to manage the economy and devise workable complex public programs. As America's love affair with technology became more complex, renewed concerns about the natural world were emerging. Earth Day began in 1970, symbolizing an attempt to place ecological issues at the center of the public agenda. The old status quo was fading, and new possibilities were arising.

Today "the sixties" are routinely attacked as an aberration, best denounced but never examined. However, the challenges that era raised were neither rebutted nor outgrown. Instead they were denied and suppressed. Nor have its achievements been credited. Millions of women benefited from the victories won by feminists, but today many women cringe at the thought of identifying with feminists. Millions of young men no longer fear the draft, while looking down on those responsible for their lack of fear. Millions have benefited from the cleaner air, water, and land made possible by the environmental movement that arose during this time, and many now look down on environmentalism. Silicon Valley is the strongest evidence that America is still a creative culture economically; its roots in the counterculture are unacknowledged and usually unknown.

Few Americans today are optimistic. If religious, the culture warriors who dominate public debate mostly look forward to a "rapture" that will leave most of us behind or to an Armageddon that will destroy what exists. If secular, they envision a universal empire enforced by a perpetual war machine, as our "vital national interests" now include every inch of the globe. Almost without exception, everything politicians of either party say is wrapped in the language of fear and resentment. Barack Obama, who campaigned on "Yes We Can!" has governed mostly with "No We Can't." The culture of distrust and the politics of fear have largely replaced the culture and politics of opportunity.

Decades of sustained efforts by right-wing think tanks, right-wing Christians, and corporate media have succeeded in obscuring America's recent history and making words such as *liberal, feminist,* and *environmentalist* terms of derision in the eyes of those who benefited most from their accomplishments. What these groups teach about that time is as accurate as Southern depictions of the Civil War as having nothing much to do with slavery.

So what did happen?

SETTING THE STAGE

The sixties emerged from many causes, but three were dominant: higher education, America's founding ideals, and television.

Returning soldiers from World War II benefited from the GI Bill, which offered them substantial financial assistance in going to college. This government program succeeded wonderfully in transforming millions of lives. The soldiers' children, the future sixties generation, generally grew up expecting they could follow in their parents' footsteps.

By the late fifties the United States was establishing many new universities, and the number of students attending them expanded rapidly. In 1960, 22.3 percent of 16.2 million Americans between eighteen and twenty-four attended college; in 1970, 35.2 percent of 24.4 million young Americans did. College was no longer the goal of only a small percentage of young people, and as the size and number of campuses grew, the stage was set for ideas that had once influenced only a small intellectual elite to involve millions.

Colleges and universities came to complement churches as places where morally engaged people could gather to discuss common problems. Historically, political and social reform efforts often originated in America's churches, creating, in Barbara McGraw's words, a "Conscientious Public Forum."[20] During the cultural ferment following the War of 1812, churches had served as college campuses later did. Abolitionism, women's suffrage, abolishment of child labor, and temperance were early examples of reform movements relying on church membership for much of their support. Only in church did many people gather for reasons related more to moral values than to economic gain or sports. It was easy for businessmen to organize their relatively few interests by meeting in clubs and professional associations. Except for churches, for most of our history engaged citizens had no equivalent gathering place. Mass higher education created a new venue where large numbers of people could gather without immediate concern about their economic affairs.

The second cause was the enhanced attention given to our founding values. During the Cold War schools emphasized our country's liberal ideals as setting us apart from the totalitarian despotisms of the Communist world and the recently defeated fascists. I and many others were taught to believe our society was morally superior to the Communist world because the midnight knock on the door was unknown, torture did not exist, we were all equal under the law, trial by jury was guaranteed, and our government supported democracy everywhere. By teaching American ideals, colleges unintentionally encouraged and provided forums for critics who reminded the country and its citizens when they failed to live up to their professed values.

Students' freedom to think was further enhanced because they had not yet taken upon themselves the responsibilities of raising families and making a living. College students combined a relative maturity with a relative openness to new information and little need to limit their involvement on issues important to them because of others' dependence on their support.

Television was the third development contributing to this period. Television has two dimensions: its technical qualities and who controls their use. The first explains its unusual power during this time, while the second explains its role in energizing citizens then and discouraging them now.

Television uses moving pictures, rather than the voice or the printed word, to tell stories. We are visual creatures, and words alone cannot compete with visual images. Television proved unparalleled at bringing events home in ways that powerfully impact people emotionally, be they Vietnam body bags, Haight Ashbury flower children, the Kennedy assassinations, or police dogs unleashed on peaceful civil rights marchers. Television gave us the emotional impact of what was happening even if it could be weak in providing the context needed to deeply understand events.

Until relatively recently a television program could not easily be re-viewed. First impressions were the only impression. John Kennedy outwitted Richard Nixon in their first presidential debate by wearing makeup after seeming to reject it, thereby calling attention to Nixon's five o'clock shadow. Those who saw the debate on television generally said Kennedy won; those who heard it on the radio more often thought Nixon did.[21]

In the early sixties television had become ubiquitous in American households but was still a relatively new technology. Despite Kennedy's insights, on balance people of power and wealth had not yet learned how to manipulate it. In-depth manipulation of the visual news would not be thoroughly established until two decades later when a shrewd politician and former Hollywood actor became president.

Initially television news broadcasts relied on people who had made their reputations in print journalism and had risen to prominence within an institutional setting that insulated news reporting somewhat from commercial values. The first nationwide news broadcasters, men like Edward R. Murrow and Walter Cronkite, had earned their stripes in print media, where reporting context and doing so in depth mattered. The time of news "personalities," corporate agendas, and tabloid priorities was still to come.

Television networks of the time followed newspapers' practice of insulating news reporting from commercial pressures. News programs were not expected to be profit centers. Consequently, television did a better job of

informing Americans as citizens then than it does today when corporations have subordinated every value to making money and politicians script
every occasion.

Of course television can still provide good and insightful reporting.
Independent producers have long done so, the best known being Bill
Moyers. However, networks cannot risk boring their viewers, because
disengagement invites channel switching, lowering advertising rates and
corporate income. As a result, while there are many television broadcasts,
virtually all are subject to corporate logic, and corporate logic is compatible with politicians' desire to substitute entertainment and sound bites for
political analysis.

In television newsrooms during the sixties journalistic standards still
counted. Politicians had just begun to discover television's importance and
had not mastered its manipulation. Consequently, on balance television
strengthened citizens and weakened centers of power, as does the Internet
today.

So the immediate roots of the sixties can be traced to these relatively
few factors—the addition of universities and colleges to churches as places
where morally concerned people could gather and discuss contemporary
issues; the political idealism among interested Americans inculcated by the
Cold War; and television's unparalleled power to make the distant near and
personal in a way that had never before existed. A sit-in at a Woolworth's
lunch counter one winter's day in Greensboro, North Carolina, provided
the final piece. (See "The Civil Rights Movement," http://dizerega.com/
faultlines/appendices/.)

The civil rights movement began the neo-Confederate South's flight from
the Democrats to join the Republicans and ultimately serve as the center of
gravity for the contemporary antiliberal right.

The next defining political issue of the time was the Vietnam War. As
with the Mexican-American War, the Vietnam War split the public because
the country's interests were not at stake. But the protestors faced not the relatively small federal government of James K. Polk but the enormously more
powerful and militarized government President Eisenhower had warned

of. (See "The Vietnam Protest Movement," http://dizerega.com/faultlines/appendices/.)

During the civil rights movement national leaders were sometimes sympathetic to Americans protesting legalized racism by the states. Consequently, southern states were somewhat restrained when defending their oppressive laws. When they weren't, television often showed the brutality of the police and racist mobs for all to see. These constraints on official misbehavior weakened during the Vietnam protests.

Vietnam protesters opposed the national government, not the city of Birmingham or the state of Alabama. All the stakes were raised. Politicians' incessant lies over Vietnam encouraged many people to question much they had taken for granted in American culture. Even so, for nearly all protestors this rejection of corrupt politicians and the companies that grew wealthy on the deaths of others was in no way a turn to Marxism or other anti-American values.

This tension between equally patriotic choices was magnified by a deliberate act of the Nixon administration. Pat Buchanan was a trusted insider, having arrived as an ally of Vice President Spiro Agnew. When Agnew's corruption became known and he was forced to resign, Buchanan stayed on as a strategist for political battles against the administration's foes. No respecter of legality, he had previously urged the government to use the IRS to harass its political opponents.[22]

Buchanan sent a confidential memo to Nixon about how to deal with his political opponents. At its end he wrote, "This is a potential throw of the dice that could bring the media on our heads, and cut the Democratic Party and country in half; my view is that we would have far the larger half."[23]

Good leaders strive to harmonize the multiple dimensions of love of country. Those seeking only personal power do not care and use the divisions caused by their policies to impugn the loyalty of their opponents, setting American against American and tearing families, communities, and ultimately the nation apart to get "the larger half." Deliberately tearing the country in two for political gain was Pat Buchanan's image of patriotism, as it still is.

THE REVOLUTIONARIES

In the sixties the ideal of masculine domination was often as strong on the authoritarian left as it still is on the political right. Some leftists proclaimed that a woman's place in "serving the movement" was "on her back." The most extreme fantasists postured as leaders of a coming violent revolution and kept posters of Che Guevara, Mao, Lenin, and other revolutionaries on their walls. They considered themselves a vanguard that would ultimately lead the masses to final victory. They made up for their lack of numbers with an arrogant confidence in their own rectitude, along with a seemingly endless ability to organize and to try to manipulate others.

For most antiwar students and their allies these people's manipulative fanaticism was a turnoff. I remember when Mark Rudd gave a talk at the University of Kansas. Rudd, who later joined the Weathermen, a violent SDS offshoot, urged us to try to get people hurt by the police, thereby "radicalizing" them. Most of us concluded he was a jerk.

The Nixon administration loved to point to these people as the real leaders of the antiwar movement, feeding the fantasies of *both* groups of power addicts. The revolutionaries felt they really were powerful, while their rightwing opponents could fantasize they were all that stood between America and a communist dictatorship.

This self-proclaimed revolutionary vanguard announced what were supposed to be the "Days of Rage" in Chicago. Their goal was to lure 20,000 radicals to the city to begin the revolution. Three hundred people showed up.

Two months before the Days of Rage, around 400,000 young people participated in a peaceful gathering of mammoth proportions at Woodstock. A week after the fizzled Days of Rage *millions* of Americans across America participated in the peaceful antiwar moratorium.[24]

The revolutionaries did better work for Nixon than they ever did opposing the war. Some like David Horowitz later turned into right-wing manipulators, changing their packaging but not their tactics. Others blew themselves up making bombs.

While there were few genuine revolutionaries, young people caught up in the spirit of that time still shared human weaknesses. Everything humans do can and almost certainly will be abused by someone. The sixties were no exception. We were naive about the barriers to be confronted and the challenges to be overcome, in ourselves as much as external.

But the fact that foolish and sometimes harmful actions are committed in the name of something is not in itself an argument against it. Cars, guns, political and parental authority, and particularly the Bible have all been abused, but those attacking the sixties for its excesses shift their standards mightily in these other cases, blaming only the individuals doing the abusing. But regarding the sixties, they attack the *values* rather than the abusers.

Pat Buchanan argued that the young people of the sixties should be attacked to help split the country and solidify Nixon's power. Buchanan has never similarly denounced his church for the child abuse by pedophile priests, nor has he argued that the dissembling and deceitful bishops who covered for them are evidence the church is irredeemably corrupt. Nor do Pat Robertson and his many clones tell us that hundreds of years of religious war and millions of deaths in the name of Christianity is evidence that scripture is irredeemably flawed. Supposedly this bloody record is not evidence of something amiss, whereas college students carried away with new insights, and sometimes doing foolish or dangerous things with them are evidence of fundamental error.

The Counterculture

This book argues that the counterculture is more important than the New Left.[25] The sixties political movement addressed America's problems within traditional logocentric frameworks. Whether homegrown radicals nurtured on C. Wright Mills, Paul Goodman, and the civil rights movement, anarchists inspired by Peter Kropotkin, Emma Goldman, and the IWW, or Marxists reading Herbert Marcuse spiced with a sprinkling of Fidel Castro and a little Lenin, all largely thought within the same logocentric intellectual framework as the managerial liberals, conservatives, and others they opposed. Whether they identified with America's founding principles, as most did, or with the European Marxist and anarchist critiques of liberalism, their major spokespeople were intellectually children of the Enlightenment.

The counterculture was different. It also had deep native roots, as we saw in our overview of America between the War of 1812 and the Civil War. Like its nineteenth-century predecessors, it was primarily oriented toward cultural change and personal growth and only tangentially engaged in political activism, notably in the movement against the Vietnam War.

The counterculture and the New Left inhabited two intellectual centers of gravity within the universe of the sixties generation. Probably the most influential non-American writers on the counterculture were Alan Watts and Herman Hesse, who introduced many Americans to Asian insights. Many in the counterculture also sought inspiration from what they knew or imagined about Native American traditions. Traditional Native Americans such as Rolling Thunder were widely respected as teachers.[26]

The counterculture was not antiscience so much as against scientism, the view that only science gave us truth. As Berkeley physicist Jack Sarfatti put it in 1976, physics "needed more 'Mythos' to leaven the 'Logos.'"[27] This stance helped open up an appreciation of insights able to heal the nihilism undermining the West.

In a book popular at the time, Philip Slater compared mainstream America to the counterculture: "The old culture, when forced to choose, tends to give preference to property rights over personal rights, technological requirements over human needs, competition over cooperation, violence over sexuality, concentration over distribution, the product over the consumer, means over ends, secrecy over openness, social forms over personal expression, striving over gratification, oedipal love over communal love. . . . The new counterculture tends to reverse all of these priorities."[28] Slater can be criticized for oversimplifying both the dominant and the counterculture visions of America, but he touched on genuine differences and described aspirations many in the counterculture shared.

For my purposes, almost every one of Slater's dichotomies contrasts a masculine mainstream value with a feminine countercultural alternative. In its basic values the counterculture was strongly feminine, as Charlene Spretnak observed: "Although gender roles remained largely traditional, with women baking bread and men building houses, the abiding values of the counterculture were those usually considered 'feminine,' relational, and ecological. From that perspective the hypermasculine mood of the postwar years seemed bizarre and dehumanizing."[29]

The mainstream masculine culture picked up on this quality, sometimes with amusing results. Long hair on men was derided as feminine, although it was usually accompanied by beards and moustaches, both absent from the closely shaved faces of bankers and frat boys.

When the draft ended, the war wound down, and the killings at Kent State demonstrated the lengths established power would go to dominate, the political movement lost steam. With its more deeply probing criticism of American culture and its attempt to provide alternatives, the countercul-ture proved more lasting.

Today alternative and holistic healing methods are pursued by an enormous public, even when not covered by insurance. Alternative spiritual traditions have become very visible in the country's urban areas as well as in the cultur-ally "bluer" parts of rural America. Farmers' markets are common nation-wide, offering small-scale agriculture a way of prospering at a time when many had been predicting its demise. Their values of buying locally and sup-porting local economies are also spreading. The Rainbow Gatherings attract as many as fifteen thousand, and the better-known Burning Man numbers nearly fifty thousand. Environmentalism continues strongly and creatively, and for many the insights offered through altering consciousness continue; marijuana has been legalized, at least for medical use, in many states.

Counterculture women played a disproportionate role in many of these currents. As Gretchen Lemke-Santangelo observed, "By the late 1970s coun-terculture women . . . were using the notion of female difference to carve out spheres of influence in emerging movements: New Age spirituality, holistic health, ecofeminism, antinuclear and peace activism, and food politics. . . .

Hippie women's influence, as agents of cultural transformation, increased and extended well beyond the 1960s and 1970s."[30] These women helped lay the foundation for an alternative to the secular and spiritual nihilism eating away at liberal America.

And the center of it all was California, a state named after a Spanish novel about a utopian society run by women.[31]

California Dreamin'

The student movement and the sixties counterculture that followed first emerged in California. It is probably no accident that much of the increasing interest in feminine values and the divine feminine initially occurred on the American West Coast, far removed from the intellectually complacent and ingrown cultural world of the East Coast or the equally embedded and vastly more ingrown cultural and religious conservatism of the South. There lay the cultural yeast that would grow to challenge a nation. California, especially the San Francisco Bay Area, became the epicenter for this alternative vision of human potential. To be sure, California was not alone, and certainly the state had its share of defenders of the status quo. But California was the center for the sixties cultural and political rejection of the managerial liberal political establishment.

California had long been a mecca for people seeking to explore alternative spiritual traditions. The Russian River area north of San Francisco had been a center for American adherents of George Gurdjieff's philosophy and Rudolf Steiner's anthroposophy since well before World War II. The Rosicrucian Museum in San Jose had the western United States's largest collection of ancient Egyptian artifacts. Asian spiritual influences had long been present up and down the coast, with the Theosophical Society located in Pasadena and Jiddu Krishnamurti living in Ojai. After World War II westerners evidenced a growing interest in Zen Buddhism, initially in the San Francisco Bay area, particularly after the rise of the Beats in 1957. Other Buddhist traditions also began putting down roots outside Asian immigrant communities, again often beginning in California.

Culturally, California disproportionately attracted people seeking to explore beyond traditional social definitions of success. The sixties counterculture arose within this well-established tradition, spreading even into high technology, where many young engineers, particularly near Stanford, turned against the dominance of computing by huge mainframe IBM machines and the conformist hierarchical culture they symbolized and supported. These young people's vision was to make computing so accessible that anyone could do so, free from corporate dominance. The personal computer was the result.[32]

Across the Bay, in Berkeley, the counterculture was influencing physics, which had become almost completely absorbed into technical research for the military and business, never looking at the deeper implications of the strange new reality it was encountering. There the Fundamental Fysiks Group turned the attention of many young physicists toward exploring these implications. Many later became major interpreters of physics to the general public and future graduate students alike, while their focus on the more unusual and arcane implications of quantum theory opened new avenues of insight toward new technologies. As physicist David Kaiser writes, "They were among the first to ask the big questions again, to return to a spirit of doing physics that had animated Einstein, Bohr, and their generation."[33]

In 1911 George Santayana observed, "I am struck in California by the deep and almost religious affection which people have for nature and for the sensitiveness they show for its influence."[34] In 1864 Congress had donated Yosemite Valley and the Mariposa Sequoia Grove to the newly admitted state as a park. Later Sequoia and Yosemite, our second and third national parks, were established in the state's mountains. The Sierra Club, America's largest environmental organization and one of its oldest, was founded in California. This long-established California tradition grew and flourished with new energy beginning in the sixties.

Berkeley became the national symbol for the student movement, San Francisco became the symbol for the counterculture, and the San Francisco Peninsula became the primary focal point for the brewing technological revolution. The Bay Area as a whole was a center of environmental awakening. From the Esalen Institute at Big Sur to Marin County and fading into the rain-drenched redwoods to the north, the Bay Area and its surroundings became a center for psychological, artistic, religious, technological, and political experimentation. Culture warriors hate the Bay Area for a reason.

SPIRIT AND THE SIXTIES

Camille Paglia argues that the sixties was one of America's "Great Awakenings," a period of enhanced spiritual concern and increased personal spiritual experience.[35] I suspect there were many causes for the upwelling of spiritual interest and commitment at this time. Perhaps the role played in the civil rights movement by many synagogues and Christian churches helped demonstrate spirituality's practical importance, as did opposition to the Vietnam War by many religious Americans. Vatican II gave many hope that Catholicism was entering a time of greater religious openness and tolerance. The nationwide worry about annihilation through nuclear war reminded thoughtful people that wealth and power were far from ultimate goals and could end in a flash. I think the working of spirit was also involved. Whatever the causes, many of the people who helped shape the sixties possessed strong spiritual motivations.

The sixties counterculture forms a psychocultural unity. Increasingly its cultural and spiritual trends reflected feminine yin values rather than masculine yang ones, coming together as a style of relating with the world and others that was receptive, intuitive, connective, sensuous, nonlineal, and experiential. Whether symbolically, as with long hair, viscerally, as with rock and roll, internally, as with the growing interest in entheogens, or explicitly, as with environmentalism and feminism, there was a shift to honoring the feminine, the physical, and harmony with nature rather than fantasizing about dominating the world or conquering space. For many Americans, Leonardo's vision that knowledge led to love began to compete with those of Bacon and Locke. Spiritual interest increasingly emphasized personal experience rather than theology, ritual rather than sermons, the sacred in the world rather than a transcendent deity.

Before the sixties America was largely a spiritual monoculture defined by transcendental monotheism. The First Amendment had established religious liberty, although in practice Indians were not included. The only religions anyone knew much about were Christianity and Judaism. As Americans engaged in military conflicts outside the European context, Asian spiritual traditions became an increasingly noticeable cultural presence, especially on the West Coast. In the sixties this influence increased, as did that of many previously suppressed Native American traditions. Neo-Paganism made its first semipublic presence known in the United States.

In 1977 the English Episcopal theologian and historian Ninian Smart observed, "Today in the Western democracies particularly, and California more intensely, men . . . shop around for faiths, and are liable to make experiments in living undreamed of thirty years back. . . . One needs to sift wheat from chaff. But the fact is that we have a great new meeting of cultures and forms of spirituality." The only previous period to compare, Smart wrote, was the late Roman world that ultimately gave rise to Christianity.[36]

One connecting thread consistently stands out: recognizing the feminine face of the sacred. This recognition was the deepest spiritual hope and promise the sixties injected into American society. Ever since, a complex interweaving of liberal Christian, Asian, Native American, and Pagan spiritual currents has influenced American religion. This feminine current also provided a way to harmonize religion with science, transform women's spiritual status, and shift spiritual attention from a transcendent God separate from the earth to a divine immanence expressing itself in and through our world.

Before we can really understand what that period offered and continues to offer, we need look more closely at the right-wing reaction, particular by the culture warriors.

Chapter Seven

The Culture Warriors

No stages. This is total war. We are fighting a variety of enemies. There are lots of them out there. . . . If we . . . just wage a total war . . . our children will sing great songs about us years from now.

—Michael Ledeen

If God is king, men have a duty to try, as best they can, to conform their lives to his will and shape society in accordance with his law. Defection and indifferentism are not options. We are commanded to fight.

—Pat Buchanan

America's Democratic liberal elite split over the Vietnam War, some siding with the antiwar movement and some resolutely against it. Subsequent economic difficulties ate away their confidence in managing the economy in the way Kennedy's New Frontiersman had fantasized. American liberalism's strongest expression was weakened, opening an opportunity for new political forces.

At the same time a major division within the least liberal elements of American society was being dissolved. Southern culture had been deeply challenged by the sixties, its old Democratic Party coalition seriously weakened. Many Southerners' loyalty to a Democratic Party dominated nationally by northern liberals was up for grabs.

Seeing an opportunity to weaken the Democrats permanently, in 1971 Pat Buchanan advised Richard Nixon that he needed to split the country to win Southern support. Nixon and all subsequent Republican administrations and presidential candidates acted on Buchanan's advice. Their Southern strategy paid off at the polls, for the managerial, technocratic orientation of the Democrats eschewed talk of values—yet ultimately politics was about what values should predominate in a society.

Republicans courted the old neo-Confederate counterculture, welcoming it into the Republican Party. Today sitting Republican legislators defend slavery and praise John Wilkes Booth.[1] The Republican Party represents America's first true counterculture. (See "America's First Counterculture," http://dizerega.com/faultlines/appendices/.)

While Republicans hoped to co-opt their Southern partners, their new allies had plans of their own. In 1979 Jerry Falwell formed the Moral Majority. Over time it and subsequent organizations got ever better at winning internal political battles. Today they easily ally with secular neoconservatives and dominate the Republican Party in ways both Nixon and Ronald Reagan would have opposed.

In their current guise as Tea Partyers the culture warriors dominate one political party in a country whose electoral rules make it almost impossible to have more than two. Even if most Americans dislike their positions, they are the only alternative available to an increasingly corrupt Democratic Party. And many voters vote for or against the incumbent depending on how their lives are going. Culture warriors benefit from electoral rules designed for a country without parties.

The Founders lived before political parties existed. Initially they had envisioned elections between many independent candidates.[2] Plurality rules seemed reasonable when there were many candidates and no experience with runoffs, but once parties arose they generated a two-party oligopoly almost impervious to outside challenge.

So long as America's parties were internally diverse and decentralized and issues relatively few and easily compromised, this arrangement worked reasonably well. Its only serious breakdown was just before the Civil War, a breakdown leading to the current Democratic and Republican Parties. Even after the federal government grew larger under New Deal reforms, so long as issues were primarily over allocation of resources determined by internally diverse parties the American system managed well enough.

However, as the Republicans became more monolithic, Republican representatives began voting in lockstep, fearing primary challenges if they did not. In 2010, Senate Republican Leader Mitch McConnell boasted, "The single most important thing we want to achieve is for President Obama to be a one-term president."[3]

Longtime conservative senator Richard Lugar lost a 2012 primary election to a Tea Party challenger because his willingness to work with Democrats was held against him. Pat Buchanan put the issue bluntly: "We no longer inhabit the same moral universe. We are no longer a moral community. We are two countries. One part of America has seceded, and the other has no interest in re-establishing the Union."[4] The democratic value of a loyal opposition was explicitly abandoned.

A powerful American version of the European revolutionary right has emerged. America's revolutionary right is complex, with powerful secular and religious components. But regardless of the variant, a focus on domination, hierarchy, and pathological masculinity exists in them all. (See "Are They Fascists?" http://dizerega.com/faultlines/appendices/.)

PROPHETS OF HEGEMONY

In praising neoconservative Michael Ledeen's foreign policy views, *National Review* editor Jonah Goldberg described the "bedrock tenet" of the "Ledeen Doctrine": "Every ten years or so, the United States needs to pick up some small crappy little country and throw it against the wall, just to show the world we mean business."[5]

Goldberg was young enough to serve in Iraq when he wrote his bold words, but he had more comfortable priorities, and Ledeen remained in graduate school during the Vietnam War. These men are typical of today's warrior-intellectuals, most of whom call themselves neoconservatives (See "Paradoxical Origins of Neoconservatism," http://dizerega.com/faultlines/appendices/.)

Neoconservatives are secular nihilists who have embraced the culture war as a path to power and domination. Shadia Drury describes neoconservatism as "an expression of modernity, and of the radical and immoderate spirit of our times. It fits . . . 'the politics of faith'—not for its religiosity, which is suspect, but for its conception of politics as a mode of conduct that seeks to bring all human activity within its domain of control."[6]

Once Communism collapsed and America ascended to unrivaled global political and economic preeminence, many neoconservatives wanted to make American dominance permanent. The new American empire was to be in the name of American values. In 1996 William Kristol and Robert Kagan argued in the elite journal *Foreign Affairs* that the role of America should be "benevolent global hegemony": "The aspiration to benevolent hegemony might strike some as either hubristic or morally suspect. But a hegemon is nothing more or less than a leader with preponderant influence and authority over all others in its domain." When Kristol and Kagan wrote, our military budget dwarfed all others in the world, despite our having *no* militarily threatening enemies. Yet the authors demanded big *increases* in military spending. We begin to see what benevolent hegemony really implied when they criticized "the admonition of John Quincy Adams that America ought not go 'abroad in search of monsters to destroy.'" "But why not?" they ask. "Because America has the capacity to contain or destroy many of the world's monsters, . . . a policy of sitting atop a hill and leading by example becomes in practice a policy of cowardice and dishonor."[7]

Note the manly terminology and eagerness to rely on violence to realize their vision, despite the fact that, like Ledeen and Goldberg, neither Kristol nor Kagan ever wore his country's uniform. Yet, agreeing with their repudiation of America's defining principles is an act of bravery and a commitment to honor, while disagreement is cowardice and dishonor.

Irving Kristol, William's father and a founding eminence of neoconservatism, asks, "What's the point of being the greatest, most powerful nation in the world and not having an imperial role? . . . It would be natural for the United States . . . to play a far more dominant role in world affairs. Not what we're doing now but to command and to give orders as to what is to be done. People need that." He complains that the Republican Party is "tying itself into knots" over prescriptions for elderly people. "Who gives a damn? I think it's disgusting that . . . presidential politics of the most important country in the world should revolve around prescriptions for elderly people."[8]

Like Goldberg, the Kristols, and Kagan, Michael Ledeen advocates American hegemony. "Creative destruction is our middle name, both within our own society and abroad." The result is war with traditional peoples. "They cannot feel secure so long as we are there, for our very existence— our existence, not our politics—threatens their legitimacy. They must attack us in order to survive, just as we must destroy them to advance our historic mission."[9]

With respect to the many deaths and ruined lives that arise from pursuing our "historic mission," Ledeen observed, "I think the level of casualties is secondary. I mean, it may sound like an odd thing to say, but all the great scholars who have studied American character have come to the conclusion that we are a warlike people and that we love war."[10] Noted neoconservative scholar Harvey Mansfield agrees: "War is hell but men like it."[11] One wonders why these lovers of war have so assiduously avoided the military, why the country has almost always had large peace movements, and why we need a draft or an underclass of poor Americans who see the military as their ticket out of poverty.

From a liberal standpoint war is a last resort, not least because of its impact on any society waging it. Like chemotherapy, war sometimes is necessary. But chemo always weakens the cancer sufferer's body and needs careful administration in measured doses. Eternal war, like eternal chemo, guarantees the patient's death.

Our Founders believed a free society was incompatible with frequent war. Alexander Hamilton, who has *never* been accused of being soft on executive power, wrote, "It is of the nature of war to increase the executive at the expense of the legislative authority." If these conditions were prolonged, "we should, in a little time, see established in every part of this country the same engines of despotism which have been the scourge of the Old World."[12] But as we shall see, neoconservatives admire one-man rule.

Neoconservatives' ignorance of Hamilton's argument that frequent war erodes a free society reflects their illiberal European intellectual heritage.

Some they picked up from their parents, many of them former Marxists. Much of the rest grew from Straussian teachings they encountered in college, teachings locating ultimate authority in a hierarchical conception of politics with the elite at the top, whereas Locke and the Founders located it in the people considered as equal citizens.

James Madison wrote that the Constitution established a government "limited in its sovereignty as well with respect to the means as to the objects of its powers; and that to give an extent to the former, superseding the limits of the latter, is in effect to convert a limited into an unlimited Government."[13] With popular sovereignty, government is properly the people's servant. When government is sovereign, it is their master.

For neoconservatives national greatness and campfire glory count for a lot.[14] For our Founders, prosperous cities and farms and a people at peace counted for much more, as would affordable prescriptions for the elderly. In their place Irving Kristol offers the opportunity "to command and to give orders as to what is to be done."

THE APOTHEOSIS OF MASTERY

Proving Hamilton's point from the other side, Harvey Mansfield underlined the neoconservatives' rejection of American democratic traditions. "In quiet times" he writes, "the rule of law will come to the fore, and the executive can be weak. In stormy times, the rule of law may seem to require the prudence and force that law, or present law, cannot supply, and the executive must be strong."

Mansfield correctly argues that the president was intended to provide "energy" in the execution of his office. That is why the Founders rejected a plural executive as too indecisive and difficult to hold responsible for its decisions. But Mansfield then writes: "One man . . . will be the greatest source of energy if he regards it as necessary to maintaining his own rule. Such a person will have the greatest incentive to be watchful, and to be both cruel and merciful in correct contrast and proportion. We are talking about

Machiavelli's prince, the man whom in apparently unguarded moments he called a tyrant."[15]

Michael Ledeen agrees: "Properly led, we can achieve glory. But the task is hard and never-ending, for we must overcome our own ruinous impulses as well as thwart those who seek to dominate us for their own satisfaction. And since we will do anything to satisfy our ruinous impulses, all manner of nastiness may be required to keep us under control, and to defeat our enemies."[16]

In 1999, when the United States was at the height of its economic and military power, Ledeen fretted, "If new and more virtuous leaders do not emerge, it is only a matter of time before we are either dominated by our enemies or sink into a more profound crisis." What does this leadership look like? "Paradoxically, preserving liberty may require the rule of a single leader—a dictator—willing to use those dreaded 'extraordinary measures, which few know how, or are willing, to employ.' . . . Just as it is sometimes necessary temporarily to resort to evil actions to achieve worthy objectives, so a period of dictatorship is sometimes the only hope for freedom."[17] Love of political authoritarianism is a defining feature of neoconservatism.[18]

Alexander Hamilton warned us of such men. So did President Eisenhower.

Mansfield might object that his recommendation applies only in "stormy times." But if suicidal attacks by nineteen terrorists armed with box cutters and unsuccessful attacks by guys with exploding shoes and burning under-wear justifies setting aside our two-hundred-year-old constitutional system, *anything* can. Using Mansfield's logic, we would have been justified in abandoning the rule of law during both world wars and the Cold War.

As I finished this manuscript Jonah Goldberg, who looks forward to attacking small countries to prove we can, had this to say about how con-servatives should deal with young voters who disagree with them: "The fact that young people think socialism is better than capitalism. That's proof of what social scientists call their stupidity and their ignorance. And that's something that conservatives have to beat out of them, either literally or figuratively as far as I'm concerned."[19]

Domination abroad and at home is the essence of neoconservatism.

THE RELIGIOUS RIGHT AND THE GOD OF DOMINATION

Neoconservatives are closely allied with the Christian right. At first this alliance seems strange because neoconservatives are mostly secular modernists. They praise right-wing Christianity for its ability to maintain social and political hierarchies, not for its claims to spiritual truth.[20] But each sees the other as a useful tool in their quest for absolute power.

The religious right largely grows from three Christian traditions long at odds: Southern Baptists, Pentecostals, and Catholics. But it should not be equated with all the people within any of these groups. The Southern Baptists and Pentecostals are very diverse. Jimmy Carter was a Southern Baptist; Bill Clinton still is. Both Baptists and Pentecostals identify themselves as evangelical Christians but many evangelicals are far from being members of the religious right.[21] Right-wing Catholics are a tiny portion of American Catholics.

The religious right consists of that portion of these and other Christian communities who ignore Jesus's warning that his kingdom is not of this world and consider themselves the troops by which this world can be conquered in God's name. Let us turn to Pat Buchanan's 1999 outburst announcing the culture war, a portion of which heads this chapter: "In politics, conservatives have won more than they have lost, but in the culture, the left and its Woodstock values have triumphed. Divorce, dirty language, adultery, blasphemy, euthanasia, abortion, pornography, homosexuality, cohabitation and so on were not unknown in 1960. But today, they permeate our lives. . . . The culture war is at its heart a religious war about whether God or man shall be exalted. . . . With those stakes, to walk away is to abandon your post in time of war."[22]

What Buchanan asserted for conservative Catholics was echoed by Southern Baptist Jerry Falwell and immediately confirmed by Pentecostal Pat Robertson. After 9/11, Falwell said on Robertson's television show, "What we saw on Tuesday, as terrible as it is, could be miniscule if, in fact, God continues to lift the curtain and allow the enemies of America to give us probably what we deserve." He pointed to those "who have tried to secularize America"—pagans, abortionists, feminists, gays, lesbians, the ACLU, People For the American Way—for helping it happen. Robertson replied, "I totally concur."[23]

According to Robertson and Falwell, God allowed America to be attacked and thousands to die because he did not approve of whom some Americans slept with. Southern Baptist John Hagee believes his God devastated the Gulf Coast via Hurricane Katrina because New Orleans was going to have a gay parade.[24] Religious southern Mississippi also got walloped, part of the Lord's collateral damage. Rather than following the Christian view that God's innocent son died to save the guilty, the religious right's deity killed many innocents to punish the guilty, but left many of the guilty still alive.

From this religious right's perspective, other religious views serve evil either deliberately or through confusion. Rick Joyner of the New Apostolic Reformation explained that godly rule at first "may seem like totalitarianism," but "the kingdom will move from a point of necessary control while people are learning truth, integrity, honor, and how to make decisions, to increasing liberty so that they can."[25] These sentiments are far closer to Lenin and Mao than to anything from Jesus. Many Christian-right groups seek to obtain total political power.

Of course there have always been Christian groups that sought political domination. But since the Enlightenment advocates of religious intolerance and theocratic rule have been in retreat in the West. Do they really matter today?

If we were a multiparty democracy, they would be an irritant. But by dominating one of two parties when people often vote based on the incumbent's record rather than the alternative's platform, the issue takes on a darker hue. Do they matter? Yes, they do.

Family Values and Christian Rule

Consider a group that includes Tom Coburn, Jim DeMint, Lindsey Graham, Chuck Grassley, Jim Inhofe, and John Thune, a sizeable minority of the Republican senators, and Mark Pryor, a Democrat. Along with being senators they are all members of "the Family."

The Family is a secretive group whose members also include many in the House of Representatives and probably elsewhere in government and the military. They are influential in right-wing circles in Washington, where many of them live in the Family's C Street residence. Jeff Sharlet, who has done the most to illuminate these people, describes the group as "followers of a political religion that embraces elitism, disdains democracy, and pursues power for its members the better to 'advance the Kingdom.'" He quotes the group's "spiritual leader," Doug Coe, preaching on the meaning of Christ's words: "You know Jesus said 'You got to put Him before father-mother-brother-sister'? Hitler, Lenin, Mao, that's what they taught the kids. Mao even had the kids killing their own mother and father. But it wasn't murder. It was building the new nation. The new kingdom."

This incident was not an isolated one. Sharlet describes how Coe's son and heir apparent, David, explained what it meant to be a divinely chosen leader. He told a young follower that even if he raped three little girls, "as a member of the Family, he's among what Family leaders refer to as the 'new chosen.' If you're chosen, the normal rules don't apply."[26] These views agree with a fifth-century Christian fanatic's claim that "there is no crime for those who have Christ."[27]

Aggressive amorality is what passes for Christianity within an important part of the religious right. Pryor is quoted as saying, "Jesus did not come to bring peace. He came to take over."[28] The Family is not a fringe sect operating out of a storefront. It initiated Washington's annual Prayer Breakfast, attended even by the president. Through its public and secret members, the Family extends throughout the government.

Rick Joyner, who endorsed divine totalitarianism, is a member of the New Apostolic Reformation, a more recently formed Christian dominionist group also wielding considerable influence at very high political levels. In 2008 C. Peter Wagner, its primary intellectual force, published *Dominion!* arguing that the "apostles" are to be "the generals in the army of God."[29] Apostle Lou Engel, influential in Christian-right circles, has said, "We are called into the very image of the Trinity himself, that we are to be His friends and partners for world dominion." Rachel Tabachnick, who extensively researched the New Apostolic Reformation, writes, "It sounds so fringe but yet it's not fringe. They've been working with Sarah Palin, Newt Gingrich, Michele Bachmann, Sam Brownback, and now Rick Perry."[30]

In 2012 Katherine Stewart reported that in the fall over 100,000 elementary school students in American *public* schools would receive explicit coaching on the scriptural justification for killing unbelievers. The instruction would come from the Good News Club, an afterschool program sponsored by the Child Evangelism Fellowship, which seeks to convert young children to Christian fundamentalism and use them to attract other children. Most distressingly, the teachings would focus considerable attention on the literal intent of biblical commands to kill every nonbeliever, basing its teachings on 1 Samuel 15:2–3 commanding genocide against the Amalekites. Why the slaughter? The lesson plan reads, "The Amalekites had heard about Israel's true and living God many years before, but they refused to believe in him. The Amalekites refused to believe in God and God had promised punishment." Further, the children would be told it was vital to obey God literally. Saul was punished by God because he did not slaughter everyone. The instruction manual continues, "If God tells you to kill nonbelievers, he really wants you to kill them all. No questions asked, no exceptions allowed."[31]

We see here a pattern in results if not intention between the amoral teachings of the Family, including its apparent endorsement of the legitimacy of destroying families and children killing their parents, and the Good News Club instilling the idea of total obedience and killing nonbelievers in small children. Hierarchy, subordination, and ruthless obedience are the substance of a religion that claims its scripture teaches, "Whoever does not love does not know God, because God is love" (1 John 4:8).

But could this really happen? An important experiment conducted in Switzerland shows how it could. Selected groups of people, mostly students, engaged in a series of opportunities to split fairly a money reward or to keep most of it. Later the second player could "punish" the first by deducting units from the first, but at a cost. For every three units deducted the punisher lost one. Members of a religious group were no more punishing toward others than any other group *unless they had recently been shown subliminal religious messages*. They then became the most punishing of all, even at a greater cost to themselves.[32] Citizens unlikely to act against others might be motivated to do so if given a religious context to justify such action. When religious differences become potent political issues in a time of stress and turmoil, the mix can be very dangerous under manipulative leaders. There are plenty of such leaders in positions of surprising power and influence.

In today's world, views such as these cannot be easily defended because a liberal respect for people has deeply penetrated our culture. Most Americans believe our common humanity trumps our individual differences. But if differences between people can be inflated in the public's eye to appear more fundamental than their similarities, that liberal insight can be overridden for many. Those who seek dominion seek incessantly to divide the country along lines of false dichotomies: one wedge issue incessantly follows another. Pat Buchanan's memo to Nixon urging him to divide the country is now standard operating procedure for the religious right and their political allies.

Christian rule in America may sound attractive to some conservative Christians with little knowledge of history. But who counts as Christians? Some who think of themselves as Christians might be surprised to learn they don't qualify. As Pat Robertson explained, "You say you're supposed to be nice to the Episcopalians and the Presbyterians and the Methodists. . . . Nonsense. I don't have to be nice to the spirit of the Antichrist."[33]

Would Robertson describe Catholics or Mormons any differently than he did Episcopalians, Methodists, and Presbyterians, were they not important in his political coalition? John Hagee identifies Catholicism as "the Great Whore of Revelation 17."[34] Mormons fare no better with this crowd. Apostle Doug Stringer observed, "In fact, if you look at the original founder of the Mormon Church, Joseph Smith, he had a huge influence by Masonry. Bottom-line, anything that is so secretive that has to be hidden in darkness . . . is not biblical."[35] But currently Mormons and Catholics are useful.

Conservative Catholics return the favor. Right-wing American Catholic bishops are forcing laypeople active in the church to sign loyalty oaths, which include pledges on whom they will or will not vote for—the opposite of John Kennedy's 1960 pledge that his religion was not relevant. Right-wing Catholic Rick Santorum said that he "almost threw up" after reading Kennedy's speech.[36]

The religious right argues that bad things happen because we do not appropriately honor their God. To prevent bad things, their God wants them to enforce their vision of what is good and bad over the rest of us. As their God dominates them, so they get to dominate us. Christian Dominionist George Grant puts it this way:

> But it is dominion we are after. Not just a voice.
> It is dominion we are after. Not just influence.
> It is dominion we are after. Not just equal time.
> It is dominion we are after.[37]

Despite their fanaticism, Michael Ledeen endorses the Christian right because "good religion teaches men that politics is the most important enterprise in the eyes of God." Further, "American evangelical Christianity is the sort of 'good religion' Machiavelli calls for. The evangelicals do not quietly accept their destiny, believing instead they are called upon to fight corruption and reestablish virtue." Ledeen tells us, "The combination of fear of God and fear of punishment—duly carried out with good arms— provides the necessary discipline for good government."[38]

A Case Study in Pathological Masculinity

Harvey Mansfield was William Kristol's mentor at Harvard. In 2006 Mansfield published *Manliness* to empower supposedly emasculated American men into regaining their manliness. What Mansfield produced is a classic example of the pathological masculinity underlying neoconservative ideology.[39] (See "Neoconservative 'Manliness,'" http://dizerega.com/faultlines/appendices/.)

For Mansfield, "manliness is knowing how to be confident in situations where sufficient knowledge is not available." It is aggression, but not purely selfish aggression. "It is aggression that develops an assertion, a cause it espouses." Mansfield distinguishes the aggression associated with animals from manliness because assertion combines our natural aggression with higher claims. Nature *and* nurture meet to differentiate manly assertion from animal aggression. Assertiveness seeks to prove a point to others.[40]

In the case of manliness, aggressive assertion demands that others "pay attention to *me*." The manly man "is stubborn for the sake of something and yet also and always on his own behalf." The "manly man thinks and asserts that he matters."[41] Risk is therefore inherent in manly action because it challenges others, for, if nothing else, by demanding their attention he runs the risk he will be ignored.

Mansfield grants that we all "accept risks in small things"—for example, "the smaller, piecework enterprise of reproducing." But manly types "who welcome risk in large enterprises do the rest of us a great benefit." Supposedly these benefactors free us from being "determined by outside forces however beneficent; they represent human freedom."[42]

Mansfield admits that "not all men are like this." But to the degree they are, aggression is transformed by being subordinated to "honor," which is "a claim to protect one's person, family, and property—and the beliefs embodied in them." Crucially, Mansfield argues, "The claim to protect is the claim to rule. How can I protect you properly if I can't tell you what to do?"[43] Here Mansfield's manliness abandons liberal principles for the principle underlying chivalry and serfdom that allowed honor-bound aristocrats to rule over peasants they occasionally protected from depredations by other honor-bound aristocrats. But unlike the older ideologies of domination, Mansfield's rule is not justified by reference to a higher moral order.

In modern times, when meaning is challenged by nihilism, manliness is "the assertion of meaning when meaning is at risk."[44] Here we find the neoconservative counterpart to the pre–WWII European right's emphasis on will and power as a response to the ultimate meaninglessness of reality.

Meaning exists because I say it does and seek to impose it on others. This is a philosophy of domination for its own sake.

Women in childbirth take a significant risk. For most of our history childbirth was a leading cause of death for women. Even today the risk is not trivial. Without modern medicine at least one dear to me would have died giving birth, and I am hardly alone. Voluntarily taking life-and-death risks and accepting the inevitability of great suffering to achieve a valued goal describes *every* woman who chooses to be a mother. Long ago Euripides had Medea say, "Men say we lead an easy life, safe at home while they risk all at the point of a spear. What do they know? I would rather stand three times in battle with shield and spear than give birth once."[45]

Mansfield turns risk from a personal venture confronting high stakes into a *spectator sport* in which "manly men" seek to be noticed by others through doing great deeds. For Mansfield, manly success apparently depends on the eye of the beholder, a more sophisticated case of little boys showing off to be noticed. But no one mistakes boys for men. Mansfield manages *simultaneously* to devalue both what women do that no man can *and* masculine personal courage. This move is crucial to his position, even if unsustainable by logic, evidence, or decency.

Mansfield appears to praise the great man alone, the hero, the duce who seeks to transform a society. Here we find the manly princes Machiavelli hoped would unite Italy to throw off the oppression of northern barbarians. Manliness becomes "wholesale" greatness, unlike womanly piecework. Most men are relegated to irrelevance, except in their roles as audience and natural resources for the manly.

Mansfield's arguments about protection and ruling strike at the heart of free societies. People hire night watchmen *all the time* to protect them without making night watchmen their rulers. Just as watchmen are not our rulers, neither should be generals responsible for leading armies, policemen, or the agents people elect to serve them. All are public *servants*.

In the last letter he wrote Thomas Jefferson said, "The mass of mankind has not been born with saddles on their backs, nor a favored few, booted and spurred, ready to ride them legitimately by the grace of

God."[46] Liberals hold that *no one* should rule society, that *no one* should simply be the raw material for others' dreams and desires, that *no one* is wise enough to remake a people. Liberals hold that individual freedom trumps the power fantasies of privileged Harvard professors like Harvey Mansfield.

According to Mansfield, "Manliness is best shown in war." He "makes war or conflict central to politics and manliness the inspiration of both." Politics is like war in that it "is always intentionally divisive, our group against yours." Lenin, Mao, Castro, and Mussolini would be at home here, but not Jefferson or Hamilton. Mansfield attempts to evade too close an association with these people by admitting there can be too much manliness. He grants that "manliness is both good and bad." To avoid the "altogether bad," manliness must be tempered by moderation.[47]

But moderation is more likely if women are subordinated to men. Manly men need womanly women to keep their aggressiveness under some control. According to Mansfield, women prevent manly barbarism only if they behave appropriately. By accepting a subordinate role, women can use men's emotional dependence on them to criticize their bad behavior in private. Subordination is inevitable for most women anyway due to their physical weakness and the habits of mind it inculcates. To accomplish their civilizing role, however, women must be wily, relying on "cunning and deceit."[48] They are "not in a position to ask for something directly. They're either obliged to smile a lot and persuade, or make a scene."[49] But in so doing women help civilize men who are too manly and so help preserve what Mansfield calls civilization. In terms of my analysis, Mansfield's cure for the excesses of Mansfield's manliness is *pathological* femininity.

What is most striking about neoconservatives' manliness is how psychologically impoverished it is. Manliness is reduced to willful self-assertion, which they equate with domination. In common with European fascists, they denigrate women and the feminine along with elevating will and power. Mansfield considers it normal for manly men to "look down" on women's work and seek to dominate them.[50]

Mansfield argues that manliness is "responsible for our individuality. And because individuality must be asserted to, and against, other people, its creation is essentially a political act." He also claims that many men do not suffer from an overabundance of manliness; rather, they are not manly.[51] By his logic, men deficient in manliness and most women are not very individuated. Yet the individuality of the manly depends on the judgment of these others who do not themselves count for much as individuals.

In fact, Mansfield argues manliness is an "aristocratic" quality.[52] Most men cannot exercise much manliness because only a few can rule. They will necessarily be dominated, but they can still find self-respect by being able at least to dominate women.

Liberal societies have found a far more appropriate institution for dealing with manly men who lack sufficient self-control to behave themselves. Jail.

MISSING VIRTUES: FRIENDSHIP, LOVE, AND COURAGE

What is lacking in neoconservative manliness is revealing. Male friendship is basic to healthy manhood. Friendship is between equals, not in the sense that friends see one another as identical, but rather that they see one another as *intrinsically valuable* and worthy of equal respect. Among friends, difference need not imply hierarchy. Mansfield never explores friendship's implications for manliness because he does not understand relations between equals.

A similar point applies to Mansfield's discussion of love. Again, he seems able to think about love only within hierarchical relationships. He is appropriately dismissive of what he calls the "masculine view of sex according to which love goes from high to low, the lover being superior to the beloved," but he can only contrast it to the Platonic view, "the true one," in which sex (equated here with love) goes "from low to high, the beloved being superior." Love is "enslavement."[53]

There is no appreciation for loving relationships between two people treasuring the *intrinsic value* each sees in the other. In contrast to enslavement, which better describes infatuation, this kind of love can be described as a *knowing* devotion to and delight in the other. The lover's self is expanded or fulfilled by the relationship rather than enslaved. This love partially shares a key characteristic with divine love, which has never been described as God's enslavement to the person loved.

On *Fox News Sunday* William Kristol observed, "White women are a problem, that's, you know—we all live with that."[54] For his part Mansfield finds women who do not live to his standards sexually undesirable: feminists "show themselves to be very unerotic."[55] In these attitudes these men typify neoconservatives as a movement.[56]

Mansfield, Kristol, and their like appear to be a minority among Americans. In her history of marriage Stephanie Coontz reports that today marital equality is associated with greater marital happiness for both sexes. In interviews of Americans who matured in the 1980s and 1990s, Kathleen Gerson reported that only one-third of men wanted a traditional marriage, whereas most young men and women alike wanted egalitarian and loving marriages.[57] These insights hold more widely. Garry Wills cited a University of Chicago study of 27,500 adults between the ages of forty and eighty living in twenty-nine countries. The research studied sexual satisfaction in relationships, reporting a substantial difference between "gender-equal regimes" and "male-centered regimes," with happiness greater among *both* women and men in more gender-equal relationships.[58]

Martha Nussbaum looked at courage as shown by people who rescued Jews during the Holocaust: "The rescuers had all been brought up to think that people ought to care for one another, and that it was unacceptable to shirk responsibility for someone else's suffering if one could do something about it." Rescuers were of both genders, but in terms of what Nussbaum describes as "common gender stereotypes," in her judgment the key traits were more feminine.[59] I would say they exemplify balance, as a strong sense of responsibility has a feminine side (others matter) and a masculine side (I can do this). People such as these, among the bravest of our time, did not claim that their courage led to the right to rule those they protected.

THE "WAR ON THE FEMININE"

Whether in secular or religious guise, the lust for dominion cannot handle equality, which for it is *always* suspect. Women are obviously different from men, so if they are equal, this insight can be expanded to undermine all other relations of domination. It opens the door for examining subtle forms of domination so integrated into a culture as to have long been invisible to dominator and victim alike.

I believe this dynamic is why all movements rooted in visions of eternal hierarchies of spiritual domination have been so vividly antifeminine. Consider Bruce Ware, professor of Christian theology at Southern Baptist Theological Seminary. Ware believes that while abusing wives is a sin, *unsubmissive* wives often bring on this abuse, and their lack of submission is *also* a sin. "A woman will demonstrate that she is in fact a Christian, that she has submitted to God's ways by affirming and embracing her God-designed identity . . . as wife and mother . . . rather than wanting to be a man, wanting to be in a man's position, wanting to teach and exercise authority over men."

Ware and those like him confuse honoring the sacred with honoring their egos and desire to dominate with God's will. To quote Ware again, "If it's true that in the Trinity itself—in the eternal relationships of Father, Son and Spirit, there is authority and submission, and the Son eternally submits to the will of the Father—if that's true, then this follows: It is as Godlike to submit to rightful authority with joy and gladness as it is Godlike to exert wise and beneficial rightful authority."[60] As Ware describes it, submission is a relation of power; it is not based on any recognition of superior wisdom or goodness.

This image of a divine baboon troop is blurred with reminders that just as God loves us so men should love women. But power and subordination are God's primary relationships to men and, in this view, of men to women. Love is nice but secondary. If a man is unloving, the command for the wife's subordination to him remains, and she sins if she does not submit, just as the reason for our submission to God is not love, but divine will backed by omnipotence. Like neoconservatives, Ware blames women for men's misbehavior. (See "Strange Bedfellows," http://dizerega.com/faultlines/appendices/.)

Leaders of the Christian right lay claim to American religious and moral leadership. Their targets are liberal modernity and feminine values, wherever they might appear. The religious right's attack on women and the feminine is prettied up in lofty moral rhetoric about "life" and "families," but a closer look reveals a much different agenda, an agenda that takes precedence over addressing the nation's severe economic difficulties, as the behavior of the Republican Congress in 2010 and 2011 demonstrates.

The morally complex issue of abortion is only an entering wedge, a way to begin to get at their real target: women and the feminine in any of their strong aspects. The only acceptable forms of female power are women actively defending the superiority of masculine values, such as Ann Coulter, Michelle Bachmann, and Sarah Palin. The life of a fetus *consistently* takes second place to bringing women under greater subordination, as the life of the woman increasingly is subordinated to that of the fetus, or even a zygote. (See "Abortion and the Irrational," http://dizerega.com/faultlines/appendices/.)

Consider sex education. Many studies indicate that sex education significantly lowers unwanted pregnancies, yet the religious right opposes sex education and advocates abstinence-only programs that demonstrably do not work.[61] The result of their opposition is to *increase* abortions. Only someone who did not care much about life could support these programs.

The religious right also opposed Plan B, which prevents ovulation and therefore fertilization. By their own logic no human life is at risk. No egg is fertilized, no zygote dies. However, Plan B enables women to exercise greater control over their bodies, expanding their freedom, which is its real shortcoming for the religious right.

Similarly, the religious right opposes distributing condoms or making contraceptives available. Condoms and contraceptives prevent many abortions and cause none.[62] For the religious right it is *better* to have abortions, legal or illegal, than to have educated women exercising informed control over their reproductive futures.

The most recent studies I have encountered indicate the percentage of pregnant women having abortions is constant whether abortions are legal or illegal, but women's death rates are far lower when the procedure is legal. In South Africa, once abortion became legal there was a 90-percent decline in women's death rates. The best available evidence also indicates that by reducing the number of pregnancies contraception reduces the number of abortions.[63] Certainly it decreases the number of innocents God kills through miscarriages and failures of fertilized eggs to implant.

The religious right also fought the HPV vaccine that reduces the chances of a woman getting cervical cancer.[64] They did so, they said, because the vaccine might encourage some unmarried women to have more sex than they otherwise would. Better more cancer and less sex.

States with strong antiabortion laws provide less funding per child for foster care, smaller stipends for parents who adopt children with special needs, and smaller payments for poor women with dependent children than states with strong abortion rights laws. In 1999 Louisiana had America's most stringent antiabortion laws and spent $603 annually for each poor child, compared to $4,648 for liberal Hawaii. Almost half the states with the strongest antiabortion laws did not make it a crime, in a no-abortion context, for a third party to kill a fetus of *any* gestational age. But six of the strongest antiabortion states that do not criminalize fetal battering prosecute women for prenatal drug use.[65]

There is a connecting thread here, one having nothing to do with being pro-life: a single-minded effort to eliminate women's control over their bodies through abolishing abortion, contraception, and sex education and in the worst cases even denying women abortions when their health is at stake or they have been raped. Alabama and Mississippi now allow miscarriages, God's own little abortions, to be investigated by the police, in case the woman might be an accessory to God's actions.

From this perspective women's primary function is breeding. Culture-warrior Zell Miller bluntly explained why. In 2007 the former senator from Georgia charged that abortion has contributed to our military's manpower shortage. Babies are needed so they can grow up and become soldiers;

besides, more American babies would mean more Americans to do the minimally paid jobs Mexican laborers seek.[66]

We look in vain here for rationality or compassion. There is none. Nor will we find charity or love, which are equally absent. The religious right's real target is to roll back the freedoms women acquired during the sixties, when the pill first became available, and, with it, all the cultural changes it made possible. Worshipping a deity of domination, they want to strengthen and reestablish domination where it has been expelled from our lives. Women and the feminine are their major target because feminine values undermine domination in whatever guise it emerges.

The culture war is a war of nihilism against civilization, domination against humanity, and power against reason. To use a phrase from George Orwell's *1984*, its vision is a boot stamping on a human face for eternity.

A great bifurcation is happening in America today, one side using fantasies of the past in service to domination and a pathological masculinity, the other offering a way out of the moral and intellectual cul-de-sac to which the Enlightenment project led us.

CHAPTER EIGHT

FEMINISM

When we have moved beyond the desolation of all our male vanities,
from the stock market to the stock pile of rockets, we will be more open
and receptive. Open and bleeding like that archaic wound, the vulva,
we will be prepared to receive the conception of a new civilization.

—William Irwin Thompson

In 1961, along with professor C. Lee Buxtom of Yale's medical school, Estelle Griswold, executive director of Planned Parenthood of Connecticut, opened a birth control clinic in New Haven. Other than by the rhythm method, preventing conception was illegal in Connecticut. Griswold and Buxtom were arrested. The case reached the Supreme Court, which ruled in their favor in *Griswold v. Connecticut*, establishing a right to privacy. By establishing this right, *Griswold* ultimately gave women control over their own bodies and shifted American feminism from a narrowly liberal perspective toward a larger, more inclusive, and more completely human context. In the process cultural feminists made a case for the intrinsic value of human beings free from the debilitating vulnerabilities that had undermined earlier liberal arguments.

Stephanie Coontz describes the roughly twenty-year period from the end of World War II to the renewed rise of feminism as the traditional liberal marriage ideal's "golden years": "Never before had so many people shared the experience of courting their own mates, getting married at will, and setting up their own households."[1] Unlike in all previous Western history, marriage increasingly resembled John Locke's vision of partnership between equals. People married because of love and hopes for personal fulfillment rather than from economic necessity, the duty to procreate, the politics of family alliances, or the shotgun.

Conservatives criticized this modern ideal as destabilizing because its foundation was too dependent on the instabilities of individual happiness. Initially their worries seemed overblown, since it was still taken for granted that marriage would always occur within a male breadwinner family. In postwar America the new model seemed to flourish. In 1957, 47 percent of married couples declared themselves "very happy." A 1962 Gallup poll indicated that American women were very satisfied with their lives.

In retrospect, conservatives had a point. In the same Gallup poll, only *10 percent* wanted their daughters to have the same lives they did![2] Under the surface there was considerable dissatisfaction but not yet a language to describe it, even to the women themselves.

Growing postwar prosperity had opened new possibilities for women to take jobs if they wanted, while the new ready-to-eat foods, household appliances, and low-maintenance clothes made the required adjustments to family life much smaller than they would have been earlier. Horizons were widening for women. They widened further when the Pill gave them more control over their sexuality than had ever before been the case. Starting in the sixties and extending into the seventies, legal changes further equalized the marital standing of husbands and wives. Shortly afterward a growing need arose for two-breadwinner families, even when the wife would have preferred to stay at home. As more women worked, traditional disparities in wages between the sexes increasingly appeared illegitimate.

Women exploring their growing opportunities encountered long-established cultural, religious, and political barriers, but they did so with less acceptance or resignation than before. These changing circumstances coincided with rising political engagement rooted in basic liberal values such as equality before the law and equality of opportunity. It is no surprise that feminism became part of the sixties' waves of change. What was a surprise was its increasing shift for many women and men from liberal to cultural feminism, from first wave to second.

Feminism was traditionally liberal. However, during the sixties and later new modifiers became increasingly prevalent. The terms *radical, socialist, Marxist, libertarian, eco,* and *cultural* identify particular sixties-rooted feminist approaches to understanding women's issues.[3] Almost all shared a common grounding in the masculine Enlightenment view of knowledge as a liberating power to manipulate things to our purposes. Except for cultural feminism and later ecofeminism, all were variants of liberal feminism or critiques of liberal feminism as not going far enough in its own terms.

With its roots in the counterculture, cultural feminism was different. Cultural feminism's criticisms of liberal feminism applied with little modification to socialist, Marxist, libertarian, and radical feminism as well. The exception is ecofeminism, which emerged from cultural feminism. It will be discussed in the next chapter.

LIBERAL FEMINISM AND CULTURAL FEMINISM

Liberal feminism is based in the ideal of equal rights for all. In contrast to the prevailing beliefs of his time, Locke had argued that mothers properly had as much authority over their children as did fathers, that marriage should be based on equality between men and women, and that any woman had the right to leave her marriage if she so chose.[4] In addition, married women should continue to own their property. Marriage should not lead to the loss of any rights. Locke's one concession to traditional attitudes was that when husband and wife disagreed the man should decide because he was "abler and stronger." Even then, Locke would have argued that women's right to keep their property and leave a unsatisfying marriage would keep any abuses under control.

Three hundred years later liberal feminism's transformations are still making their way through American and many other cultures. Liberalism delegitimizes domination, the principle that some people are uniquely fitted to command others. Without this crucial step the ones that followed would have been inconceivable. The *principle* of domination must be successfully challenged before people can move on to uncover the many ways it distorts our thinking.

Liberal feminists target discrimination against biological women as individuals rather than challenging the denigration of the feminine in women and men alike. Consequently, liberal feminism emphasizes individual equality: women are just as good as men in the traditional values our society espouses. In *My Fair Lady* Henry Higgins asks his friend Pickering, "Why can't a woman be more like a man?" The liberal feminists answered, "She can."[5]

Liberal feminism's position was not wrong; it was incomplete. Locke offered a powerful defense of gender equality based on masculine styles of thinking and masculine values. When making their case for relations free from domination, liberals emphasized the necessity *and sufficiency* of universal abstract rights, the moral inviolability of our bodies, and explicit contractual agreement. With their emphasis on abstract rationality as the defining human characteristic and the foundation for ethics, liberals in general have honored individuals conceived of as rational social atoms whose boundaries are inviolable.

Cultural feminists argue that feminine qualities are equal (some would say superior) to those associated with masculinity. In moving beyond emphasizing abstract equality to exploring the value of gender differences, cultural feminists deepened our understanding not just of the feminine, but also of what it is to be human. Men as well as women benefit from this deeper appreciation.

The New Left of the sixties stood squarely within the masculine Enlightenment tradition, as did its expressions of feminism. The left's radical feminism considered gender a social construct, building off two basic Lockean principles: that people are morally equal and that the human mind is a *tablua rasa* upon which experience writes its text. The first principle is the core of liberalism, the second a clear expression of logocentrism. Feminisms of the left incorporated the idea that we are distinct from nature and able to sculpt it to our desires, even refashioning our own nature. In the best society, women have and exercise the same rights as men and do so in the same ways.[6] Given their dependence on these assumptions, these radical feminisms were ultimately vulnerable to the ethical dilemmas undermining liberalism itself.

As it emerged in the sixties counterculture, feminism was different. Gretchen Lemke-Santangelo observed, "Most hippie women adopted a feminism that affirmed and celebrated 'natural' or 'essential' female characteristics."[7]

Theirs was a new perspective, and it was new in transformative ways. Charlene Spretnak observed that the counterculture was the first broadly based genuinely postmodern cultural movement: "Modernity situates humankind in a box *on top of* nature. . . . To be truly *post*modern is to reject that discontinuity by opening the box to connect anew with our larger context: the Earth, the cosmos, the sacred whole."[8] By contrast, later academic postmodernism is simply an extreme distillation of modernity.

The counterculture not only encouraged re-envisioning feminism to bring it into greater harmony with the feminine but also provided broadly supportive community spaces within which these ideas and values could be lived, explored, and refined. Insights earlier possible only as relatively isolated personal protests against the dominant culture could be nurtured and developed. And they were.

Rights and Relationships

Liberal feminism set the stage for cultural feminism. In fact, it built the stage. Domination-based societies went to great lengths to distinguish people using some hierarchy of qualities that mattered more than any common shared humanity. Liberalism challenged this ethic with its principle of abstract equality. Hierarchy still could exist, but subordinated to an ethic applying equally to all. Hierarchy had to justify itself to others *in their common capacity as equals*. If it could not do so, it was illegitimate.

For cultural feminists, liberal feminism was a good start, but left too much unexamined. While liberal feminism vindicated women's equality in terms of masculine values, it did not challenge domination of masculine values over feminine ones. *Cultural feminists argued that claiming women could be as good as men in men's terms devalued what it was that made them women.* They held it was important to revalue feminine values themselves, and therefore women as distinct from men and not just as abstract individuals. In response to Henry Higgins's lament "Why can't a woman be more like a man?" cultural feminists answered, "Why should she?"

This argument takes us a step beyond basing ideal human relations on abstract qualities of rationality, a position compatible with considering masculine values superior to feminine ones. Instead, many different human traits are equally worthy of moral consideration, equally worthy of respect. From this perspective, being different need not be considered better or worse or more or less advanced. The liberal case for abstract equality is placed within a deeper context, which strengthened it by offering a solution to important weaknesses.

Abstract theories of rights have two weaknesses. First, they disguise some kinds of domination. Second, they are too weak to provide strong safeguards even in many instances where they can recognize the oppression of others.

Abstract theories of rights have been used to justify egregious practices by the powerful toward the weak as long as some formal preconditions could be abstracted sufficiently to resemble the liberal ideal of voluntary agreement. Because only impersonal abstractly equal relationships received foundational status in most liberal morality, the liberal attack on domination proved too blunt an instrument to comprehend how domination often manifests in daily life. People did not create equal relationships within a Lockean state of nature and then proceed with their lives; they sought to establish equality within and growing out of a previously existing condition of domination and mastery that had shaped the society. Preexisting inequalities enabled those who once dominated often to preserve the substance of their mastery even within "formally equal" conditions.

Moreover, pure abstractions, such as universal human rights, are weak barriers to strongly felt beliefs. The concrete good supposedly served by denying an abstract right often easily overwhelms that right. Many Americans' acceptance of torture is a tragic example. So also is the frequent finding that many people uphold freedom of speech and association as slogans but oppose them when confronting someone with views they strongly dislike. We need a degree of empathy and respect for others to honor their rights when we are tempted not to.

By themselves liberal rights are too intangible to maintain a free society's foundations. It is hard to empathize with an abstraction. Fundraisers have long known that pictures of cute children or baby animals generate more donations than references to starving children or endangered species.

The liberal penchant for emphasizing the abstract ignores context in favor of general principles applying equally to everyone. Liberal morality focuses on the abstract individual alone as morally considerable and in a just society fully autonomous. Individuals are foci of absolute value and should all count equally, like grains of sand, when we weigh up collective happiness. There is important truth in this outlook, but something important is also missing.

To see what that something is, consider an example with which many of us are familiar or can readily identify: I have an argument with my beloved. I lose my temper. She replies sharply, "Don't talk to me that way."

If I am a (very dense) liberal, I might answer, "I have a right to speak as I please."

She might then reply: "Yes you do. Goodbye." Whatever my rights might be, I was no longer acting as an intimate.

More wisely I might apologize, saying, "I had no right to speak to you that way." I had an abstract human right to do so, but in the context of a particular kind of concrete relationship, *that right has no validity*. Rights are context specific. In practice, morality is a quality of relationship.

Abstract rights are not the form morality takes among intimates. This insight illuminates the hole in liberal conceptions of rights. It envisions society as composed of strangers engaged in impersonal and instrumental relationships, but does not adequately describe how we should relate when we are more knowledgeable about others.

For example, do I violate my friend's property rights when I take his keys away because he is drunk? The true friend would take the keys if his drunken companion insisted on driving and drive the person home or call a cab. In seeking to apply abstract principles to life, the intricacies of context and relationship must be considered. As they are, the rights-holding atomistic monad increasingly becomes a social being immersed in a network of concrete relationships.[9]

Rights are the form respect takes when dealing with strangers about whom I know little beyond our common humanity, which is why they are such important political principles.[10] But as we enter into more complex or intimate relationships the language of abstract rights fits increasingly poorly. In a caring relationship I do not have a right to say whatever I want without taking the other's feelings into consideration. That right is incompatible with a caring relationship.

John Locke was far ahead of his time in applying the logic of equal rights to marriage, enabling a decisive break with domination in a society that conceived virtually every relationship hierarchically. But no marriage is primarily shaped by rights equally applicable to strangers. A marriage between equals becomes increasingly based on love and affection, shifting its center of gravity toward the quality of the relationship, not the validity of its legal status. That gay marriage is now increasingly accepted illustrates this fact.

We are *always* in relationships and always exist within ethically important contexts. As with the Daoist yin-yang symbol, sometimes the relationship is more important than the individual considered in isolation. At other times the opposite holds. But neither is ever fully absent. Abstract relationships among strangers are one end of a continuum whose other extreme is love.

When carefully considered, liberal feminism led people toward a greater sensitivity to other forms of domination and ultimately toward affirming the feminine as coequal with the masculine. Care and respect continually solve problems of normal life the principles of abstract rights cannot even grasp. They also enable people to distinguish domination and exploitation where the abstract language of rights could not distinguish between theoretical perfection and the reality of societies culturally shaped by centuries of exploitation. In elevating the legal and moral status of biological women, liberals ultimately elevated the feminine as well.

Here, I think, is an important reason why culture warriors attack both feminism and liberalism. These traditions are linked. Cultural feminist insights grew out of and complete liberal ones. Collectively they form a moral and intellectual center of gravity that rejects domination and the primacy of hierarchy, and at its root preserving domination and the primacy of hierarchy is what the culture war is all about.

SHIFTING CONSCIOUSNESS

In her study of a feminine "ethic of care," Nell Noddings argues that neither empathetic caring nor objective rational thinking is superior to the other. "What seems to be critical," she writes, "is that we retain the ability to move back and forth and to invest the appropriate mode with dominance. When we give over control to the inappropriate mode, we may properly speak of a degradation of consciousness; in the one case we become irrational and in the other unfeeling and unseeing."[11] Both failed states of mind remove our hope of gaining understanding of others, our world, and ourselves.

Noddings emphasizes that an ethically competent person is able to *shift* consciousness laterally in "moves which are neither up nor down." Far from arguing that these modes of consciousness are limited to one gender or the other, she emphasizes, "Both men and women may participate in the 'feminine' as I am developing it."[12] Human beings are *naturally* consciousness changers.

Chapter 3 recounted Mihaly Csikszentmilhalyi's discovery that psychologically androgynous people in effect double their repertoire of responses and can interact with the world in richer and more varied ways.[13] Noddings argues that the same capacity is critical for any genuine understanding of ethics.

By arguing for the equal status of feminine with masculine values, cultural feminists raised the status of the concrete, of experience, feelings, and empathy, and made relationships central. Our immersion in society and in the world received equal recognition with abstract reason that distances us from society and the world. Cultural feminism thereby legitimized different states of consciousness and the advantages of being able to participate within more than one. This recognition was a defining characteristic of the counterculture.

For many Americans cultural feminists established the importance and intellectual legitimacy of the concrete, of feelings, of empathy, of relationship. Our multisensory immersion in the world was a source of genuine knowledge and not merely subjective epiphenomena or personal idiosyncrasies. This shift opened the path for reestablishing modernity's moral foundations within a larger context embracing all of what it is to be human and potentially the world as a whole as well.

Cultural feminism also had a powerful spiritual impact. Lemke-Santangelo writes, "During the 1960s most counterculture women believed that spiritual truth was located within the self, waiting to be discovered or awakened by opening up to the individual's natural intuitive capacity to recognize the divine."[14] This openness led to reevaluating traditional religious views toward women, the feminine, and the sacred.

FEMINISM'S SPIRITUAL DIMENSION

Writing in the late 1990s, prominent theologian Marcus Borg observed that religious feminism was "the single most important development of theology in my lifetime."[15] During the sixties women's role in religion became an important question in communities throughout the country. To an unprecedented degree women began making inroads into leadership positions within mainstream American religions. This expansion of their participation was not just within Christian and Judaic traditions; it also extended into the growing Buddhist community and the rapidly expanding Neo-Pagan communities.

But cultural feminism's impact went deeper than raising women's organizational religious status, which might be considered a variant of liberal feminism, ultimately spilling over into reexamining how we thought about the sacred and our relationship to it. Conceiving spirit as feminine and immanent in the world as well as masculine and transcendental to it became easier when we no longer abstracted ourselves from our world.

As the Christian church became institutionalized during the centuries after its founding, women were increasingly devalued. The same process happened in Islam.[16] Rita Gross writes of Buddhism that historically "the male near-monopoly of the teaching role can be compared to the male monopoly of the deity role in traditional monotheism."[17] Feminism challenged this universal disparaging of women and the feminine among the major Axial Age religions, increasing awareness of our need to free our understanding of the sacred from dependence on the rigid structures of masculine logocentric theologies.

Judaism and Christianity

When she entered the University of Chicago Divinity School in 1965, Rita Gross writes, "There was a huge influx of female students . . . twelve women among four hundred students."[18] As women increasingly entered seminaries, the spiritual role of women and the feminine became an issue. The stage was being prepared for a spiritual transformation that would deeply impact Christianity and Judaism.

These women's defining experiences as young adults had often been in the civil rights and antiwar movements. They had learned the value of not being passive and carried these lessons into their spiritual calling.[19] Christianity and Judaism came under pressure to reexamine their traditional exclusion of women from religious offices and of the feminine from any identification with the divine.

While at Chicago Gross was a founding member of the Upstairs Minyan, which worked to transform the role of women in Jewish services. Merlin Stone observed that in Judaism "the image of the Shekhina has again risen to be recognized and revered as a result first, of Patai's the *Hebrew Goddess*, and then by the active involvement of Jewish feminists."[20] Since then this "pattern has been repeated all over the Jewish world as Jewish women acquire Jewish educations and liturgical skills they had never been taught before."[21]

Catholicism rarely accorded women genuine spiritual respect. Yet even here theologian Rosemary Radford Ruether observed, "My own trajectory of development coincided with the opening up of Catholicism in the Second Vatican Council (1962–65) and the development of liberation theologies and the birth of feminism in circles. . . . Had I been trying to pursue this path of critique ten years earlier there might have been a different outcome."[22]

Taking women to be as competent spiritually as men inevitably led to reconsidering traditional masculine images of God. The timing was good. Legitimate scholars were abandoning biblical literalism, a position that had become impossible to hold with any intellectual honesty. The Bible was seen as writings that may have reflected and reported genuine spiritual teachings but did so in the context of the times when its writers lived. It became possible again to read scripture from a perspective more open to mythic insights, opening opportunities for renewed and deeper understandings of its central message.

Women in particular began scrutinizing long-complacent attitudes that God was male, or if beyond gender somehow, most appropriately referred to as male. A more accurate conception of God required honoring divine feminine as well as divine masculine qualities. In seeking to respond positively to women's desires for inclusion, more liberal Protestant denominations as well as Reformed and Conservative Judaism ultimately ended up opening themselves to considering the feminine aspect of the sacred.

Early Jewish and Christian history was reexamined. As it was, powerful evidence for the existence of a Hebrew Goddess emerged.[23] Early Hebrew polytheism was rediscovered and reevaluated as traditional texts were read with new eyes and understanding. For example, Solomon, described in scripture as the wisest of Israel's kings, raised altars to the goddess Astarte (1 Kings 11:5).

In the Christian tradition old questions long regarded as settled were reexamined. Biblical scholars began questioning New Testament passages marginalizing women. Either material attacking women's leadership was inserted into some of Paul's epistles after he wrote them or Paul contradicted himself on a massive scale, because other letters included friendly greetings to women active in leadership roles.[24] Many early gospels rejected from the Christian canon were rediscovered. Some endorsed women exercising rightful authority in the early church, which may be *why* they had been rejected.

Carol Christ described four basic strategies women theologians employed in their encounter with what appeared to be an unacceptably male religious tradition. Least disruptive to established traditions was the attempt to interpret "male symbols of God (and Jesus) . . . in non-oppressive ways because what is oppressive is not the language associated with the male gender, but the . . . domination and oppression often associated with male symbolism." A step further was taken by theologians arguing that "God language must be neuterized or made androgynous because language associated with one sex or another inevitably is oppressive and also fails to symbolize the Transcendence of God."[25] Some denominations sought more inclusive liturgies, referring to God as the divine Parent rather than Father.

Another step from the theretofore-dominant tradition occurred when the meager female symbolism in biblical and Jewish traditions, and sometimes outside them, was "introduced alongside male God symbolism because the Transcendence or bisexuality for God is best symbolized by dual imagery."[26] Rosemary Ruether argued that the Old Testament Wisdom, or Sophia, is the feminine face of the Christian God, a face obscured by John's replacing the feminine Sophia with the masculine Logos. She also emphasized Sophia's presence in early Protestant and Catholic traditions.[27]

Carol Christ took a final step, concluding that male images of God "must be abandoned and/or deemphasized as the female God, or Goddess, returns to ascendancy."[28] Christ had made a long spiritual journey from seeking to stay within Protestant Christianity to embracing Goddess theology. Many other women who began their spiritual journey within the Abrahamic traditions of Christianity and Judaism came to similar conclusions.

As feminine values were honored additional changes unfolded. Masculine values emphasizing transcendence and separation began giving way to feminine ones emphasizing immanence and connection. Charlene Spretnak contends, "The central understanding in contemporary Goddess spirituality is that the divine—creativity in the universe, or ultimate mystery—is laced throughout the cosmic manifestations in and around us. The divine is immanent."[29] As feminine values were recognized in the sacred, divine transcendence was joined with divine immanence.

This complex rethinking from within the dominant Abrahamic traditions raised two points particularly important for my purposes. First, because these efforts originated from within, they increased Christian and Jewish communities' awareness of issues surrounding the Divine Feminine. Second, because these feminine sources were relatively meager in scripture, women often looked elsewhere for insights. In the process, traditionally hostile Christian views toward other spiritual paths were often transformed into acceptance of a multiplicity of legitimate faiths. When feminine dimensions of the sacred are recognized, the presence of the sacred everywhere seems to follow, enriching traditional emphasis on divine transcendence with recognition of divine immanence.

Rosemary Ruether once rejected Goddess theology, arguing that Catholicism offered a better grasp of transcendence and that a feminist Jesus could help us better grasp the reality of a truly transcendent God. She continues her commitment to working within the Catholic tradition but now regards Wicca, with its emphasis on a Goddess and sacred immanence as, along with other spiritual paths, "equally legitimate" with her own.[30] For Ruether the many faces of the Largest Truth There Is now extend beyond Christianity and even beyond monotheism. The logic of divine immanence accompanies and grows from awareness of the divine feminine.

Rejecting purely masculine images of the sacred did not always lead to Goddess spirituality. Sometimes it led to Asian and polytheistic Pagan spiritual traditions.

Buddhism

Beginning in the late 1960s and early 1970s, Buddhism began putting down vigorous roots in the United States.[31] Today the Dalai Lama is widely revered and respected almost everywhere except among some conservative

Christian communities, and the Vajrayana (Tibetan Buddhism) tradition he leads is well known if not well understood. Other schools of Buddhist practice, based in Mahayana (especially its Zen form) and Theravada traditions, have also put down deep roots.

Buddhism did not enter America as a feminine spiritual path. It was as masculine as the Abrahamic traditions and in its own way denigrated women as much. The Buddha is said to have told his monks, "The one thing that enslaves a man above all else is a woman. Her form, her voice, her scent, her attractiveness and her touch all beguile a man's heart. Stay away from them at all costs."[32] For many Asian Buddhists, a woman living an exemplary life positioned herself to be reborn as a man and so attain a chance for enlightenment. Senior Buddhist nuns had to bow before even novice monks and were otherwise continually reminded of their second-class status.[33]

As in the Abrahamic traditions, women's status in Buddhism had once been higher. Much in early Buddhist traditions praised the spiritual possibilities open to women.[34] For example, while Vajrayana Buddhism shares in the historical denigration of women practitioners, its early literature could explicitly teach the contrary. Padmasambhava, one of Tibetan Buddhism's most important teachers, taught:

> The basis for realizing enlightenment is a human body.
> Male or female, there is no great difference.
> But if she develops the mind bent on enlightenment,
> The woman's body is better.[35]

Western Buddhism dramatically changed the day-to-day role of women in the sangha (spiritual community). Gross writes that today "the single greatest difference between the practice of Buddhism in Asia and . . . in the West is the full and complete participation of women in Western Buddhism."[36] David Chadwick, a prominent American writer on Buddhism, told me that half the dharma teachers in the United States today are women.

Something profound is taking place in the Buddhist religious landscape as it has in the Abrahamic one. The reason appears closely connected to the cultural flowering of the sixties. During that time Buddhism was putting down native roots outside of immigrant communities. Gross observed, "Coming to Buddhism in the era of feminism, rather than in the fifties, . . . women who were attracted to Buddhism simply assumed that Buddhist teachings and practices were made for them as well as for men."[37]

Gross argues that feminism facilitates a deeper understanding of Buddhism. Cultural feminism in particular shares important similarities with the Buddhist understanding of the ego. Emphasizing the enlightened perception of self as "fundamentally relational rather than essentially autonomous" is central to Buddhism. The bodhisattva vow affirms "one's connections with others as fundamental."[38]

Historically Buddhism developed as a religion of monks requiring outside support from a traditional hierarchical society to sustain its monasteries. Monks practiced, and laypeople supported them in hopes of attaining merit toward a more auspicious reincarnation, perhaps as a monk. Today most Western Buddhist practitioners are laypeople who want more than the opportunity to gain merit by giving monks money.

In an extended meeting in Dharamsala, India, Jewish leaders told leading Tibetan Buddhists, including the Dalai Lama, that Judaism's survival depended on its having strong lay communities. Synagogues developed only after the temple had been destroyed, rendering its priestly hierarchy largely useless. Much of Judaism's survival also centered on practices within the home. The Vajrayana focus on monks and denigration of women boded ill for its long-term survival. Buddhist feminists might end up being its salvation.[39]

Buddhism has also viewed the world as a trap, with enlightenment offering final liberation. Respected Buddhists have told me we waste our time trying to improve this world. In some traditions the bodhisattva compassionately remains here after attaining enlightenment to assist "all sentient beings" in freeing themselves. Staying in the world as an act of selfless compassion is not an endorsement of bodily existence.

The Buddhist feminist perspective is different. To make this point Rita Gross quotes Starhawk's critical comparison of Wicca with Buddhism:

Witchcraft does not maintain, like the First Truth of Buddhism, that "All life is suffering." On the contrary, life is a thing of wonder. The Buddha is said to have gained this insight after his encounter with old age, disease, and death. In the Craft, old age is a natural and highly valued part of the cycle of life, the time of greatest wisdom and understanding. Disease, of course, causes misery but is not something to be inevitably suffered: The practice of the Craft was always connected with the healing arts, with herbalism and mid-wifery. Nor is Death fearful: It is simply the dissolution of the physical form that allows the spirit to prepare for a new life. Suffering certainly exists in life—it is part of learning. But escape from the Wheel of Birth and Death is not the optimal cure, any more than hari kiri is the cure for menstrual cramps. When suffering is the result of the social order or human injustice, the Craft encourages active work to relieve it. Where suffering is a natural part of the cycle of birth and decay, it is relieved by understanding and acceptance, by a willing giving over to both the dark and the light in turn.[40]

Gross argues that Starhawk's critique echoes "the contrast between Buddhism interpreted as the quest for freedom from the world and Buddhism interpreted as the quest for freedom within the world. Given feminist distrust of dualistic, otherworldly spiritualities, feminist Buddhism would sound more like what Starhawk outlines as the position of the Craft."[41]

The jury is out on what feminism's ultimate impact on Buddhism will be, but I find it very significant that the Dalai Lama has said, "I call myself a feminist. Isn't that what you call someone who fights for women's rights?"[42]

Neo-Paganism

In the 1990s Dar Williams's song "The Christians and the Pagans" was heard across the country. Williams described Wiccans and Christians in the same extended family spending a holiday together, Christmas for the Christians and Yule, or Winter Solstice, for the Pagans. That such a song could succeed points to one of the biggest changes on the American religious scene, again with its roots in the sixties.[43]

Wiccan soldiers killed during wartime now can have a pentacle on their headstones, in acknowledged respect for their spiritual path. "Witches" now appear in television shows, not just as characters in fantasy novels or as villains in some overwrought horror show but as sympathetic, even good characters.

In 1951 England abolished its antiwitchcraft laws. Soon thereafter some witches emerged from the broom closet and found a few people in the wider public interested in learning their practices. By the early sixties practicing Wiccans had crossed the Atlantic and established a tiny but growing American presence. Their timing was optimal, particularly for women attracted to immanent and feminine forms of spirituality.

Counterculture women in particular began to explore Native American, Wiccan, and occult traditions. They often liked what they encountered. In return they were welcomed.[44] Today Neo-Paganism has a rapidly growing presence in the United States and elsewhere.

Neo-Paganism has developed in many directions since the 1950s. There are no sacred texts, no organized hierarchy, and no universally acknowledged leaders, yet, beyond this surface variety, at a deeper level Neo-Pagans share much in common.

Generalizations always have exceptions, particularly among Neo-Pagans, but typically rituals reflect the phases of embodied life from birth to death and beyond. These phases are represented mythically by the phases of the moon and the annual turning of the seasons, called the Wheel of the Year. Thus sacred immanence rather than transcendence is their primary spiritual focus. Spiritual life is represented as getting into harmony with sacred rhythms rather than linear progression toward salvation or enlightenment.

In virtually all their forms Neo-Pagans honor the Divine Feminine as Goddess or as many goddesses. Traditional Wicca focuses on female-male duality along with the cycle of life and death. However, male deities are usually relegated to a secondary but still very important status. Traditional Wicca therefore attends to the Goddess and the God and their rituals usually include both a priestess and a priest.

Many within the Wiccan community distinguish between Wicca as a whole and feminist Wicca. Compared to the Western norm, *both* are feminist. Feminist Wicca often limits membership to women (Dianic Wicca) and relates only to the Goddess or goddesses. But in both forms of Wicca the sacred feminine holds pride of place, and the priestess is the ultimate decision maker or first among equals.

Some Neo-Pagan traditions are less Goddess oriented, particularly within reconstructionist traditions inspired by pre-Christian Celtic, Norse, Greek, or other peoples. But here as well female deities and women priestesses are normally central to their practice. In addition, women are disproportionately represented among Neo-Paganism's public figures, as well as leading locally within covens and the other small groups that characterize its practice.

Just how rapidly Neo-Pagan traditions are growing is difficult to discern because most Pagans meet quietly in private homes. There are few established public Pagan temples, and in many parts of the country, especially where culture warriors are strong, it is unwise to be too public. That said, the CUNY survey of American religious identification included various kinds of Neo-Pagans and concluded their numbers were increasing rapidly.[45]

Neo-Pagans appreciate both the centrality of personal encounter and the importance of different kinds of consciousness in our lives. Traditional Wiccan rituals usually focus on personal encounter with the sacred, which changes a person in ways that do not happen from adopting a new belief, being shaped by social pressure, or following someone else's attractive example. When people have powerful personal spiritual experiences they make the lesson their own.

Long-established religions such as Christianity, Judaism, and Buddhism have often confronted the challenge of recognizing the Divine Feminine by adapting Neo-Pagan symbols and practices. Pagan women such as Starhawk and Z Budapest have served as teachers and sources of inspiration for feminist theologians seeking to work within more mainstream traditions as well as for Neo-Pagans. As a result Neo-Pagans' influence in the broader American religious community far outweighs their actual numbers.

Starhawk plays a positive role in much of Catholic Rosemary Ruether's discussion of contemporary religious feminism.[46] She was also a pivotal influence on many Christian and Jewish women who left the Abrahamic traditions entirely to enter either Neo-Pagan or completely Goddess-oriented traditions. Future historians of religion may well look back on our time and identify the witch Starhawk and her book *The Spiral Dance* as pivotal players in the growing recognition of the Divine Feminine.

These developments are in fascinating accord with an unusual encounter in the late 1950s. Idries Shah (1924–96) was a prominent Sufi writer who throughout his life explored and wrote on a wide variety of spiritual and psychological subjects. He was then writing a biography of Gerald Gardner, who had introduced Wicca to the public after England's antiwitchcraft laws were repealed. Shaw told Fred Lamond he was writing Gardner's biography because he had it on "the highest spiritual authority" that Wicca would be the dominant spiritual current of the twenty-first century. Lamond explained to me that "highest spiritual authority" was how Shaw referred to "inner-planes contact." According to Lamond, Shah added, "But personally, I can't see it."[47]

"Spiritual current" refers not to a religion but to its dominant values, which in Wicca's case are the Divine Feminine and divine immanence. Perhaps Shah's contacts were correct.

African Diasporic Traditions

Beginning in the 1960s a superficially very different expression of women's central spiritual role and the sacred feminine appeared in the American religious landscape. After Fidel Castro took power in 1959, thousands of Cubans arrived in the United States as refugees from Communist rule. Many brought the African diasporic religion of Santeria with them.

Santeria blends Catholicism and African spiritual traditions that came over with the slaves. Enslaved Africans managed to preserve their own religious practices during captivity by creatively mixing them with Catholic rituals, identifying their deities as saints, and perfecting techniques of secrecy.

Music is central to these traditions. Joseph M. Murphy writes, "Santeria is a danced religion because dancing expresses the fundamental dynamism of *ashe*. Words . . . cannot express the mystery. The world is a dance."[48] *Ashe*, pronounced "ah-shay," is the basic life force that permeates all things.

Significantly for my argument, Santeria focuses on sacred immanence, the spirit that is everywhere in life and death. Its pantheon is polytheistic, in many ways resembling what we know of the gods of the Greeks and Romans. Goddesses as well as gods are vital presences in their drumming rituals, incorporating themselves into mediums who serve as their "horses" as they dance. Few if any followers wonder whether their deities exist, for they encounter them regularly and intimately.

Today Santeria attracts many non-Cuban Americans who find this spirituality more joyful and less mind numbing than what they had previously experienced. According to the CUNY survey, in 2001 there were twenty-two thousand followers of Santeria in the United States, whereas the religion had not been listed at all in 1990.[49] But more than with most such studies, accurate numbers are hard to find because so many practice in secret. In a scholarly analysis published in 1997, George Brandon argued that America's Santeria population was then probably larger than the number of practitioners in Cuba before Castro's revolution.[50] If he is correct, CUNY's numbers are far too low, because according to the University of Miami's Institute for Cuban and Cuban-American Studies, Cuba's Santeria population is at least one million and possibly up to 70 percent of all Cubans.[51]

While it is the most numerous of African diasporic religions in the United States, Santeria is far from alone. It is joined by practitioners of Haitian Voudon and Brazilian Umbanda and Candomble. Their deities are called *orixas* in Brazil, *orishas* in Santeria, and *loa* in Voudon. They share much in common.

Popularly but incorrectly called Voodoo, Voudon is probably the one Americans have heard most about. It has existed here since the Louisiana Purchase. Voudon originated in formerly French-ruled areas of the Caribbean and in New Orleans and continues to reflect that French heritage along with the African traditions transported there by French slaves. Some religious practices of Indian peoples since exterminated from the Caribbean islands also survive in Voudon.

Explicitly non-Christian and originally practiced only by Blacks, Voudon was known to others primarily through lurid tales about black magic. It did not begin to attract a significantly wider range of practitioners until well after the 1960s but now has many white devotees, as I discovered when visiting New Orleans. Having crossed the color line, Voudon is spreading well beyond its original boundaries, as to a smaller degree are Brazilian traditions.

Yet, from another perspective their influence is already powerful and pervasive, for America's most uniquely American music, jazz, blues, and rock and roll, all have their roots in African music played around "Congo Square" during slave times in New Orleans.[52]

African diasporic traditions were suppressed more briefly than were European Pagan religions. Many verbal teachings and ritual skills lost a millennium ago to Europeans remain vital parts of African diasporic traditions and practices. As a consequence, many neo-Pagans are now learning from them. Pagan spirituality's lack of claims to exclusive truth on anyone's part makes this learning easy. If Neo-Pagans have influenced the broader American religious communities out of proportion to their numbers, the same may be said for the influence of African diasporic traditions on the Neo-Pagan community.

Significantly, many leaders of Santeria, Voudon, and Umbanda temples are women, and this has always been so. The Caribbean and Brazil are hardly feminist paradises, and these spiritual traditions have been deeply influenced by the cultural dominance of a one-sided masculinity, but they do not *denigrate* the feminine. Women have long held powerful and respected positions in these traditions unmatched in even the most feminist Christian and Jewish communities.[53]

Observed from the outside, these religions' central feature is their deities' temporary entry into the bodies of human mediums, "horses." In Brazil, traditionally women and sometimes gay men incorporated these divine riders. As one Brazilian man explained to Ruth Landes many years ago, "No upright man will allow himself to be ridden by a god, unless he does not care about losing his manhood."[54] Heterosexual men preserved their boundaries intact, serving as drummers to call down the *Orixas* into mediums.

Today this disdain for heterosexual-male mediumship is breaking down, at least in the United States. Straight men are respected mediums. I suspect that the sixties played a role in altering these practices.

Feminine Spirituality

Compared to previous Western religious experience, feminist spirituality displays a striking absence of rancor over theological issues. The diversity of feminine approaches to spirituality has not been marred by the kind of struggles for doctrinal purity that have characterized transcendental monotheism.

Carol Christ describes a class on feminist spirituality taught by Gail Graham Yates at the University of Minnesota. Students divided themselves into discussion groups based on whether they were "seekers," "reformists," or "post-traditionalists." By the end of the semester the seeker group had dissolved into the other two, which continued to meet separately. "Toward the end of the semester the post-traditionalists decided to have a ritual, and they went outside, sat in a circle, and chanted to Goddess. Meanwhile the reformers decided to have a ritual, and they sat in a circle, passed an apple, and asked the blessing of Mother God." Christ quotes Graham Yates: "So much for the differences between the reformists and the post-traditionalists."[55]

The new feminist currents that arose during the sixties provide one powerful way to redress the moral and spiritual crisis of modernity. Value is intrinsic to the world. A good life is lived in harmony with it. With such insights nihilism is impossible.

THE REDISCOVERY OF NATURE

*For one species to mourn the death of another
is a new thing under the sun.*

—Aldo Leopold

During the sixties the liberal concern with conservation rooted in the self-interest of individuals and the nation, typified by Roosevelt's New Deal, developed a deeper, more feminine appreciation of nature as home. We are not isolated atoms, not a species removed from its spiritual environment or engaged in a war of all against all for survival. The modern quest for Faustian domination, whether as individuals or species, is misdirected and ultimately self-destructive. We are biologically and ecologically linked with all that is around us.

Our world is a field of value relationships, a field from which we cannot be extricated. For some environmentalists we are also energetically and spiritually embedded within a more-than-human world. Environmentalism is a perception that nature matters ethically as well as instrumentally. It offers an antidote to modernity's growing nihilism.

ENVIRONMENTALISM AND THE FEMININE

Women had always been active in the American conservation movement. The Appalachian Mountain Club, America's oldest such organization, admitted women to membership at its second meeting in 1876. From its beginning, the Sierra Club had women active within its ranks, electing its first female president in 1927. In the early part of the twentieth century the Progressives had pushed for both conservation and women's suffrage.

Favoring nature's conservation was accompanied by a greater than average acceptance of women as equals.[1]

By contrast, there was little connection between environmentalists and the major political movements of the sixties generation. The civil rights movement was initially uninterested in environmental issues even though the poor were the major victims of pollution and abuse of the natural world. Civil rights leaders tended to regard environmentalism as a white-middle-class distraction. It would be years before their descendants became interested in environmental justice, as in Van Jones' path-breaking work.[2] Many antiwar leaders also regarded environmentalism as a middle-class indulgence, even as the United States used ecological warfare massively against Vietnam. While environmentalism picked up new supporters as activists became frustrated with a seemingly endless war and whites were pushed out of the civil rights movement with the rise of Black Power, its roots lay elsewhere.[3]

Aldo Leopold was the most important American environmental thinker since John Muir. To my knowledge Leopold was not personally involved with feminist issues, nor apparently were later leaders such as David Brower, Gary Snyder, and Edward Abbey much involved. Their concerns were different. Yet compared to its predecessors the environmental movement of the late sixties and into the seventies increasingly emphasized a new feminine sensibility toward nature.

Many active in the conservation movement were shifting from the traditional conservationist emphasis on nature's utilitarian value toward emphasizing the intrinsic value of the wild. The tension between these perspectives first came to a head during the struggle over building the Hetch Hetchy Reservoir in Yosemite. John Muir, who defended wild nature, and Gifford Pinchot, who founded the US Forest Service along utilitarian lines, took opposite sides in that conflict. Pinchot won, but from the sixties on, Muir's view began speaking more powerfully to people's hearts and minds. The conservation movement was shifting from a Lockean and Baconian perspective to a sensibility akin to that of Leonardo's love born of knowledge.

During the 1980s many cultural feminists expanded their analysis from a purely human viewpoint toward one encompassing our relations with nature as well. Cultural feminists were perhaps the first to see how attitudes toward people that characterized dominator societies also characterized their relationships with the other-than-human world, giving birth to ecofeminism. Coming from different areas of initial concern and relying on different kinds of analysis, the separate currents of feminist and environmental thought arrived at remarkably similar conclusions.

This new environmental sensibility also began influencing mainstream American religion, strengthening insights prominent in religious feminism. As religion increasingly acknowledged sacred immanence, a hitherto-lacking link was forged between spiritual and secular traditions, creating the possibility for an integral worldview to replace that destroyed during the Reformation.

AMERICAN CONSERVATION

Concern with protecting wild nature was born in the United States, even as the country was amassing an unequaled record of despoiling that same nature and environment. In 1864 Abraham Lincoln protected Yosemite Valley from development, and Ulysses S. Grant followed suit for Yellowstone in 1872. In 1885 New York State created the Adirondack Forest Preserve from largely devastated land. Today Adirondack Park is larger than Yellowstone, the land healed. America's national and state parks have inspired similar efforts on every continent.

During the antebellum period, similar in so many ways to the sixties, writers such as Emerson and Thoreau emphasized the wild world's intrinsic value and described the healing people could gain from immersing themselves in it. In words remarkably resonant with William Blake's depiction of the sun quoted in chapter 2, Emerson wrote, "To speak truly, few adult persons can see nature. Most persons do not see the sun. At least they have a very superficial seeing. The sun illuminates only the eye of man, but shines into the eye and heart of a child. The lover of nature is he whose inward and outward senses are still truly adjusted to each other."[4] For Emerson the language of mythos was necessary for people to understand the land where they lived.

Bron Taylor persuasively argues that Thoreau was "the most important innovator of American environmental thought."[5] Going further than Emerson's more transcendental emphasis, Thoreau emphasized nature's immanence: "The earth is not a mere fragment of dead history, stratum upon stratum like the leaves of a book, . . . but living poetry like the leaves of a tree, which precede flowers and fruit—not a fossil earth but a living earth."[6] Beyond even beauty and sublimity, Thoreau argued, "In wildness is the preservation of the world."[7]

Influenced by Emerson and Thoreau and even more by his personal experience, John Muir described how Americans might finally begin reevaluating the modern West's myopic perception of nature and of life. Muir emphasized that what wild nature had to teach could be learned only through direct immersion: "Let the children walk with nature, let them see the beautiful blendings and communions of death and life, their joyous inseparable unity, as taught in woods and meadows, plains and mountains and streams of our blessed star, and they will learn that death is stingless indeed, and as beautiful as life. . . . All is divine harmony."[8]

Like Emerson, Muir knew the modern attitude toward nature required deadening and narrowing basic human sensibilities, a kind of cultural autism. But this mental crippling could be healed. Muir urged people to "climb the mountains and get their good tidings. Nature's peace will flow into you as sunshine flows into trees. The winds will blow their own freshness into you, and the storms their energy, while cares will drop away from you."[9]

Muir's was a feminine way of perceiving, urging people to at least momentarily give up logocentric ways of thinking and perceiving and open themselves to meaning as directly experienced. Muir had many admirers in his time, from Emerson to Theodore Roosevelt, but his message was too deeply probing for a society giddy with its growing power and prosperity.

America was firmly in the grip of liberal ideals, and these ideals insisted that the other-than-human-world was only a storehouse of resources that human creativity and effort could transform into realizing our dreams; otherwise it was "wasted."

The old word *conservation* is utilitarian: Nature consists of useful things we should not waste. We should protect resources from shortsighted waste to have more to use later on. This way of thinking reflected genuine concerns that industrial and political greed would destroy our natural heritage, for perceptive people were aware that cutover forests, enormous wildfires, degraded farmlands, and abused fisheries undermine a sustainable future for everyone.

Many conservationists also genuinely treasured their encounters with the wild, but their terminology treated people as radically distinct from nature. Protection for nature was usually advocated within ruggedly masculine styles of thought. It provided a worthy challenge to hardy mountaineers "conquering" mountaintops. Climbing mountains strengthened people's manly character softened by civilization's plenty. It enabled them to engage more successfully in the competition defining all of existence.

For Theodore Roosevelt, living in wilderness promoted "that vigorous manliness for the lack of which in a nation, as in an individual . . . no other qualities can possibly atone." TR also emphasized that "no nation facing the unhealthy softening and relaxation of fibre that tends to accompany civilization can afford to neglect anything that will develop hardihood, resolution, and the scorn of discomfort and danger." Conservationist William Kent wrote that after a hunt "you are a barbarian, and you're glad of it. It's good to be a barbarian . . . and you know that if you are a barbarian, you are at any rate a man."[10]

This one-sided masculinity was not threatened by strong women. William Kent supported women's suffrage and was married to a prominent feminist. Roosevelt's Bull Moose Party placed more women in leadership positions than ever before in American history. Roosevelt advocated women's suffrage and women's rights. No other major candidate had ever gone so far.[11] Many Progressives were liberal feminists and liberal conservationists.

In deeply personal ways Progressive conservationists brought together a utilitarian liberal worldview, a powerful love of nature, and a masculine orientation that nature was wholly other. By mid–twentieth century this one-sided attitude was being enriched by a more feminine understanding of the natural world. Aldo Leopold and Rachel Carson were the two most important influences behind the growth of this new perception.

Aldo Leopold

First published in 1949, Aldo Leopold's *A Sand County Almanac* gives many accounts of hunting and fishing. Both played central roles in Leopold's life and in his love for the wild. He was long employed by the US Forest Service, and his earliest conservation activities involved attempting to extirpate predators so hunters could harvest abundant crops of deer. Leopold began his career with the traditional masculine conservation perspective of his time and reflected it in his writing, but only to some degree.

Leopold's approach to hunting was neither utilitarian nor aggressively masculine. He hunted and fished for food, not trophies, and also, I think, for increasing the depth of his immersion in nature. Many of the ethical injunctions he defended were described in traditional terms of fairness and rewarding skill, but with a new nuance.

In the section "Thinking Like a Mountain" Leopold described his time with the Forest Service in Arizona and New Mexico, where killing predators was part of his job. He and his associates happened upon a pack of wolves and shot them up, mortally wounding the pack's matriarch: "We reached the old wolf in time to watch a fierce green fire dying in her eyes. I realized then, and have known ever since, that there was something new to me in those eyes— something known only to her and to the mountain. I was young then, and full of trigger-itch; I thought that because fewer wolves meant more deer, that no wolves would mean hunters' paradise. But after seeing the green fire die, I sensed that neither the wolf nor the mountain agreed with such a view."[12]

Leopold's capacity to blur his boundaries and perceive deeply into the nature of the wild led to an unsurpassed description of nature as a place of value and beauty quite distinct from whatever impact it might have on human beings, returning us to Leonardo's insight that "the virtues of grasses, stones, and trees do not exist because humans know them. . . . Grasses are noble in themselves without the aid of human languages or letters."[13] Anyone reading *A Sand County Almanac* cannot help but be impressed by how it is leavened with care and concern for the wild world on its own terms. "Insignificant" animals and plants, such as a mouse, grouse, or tamarack tree, play important roles in his narrative. Offering a profound alternative to the reigning utilitarianism, Leopold argued that our most unique trait was not tool making or language but the ability to care for living beings of no utility to us.

Leopold's masculine perspective was in balance with a feminine sensibility. Consequently his capacity to understand nature and communicate this understanding was unsurpassed among his generation and has been rarely equaled since. But it took the transformation of the sixties for it to become popular. By then Leopold was dead. Today *A Sand County Almanac* is widely regarded as the most influential book on nature ever written by an American, with only one competitor.

Rachel Carson

If modern environmental *understanding* owes much to Aldo Leopold, in many ways the modern environmental *movement* was sparked by Rachel Carson, an aquatic biologist for the Bureau of Fisheries, later renamed the US Fish and Wildlife Service. Assigned to edit other scientists' reports, Carson rapidly broadened and deepened her own scientific knowledge. By 1949 she had been named editor in chief of the agency's publications.

Carson also pursued her private writing, publishing *The Sea Around Us* in 1952 and her best-selling *The Edge of the Sea* soon thereafter. These books won many awards, and she was elected to the American Academy of Arts and Letters. But at the same time she was becoming increasingly worried about the impact newly developed pesticides were having on the earth and potentially on the human body.

In 1962 Carson's concerns became a book, *Silent Spring*, which challenged the complacent attitude that nature was simply a supply of resources distinct from us. The prevailing attitude was that human beings existed to conquer nature, and the new pesticide DDT was heralded as the next step in achieving her further subjugation. DDT had successfully prevented serious disease outbreaks in war-shattered Europe. Inspired by this achievement, farmers now applied it indiscriminately. In terms of saving crops from insects, the results were impressive. But life is knit together in an intricate network, and you cannot do only one thing. DDT did not do only one thing.

Carson argued that DDT ended up in the bodies of humans and other beings high on the food chain, threatening serious long-term consequences. The eggshells of sensitive bird species were already thinning, leading to broken eggs and a failure to reproduce. Brown pelicans, peregrine falcons, and eagles were at risk of extinction. Nor were we immune: pesticide residue was building up in human bodies.

Carson's description of the ecology of the body introduced many modern Americans to a whole new way of thinking, placing us within nature, not above it.[14] Our boundaries with the world were permeable, and there was nothing we could do about it. We had encountered a limitation on our power to dominate, a limitation rooted in the nature of things. No technological fix could correct it. We are not simply surrounded by a world of resources; we are a part of that world, its "plain citizens," as Leopold put it. The world was not our block of granite on which to carve our visions. If we wanted to live wisely we had to take more interests than our own into consideration. If we wanted to live in a biologically rich world, Carson argued, sometimes we needed to refrain from doing what we had the power to do. We had to act with maturity.[15]

Leopold had made a similar case but without the crucial link to what was happening in people's backyards and within their own bodies. When it first appeared, *A Sand County Almanac* had a small impact. Only after Carson's words had begun to sink in were more people ready to read him and understand the importance of his message.

Carson's argument challenged corporations' right to make money when they did not know, and often chose not to know, the impact of their actions. The case of DDT was an early example of taking a product useful for saving human lives and applying it so widely that it built up in our bodies while enabling insects and other disease vectors to develop resistance to it. Future human lives were endangered to lower the price of lettuce a few cents and increase a corporation's cumulative profit by a great deal. These companies chose to ignore DDT's long-term impact on other life forms, as they continue to do today with anything that would interfere with making a profit, unless forced to do so.

In her critique of the overuse of DDT, Carson argued that government was responsible for protecting its citizens from being poisoned by pesticides. Industry responded that there was no problem. Then as now they said they could be trusted. But unlike normal people, corporations do not care about values beyond profit. They are institutional sociopaths. Then as now, government initially took the chemical companies at their word, but Carson used the evidence of DDT's deleterious impacts on birds to make her point and energize popular support, igniting a citizen movement that ultimately forced government to act. The ethos of power and domination clashed with one of care and responsibility. Leonardo's spirit clashed with Bacon's.

In their struggle to defend their profits no matter the cost to others, corporations hit on a strategy they have since perfected. Because science explores the frontiers of what is known, corporations needed only sow doubt in the public's mind. Without strong pressure, politicians would not challenge the source of so much of their campaign funding and future wealth as lobbyists. Calling for more studies became the order of the day, and when those were done the call went out for still more. A strategy developed to prolong indiscriminate use of DDT was later followed for obscuring the harm of tobacco, the decline of salmon, the existence of global warming, and more.

But this time greed, power, and money lost. The media was not yet a wholly owned subsidiary of corporate conglomerates, and some journalists still practiced journalism. Aldo Leopold's insight about people proved more accurate than those of economists, CEOs, and most politicians. As a result, today we can see brown pelicans, eagles, peregrine falcons, and other birds the corporate world would have written off as collateral damage.

Silent Spring brought new people into a movement already energized by a successful campaign against damming the Grand Canyon. Brilliant as it had been, that campaign had been waged on familiar grounds: the desecration of a national treasure for the benefit of unneeded power. Now people were beginning to realize that nature was not just magnificent landscapes. Nature was home, in our backyards, and nature was we ourselves, in our bodies. Carson enabled the modern environmental movement to go far beyond traditional conservation concerns.

Like Aldo Leopold, Rachel Carson did not live to see her victory, dying from breast cancer eighteen months after her book was released. But by then she knew the industry-financed character assassinations had failed. Even so, it would be years before the sensibility she did so much to develop and empower manifested in the first Earth Day and led Richard Nixon and Congress to establish the Environmental Protection Agency.

Her opponents never forgot or forgave. Even now they spread the falsehood that Carson was responsible for millions of deaths due to DDT being banned. (See "The DDT Lie," http://dizerega.com/faultlines/appendices/.)

More Streams of Influence

Aldo Leopold's and Rachel Carson's influence was enriched by other developments during the sixties. The Apollo moon landing made an unexpected contribution to rising environmental awareness. The photograph of a beautiful earth rising over a lifeless lunar landscape provided millions, maybe billions, with a sense of our planet as a whole, a whole of ethereal beauty starkly suspended in the blackness of space. This insight particularly impacted astronauts and cosmonauts, changing the lives of many.

In 1983 American astronauts and Soviet cosmonauts came together to form the Association of Space Explorers. In the process they described their "enhanced reverence for the Earth as a result of their space flight experience." Cosmonaut Yuri Artyukhin observed that in space "it isn't important in which sea or lake you observe a slick of pollution, or in the forests of which country a fire breaks out, or on which continent a hurricane arises." He added, "You are standing guard over the whole of our Earth."[16]

While standing on the moon, American astronaut Edgar Mitchell experienced earthrise as "a glimpse of divinity." On his trip back Mitchell had "a very deep gut feeling that something was different . . . a nonrational way of understanding. . . . I was suddenly experiencing the universe as intelligent, loving, harmonious."[17] Upon returning, Mitchell learned meditation and founded the Institute for Noetic Sciences, which flourishes to the present.[18] Unlike culture warriors, many representatives of can-do masculine optimism were open to the feminine awareness then blossoming.

In the late sixties James Lovelock and Lynn Margulis developed a scientific theory that our planet is a self-regulating system. The initial insight had come to Lovelock while he worked for NASA, trying to determine whether life might exist on Mars. He realized the Martian atmosphere was in chemical equilibrium, whereas Earth's was far from equilibrium, but stable—suggesting there was no life on Mars. But how does Earth's atmosphere, which is produced by life, stay so constant over millions of years? That question led Lovelock and Margulis to theorize that Earth itself was a living system, a kind of organism.

In 1979 Lovelock published *Gaia: A New Look at Life on Earth*,[19] and their theory took off. Although initially ignored by the scientific community, the idea spoke to many laypeople's deeply felt need for a stronger connection with their home. Its appeal was strengthened by powerful insights many gained from their use of psychedelic substances, including direct experience of everything around them being alive.

The Gaia hypothesis ultimately influenced scientists to look at our planet from a far more integrated perspective, a perspective continuing to bear fruit.[20] It also led NASA to look for small pockets of gas on Mars that were not in chemical equilibrium. Some have been found, although it is too early to judge whether their source is from chemical processes emanating from deep within the planet or evidence of life's hanging on, survivals from an earlier time.

THE FEMININE DIMENSION

Richard Nelson wrote, "Probably no society has been so deeply alienated as ours from the community of nature, has viewed the natural world from a greater distance of mind, has lapsed to a murkier comprehension of its connections with the sustaining environment." Consequently, "We have created for ourselves a profound and imperiling loneliness."[21] Neither the popular understanding of Darwin nor traditional monotheism bridged this gap, a gap that made us lonely aliens and taught us to distrust the feelings we experience when immersed in nature. By teaching us the depth of our connection, the permeability of our boundaries, and the fragility of so much that we love, such as the birds in our backyards, ecology began to heal this separation.

As many Americans began to grasp how deeply we are a part of nature, their intellectual understanding began to reinforce many people's long-felt awareness of the earth as their home. Our earthly evolutionary heritage shows in every dimension of our bodies, bodies that are as they are because we evolved and live on *this* earth. Among many in the sixties generation and others sympathetic with them, the increasing complementarity of our intuitive and aesthetic perceptions and our intellectual understanding transformed how we perceived the natural world. Today many Americans describe nature and encounters with wildness in terms markedly different from earlier liberal conservation leaders and writers. This difference is most apparent in the new genre of literature called nature writing.

Nature writing and what is now called deep ecology have a long history in California, beginning with John Muir.[22] After the sixties it became a national literary force.

Virtually all contemporary nature writers describe encountering nature as a sensuous experience of immersion and relationship—and not usually in terms of making us more manly or overcoming personal challenges. Accounts of hunting differ in tone from William Kent's "barbaric manliness," sharing or going beyond Leopold's sensibility of hunting as relationship within the ecological community.

In *Ecomysticism* Carl von Essen describes what he calls "the hunter's trance," a mental state common among fishermen, hunters, and others who immerse themselves deeply in the wild. He described a friend's experience while hunting elk in Colorado: "I felt now their presence and somehow knew that they felt mine. As I stood there, the sense of time remarkably changed. What seemed like minutes I found later to be over an hour. At the same moment an intense feeling of the clarity of the scene swept over me. All my sense seemed to sharpen to an exquisite razor's edge. . . . I felt, amazingly, a sort of merger of myself with everything, a sense of belonging. I was connected with everything in that panorama, the grass, trees, rocks, insects, birds, the elk."[23]

Gary Snyder has been a major figure in the contemporary environmental movement and in modern poetry as well as in fostering the spread of Buddhism to the West. He writes, "An ecosystem is a kind of mandala in which there are multiple relations that are all-powerful and instructive. Each figure in the mandala—a little mouse or bird (or little god or demon figure)—has an important position and a role to play. Though ecosystems can be described as hierarchical in terms of energy flow, from the standpoint of the whole all of its members are equal. . . . We are all guests at the feast, and we are also the meal! All of biological nature can be seen as an enormous *puja*, a ceremony of offering and sharing."[24]

Snyder's Buddhism returns us to von Essen's observation that "the Zen practice of *shikan-taza* resembles the hunter's trance in that the mind is brought to a heightened state of awareness, intensely involved in the object of its attention. . . . Simultaneously the participant can be peculiarly detached, but centered into the ground of his being. . . . The hunter's trance is thus a form of meditation, but in a dynamic and primal mode that evolved from evolutionary forces that existed millions of years ago."[25]

Perhaps this phenomenon provides a common experiential core for all who have devoted much of their lives to defending the more-than-human world. Progressive conservationists realized they attained a "peaceful mind," but their one-sidedly manly vocabulary could not capture it as well as the new more feminine sensibility of open but intense connection, empathy, and relationship, shown with striking power in Terry Tempest Williams's writings on

Yellowstone: "It is time for us to take off our masks, to step out from behind our personas . . . and admit we are lovers, engaged in an erotics of place. Loving the land. Honoring its mysteries. Acknowledging, embracing the spirit of place—there is nothing more legitimate and there is nothing more true."[26]

The modern skeptic will scoff that there is too much anthropomorphism here. But the skeptic uncritically accepts the Enlightenment belief that we live alone in a world of objects.

THE BLINDNESS OF THE TAKEN-FOR-GRANTED

David Abram answers this challenge: "Are we not simply projecting our own interior mood upon the outer landscape?" He answers, "Well, no—not if our manner of understanding and conceptualizing our various 'interior' moods was originally borrowed from the moody capricious earth itself."[27] George Lakoff and Mark Johnson have shown human thought to be metaphorical at its core, and our root metaphors arise from our bodies and their relation to the world.[28] Metaphors ultimately rooted in the body are essential in enabling scientific discovery.[29] Freya Matthews points out, "We are the only model of subjectivity available to ourselves."[30] How else could we describe innerness? Our anthropomorphism is inseparable from our world.

But we have become blind to this fact. Not only do we usually thoughtlessly accept the Enlightenment view of the natural world as ultimately inert, we also have a long record of letting taken-for-granted assumptions about our superiority blind us to seeing our similarities to others. Enormous crimes have often resulted.

California today has no large Indian reservations because settlers murdered virtually all of the state's original residents who had survived European diseases. In 1853 the *Yreka Herald* told its readers, "Extermination is no longer a question of time—the time has arrived, the work has commenced, and let the first man that says treaty or peace be regarded as a traitor."[31] By 1890 the recorded population of California Indians was 15,283, a decline of at least 95 percent from 1851.[32]

Decades of oppression and murder that followed the end of slavery stand as damning testimony to the moral self-deception of those who could not see African Americans as human as themselves. The confident declarations by many whites about Blacks' innate inferiority are further evidence of how what counts as evidence is shaped by what we want to see. These people could not see the common humanity in front of their faces *every day*.

For much of recorded history men believed women were intellectually weaker. Yet men and women lived together intimately every day. Generations took for granted attitudes that now stand before us as obviously wrong. We are not any brighter than our erring forbearers, but we no longer so take for granted their old beliefs and so can more easily see the evidence they could not.

We also have blind spots. I will not see mine until someone or some event points them out—if I have the integrity to look. That's why they are called blind spots. But some I see now because others sensitized me to them.

For many today the final barrier radically separating us from animals is morality. We can be moral, they can't. This belief in nature's amorality undergirds secular nihilism. But for those who take the time to look, animals often exhibit what we would call moral behavior if a person did it, including fairness, altruism (unrelated to self-interested genes), and forgiveness.[33]

These recent findings put Aldo Leopold's observation about our ability to care for other creatures of no practical use to us in a new light. What we call morality is *intrinsic* to our world. If Leopold's observation distinguishes us from the rest of the wild world, environmentalists are *better* exemplars of our most uniquely human capacities than are their critics. To be fully human we need to be able to care about the other-than-human world. Love and compassion are emergent qualities of our world. They are the outcome of evolution, its finest human fruits but not absent in many other beings.

ECOFEMINISM AND DEEP ECOLOGY

As feminist scholarship became established, its advocates began asking questions earlier scholars had never thought to ask. Carolyn Merchant's

1980 *The Death of Nature* offered a fascinating reexamination of changing attitudes toward nature from the sixteenth century into the early Enlightenment. At the beginning of the sixteenth century nature had long been regarded as female. As nature was increasingly considered lifeless and was described mechanically, Merchant argued, these perspectives appeared in changing attitudes toward women.[34] As nature came to be viewed as passive matter acted on by external laws, women increasingly were understood as passive as well. Metaphors shaped our perceptions in both directions: nature as feminine and as mechanical, and the feminine as passive and more ruled by "mere matter" than the full masculine ideal.

According to Merchant, much of the reason for this increasing denigration of women's minds had to do with women's more obvious identification with biological life and the world of matter, whereas men could fantasize their minds as disembodied, perceiving the world from the outside.[35] In 1981 a fascinating anthropological study incorporating research from over 150 tribal societies demonstrated that Merchant's linking of attitudes toward women and attitudes toward nature possibly applied worldwide.[36] Merchant's book helped catalyze the offshoot of cultural feminism we call ecofeminism.

Ecofeminists rejected the modern ideal that disembodied abstract knowledge could give us any more adequate knowledge of the natural world than it could of women. Terry Tempest Williams gives a good description of the ecofeminist perspective: "I see the Feminine defined as a reconnection to the Self, a commitment to the wildness within—our instincts, our capacity to create and destroy; our hunger for connection as well as sovereignty, interdependence and independence, at once. We are taught not to trust our own experience. The Feminine teaches us experience is our way back home, the psychic bridge that spans rational and intuitive waters."[37]

The generic term *deep ecology* was derived from Norwegian philosopher Arne Naess's work.[38] Naess, who had been influenced by Aldo Leopold, Rachel Carson, and Robinson Jeffers, argued that we could begin to gain a more accurate understanding of nature and our place in it through reexamining what truly constituted the self. "As we mature an inescapable process of identification with others" takes place, and "the self is widened and deepened. We 'see ourselves in others.'" In terms of deep ecology, "The ecological self of a person is that with which this person identifies."[39] Naess's view harmonizes with Leopold's insight about our ability to care for other species of no utility to ourselves, for care is rooted in empathy and empathy in expanding identification. Whether in David Abram's subtle analysis of how we actually experience nature, Derrick Jensen's courageous descriptions of nature as living and passionate attacks on the modern Baconian destruction of the world, Jane Goodall's powerful and moving work on our relation to the rest of the natural world, or the writings of many others, what can be broadly called deep ecology provides some of the most insightful writing and thinking ever done by Westerners about nature.

Arriving at similar conclusions by different routes, ecofeminism and deep ecology restore us to a world of more-than-human value, a world that is not just our habitat—it is our home. We are earthlings "all the way down," and our ability to care for life other than our own is our most uniquely human characteristic. (See "Deep Ecology and Ecofeminism," http://dizerega.com/faultlines/appendices/.)

This rethinking of nature in environmentalism dovetails with the rethinking of deity within religious feminism.

THE RELIGION OF SCIENTISM

At its core environmentalism is concerned with the flourishing of life as a whole. We are neither separate from nor properly dominators of the rest of the world. We are "plain citizens" of something bigger than we are, and this something bigger is both masculine and feminine, and in its immanence, feminine.

Environmentalism directly challenged the West's dominant Faustian mythos. In doing so it was as unsettling to modern secularism as science had been to biblical religion. Because modernity increasingly failed to recognize any values other than power, and science promised ever-increasing power, the possibility that power might have to be limited removed the only veil between the modern mind and awareness of its ultimate vulnerability in a world it imagined as alien.

As science became secular modernity's substitute for religion, it embodied its hope for salvation and immortality in Faustian garb. In 1939 J. D. Bernal imagined, "It is unlikely that man will stop until he has roamed over and colonized most of the sidereal universe, or that even this will be the end. . . . By intelligent organization, the life of the universe could probably be prolonged to many millions of millions of times what it would be without organization."[40] Richard Dawkins echoes this vision: "Science boosts its claim to truth by its spectacular ability to make matter and energy jump through hoops on command, and to predict what will happen and when."[41]

Making control our goal is a hopeful response if we live in an ultimately meaningless world that left to its own devices leads to our inevitable extinction. Any insuperable limitation challenges this dream, bringing us face-to-face with the fear lurking at the heart of the modern secular belief that we live in a world without hope or escape. Secular scientistic critics such as Michael Crichton are at one with conservative evangelicals in claiming environmentalism to be a "religion" boding horrible things for the human race.[42]

Ironically, environmentalists' warnings are usually science based. The overwhelming bulk of scientific opinion says global warming is happening, the oceans are seriously depleted, forest ecosystems are declining, and so on. Objections to those warnings are couched in hysterical terms—environmentalists hate human beings or want us to go back to hunting and gathering—exposing Faustian scientism as the religion of the modern secular masculine mind. But environmentalism is not a religion because its insights are fundamental to all religious traditions.

RELIGION AND THE ENVIRONMENT

The environment is a common concern of religions worldwide, from monotheists, nontheistic Buddhists, and polytheists to Neo-Pagans and traditional Native Americans. In one form or another its core insights exist in all the major religions of which I am aware. Only some of the religious right seems immune.

Consider Job 12:7–8: "But ask the animals, and they will teach you, or the birds of the air, and they will tell you; or speak to the earth, and it will teach you, or let the fish of the sea inform you." And this, from Orthodox Christianity: "Nature is a revelation not merely of the truth about God but of God Himself. . . . If God is not present in a grain of sand then He is not present in heaven either."[43]

The core ethical insight that nature has value independent of our attitudes is expressed within the contexts of *all* the major religions existing in this country: Christian, Muslim, Jewish, Buddhist, Bahai, Hindu, Daoist, Native American, and Neo-Pagan. Depending on their theological tenets and specific mythologies, the precise understanding of why these values are important varies. But that they exist does not change. High-ranking representatives from all the world's major religions and many of its smaller ones argue that environmental preservation is a religious obligation. They adopted a common declaration of responsibility for the environment and care for the other-than-human world.[44]

A component found within all major religions cannot itself be called a religion, but it can be called *foundational to them all*. Historically concern with nature has not been a major emphasis within most of these older traditions, but until recently humanity has not had the destructive impact we now have. Nature was usually taken for granted, but the basic insight of nature's value over and above its utility to us is so common that any religion blind to it is spiritually deluded, as with right-wing spiritual nihilism.

SACRED IMMANENCE

Right-wing opponents are wrong in calling environmentalism a religion. But they are correct in picking up on something in environmentalism that challenges their worldview more deeply than simply a desire to preserve old-growth forests, clean streams, and the quiet of the hills might suggest.

Environmental values appeal to a sensibility present in all normal human beings and in all major religions, but one many Americans have lost the ability to discuss or often even identify beyond dismissing it as subjectivism. E. O. Wilson points out that more children and adults visit zoos in the United States and Canada than attend all professional sports, combined.[45]

Jules Pretty and Jo Barton found that people's mood and self-esteem benefit from what they call "green exercise."[46] Pretty said of his study, "For the first time in the scientific literature, we have been able to show dose-response relationships for the positive effects of nature on human mental health."[47] Recent research indicates that living in more complex natural environments has measurably better mental health impacts than living in simpler ones, and that both are superior to being surrounded by concrete and traffic.[48]

We all understand terms like *virgin* forest, *God's* country, *pristine* and *unspoiled* wilderness. The terms may be hackneyed, but what they refer to is not: a quality of *experience* that we can describe only poetically, metaphorically, or mystically.

In 1898 the prominent philosopher William James hiked to the top of Mt. Marcy, New York's highest peak. Later he wrote his wife of his night on the mountain: "I spent a good deal of it in the woods, where the streaming moonlight lit up things in a magical checkered play, and it seemed as if the Gods of all the nature-mythologies were holding an indescribable meeting in my breast with the moral Gods of the inner life."[49]

In 1923 the photographer Ansel Adams wrote of his experience hiking through California's Sierra Nevada. "The silver light turned every blade of grass and every particle of sand into luminous metallic splendor; there was nothing, however small, that did not clash in the bright wind, that did not send arrow of light through the glassy air. I was suddenly arrested in the long crunching path up the ridge by an exceedingly pointed awareness of the *light*. . . . I saw more clearly than I have ever seen before or since the minute detail of the grasses, the clusters of sand shifting in the wind, the small flotsam of the forest, the motion of the high clouds streaming above the peaks."[50]

Most people can immediately identify with Adams's statements. He reports a quality of the human experience on earth. Value is in nature; it is immanent and it is all around us. If I say I went for a walk in nature to help me put things in perspective, almost everyone knows what I mean. Getting out in the more-than-human world helps put my very human cares and fears and desires into context. Shopping at Target or Wal-Mart does not. And yet, the dominant streams of our culture have resolutely denied its importance while telling us that Target and Wal-Mart have made great contributions to our well-being.

Our power to care about things for their own sake, which Leonardo described and Aldo Leopold celebrated, is a superior insight into reality compared to celebrating our power to dominate them. Modern environmentalism has reintegrated a mind split asunder during the Reformation and Enlightenment while simultaneously opening it to the sacred immanent in the world, encouraging a reverence for life, and overcoming nihilism. Like feminism, environmentalism strikes at the heart of pathological masculinity, for if we are not to dominate the rest of the world, the claims of those who would dominate us are also weakened.

But why is all this happening now? Why the appeal of the feminine values of the sixties to so many Americans, and why their ability to heal the loss of the values that once gave soul to the West and to America?

THE FALL AND RISE OF SACRED IMMANENCE AND THE DIVINE FEMININE

This whole is in all its parts so beautiful, and is felt by me to be so intensely in earnest, that I am compelled to love it and to think of it as divine.

—Robinson Jeffers

Another world is not only possible, she is on her way! On a quiet day, if you listen carefully, you can hear her breathing.

—Arundhati Roy

The culture war is the most visible manifestation of the collapse of modernity's moral foundations and the consequent degeneration into a nihilism manifesting as the worship of power for its own sake. Taken together they constitute a perfect storm battering America's founding principles.

Happily there is a deeper level to this cultural, political, and spiritual crisis. Modernity's moral collapse is inherent not in liberal values but in the effort to base those values on spiritual and philosophical foundations ultimately hostile to them. Modernity's humane liberal core can be reestablished and strengthened by spiritual and ethical currents empowered by the sixties that flow below the radar of today's corrupt elites and their media servants.

THE MODERN MUTATION

Modernity is a genuine social mutation. It moved most people from the countryside to cities and from an economy rooted in human and animal power to one based on electricity and the internal combustion engine.

197

The context of human relations shifted from eternal hierarchies to a formal equality requiring hierarchies to justify themselves to all. Today even dictators and oligarchies use democratic trappings to legitimize their rule rather than claiming divine right or the inherent superiority of class, race, caste, or religion.

Family life has been transformed. Most children survive to adulthood, transforming parents' relationships with the very young.[1] Most mothers make it into old age, so single parents usually reflect failed marriages rather than a parent's death. Most parents no longer need their children to care for them in their old age. Increasingly families bond or divide on the strength of affection and love.

For the first time since the rise of cities, the poor became a minority group. Most people no longer need to farm in order to survive and so have become insulated from the uncertainties of farming life. Those who continue to farm increasingly treat it as a calling, not a fate.

Modernity's rise dramatically expanded opportunities for people to make important choices in work, friends, family, and religion, increasing their sense of being individuals rather than part of a timeless social order.

Science, the market, and democracy are modernity's most defining institutions. They are impersonal networks linking scientists, producers, consumers, and citizens, each aware of only the tiniest fragments of the whole system. By enabling them to benefit from strangers' insights to a greater degree than in any other human association, these linkages empower people in their individual projects while encouraging them to act within contexts controlled by no one.

JERUSALEM AND BENARES

A social transformation as complete as modernity's occurred only once before. Beginning about eleven thousand years ago hunter-gatherers shifted to agricultural and pastoral ways of life, passing from one way of life to another. The result was a profound disconnection between inherited ways of understanding the world and the world that had come into being. (See "Before the Farm, and After," http://dizerega.com/faultlines/appendices/.)

Agriculture made possible cities, writing, the arts, roads, and the first machines. It also made possible the rise of powerful hierarchical orders that exploited most people. Humans were more numerous, but life for most was worse than in earlier hunting and gathering societies. The bad prospered in a way they had not before.

Earlier spiritual traditions failed to address the new world brought into being with agriculture and the hierarchies it made possible. In response what are now considered the great world religions arose during what is often called the Axial Age.

The Axial religious traditions responded to the terrible conditions confronting most people in large agricultural civilizations, which inherited religions could not effectively address. Axial traditions focused on the inner self and moral reasoning because the exterior world was so obviously imperfect.[2]

Two strategies characterized how many cultures coped. Either a source of ultimate justice compensated for the worldly success of the bad, or the world itself was a trap from which we needed rescuing. In various forms these views prevailed from the classical West to India.[3] Peter Berger labels these two spiritual perspectives by the dominant cities associated with them: Jerusalem and Benares.[4] (Berger did not address East Asia's response.)

In India and the West alike, if a teaching could be interpreted as either world affirming or world denying, the more negative interpretation seemed to dominate. For example, the Hindu *maya* could be seen as an illusion in which we are trapped or as a divine game in which we participate.[5] It usually was interpreted negatively.

Meditation was practiced in the West as well as the East, for late classical teachers such as Plotinus certainly taught it.[6] Both Hindu India and classical civilization provided harmonious contexts for such a development. Meditation need not indicate something is lacking in embodied existence, but, many traditions, at least in the East, rejected the goodness of the physical world and viewed meditation as a tool for ultimate escape.

Originally the split between Benares and the West was not sharp. But in the West this common approach was eclipsed by the "religions of the Book," whose earliest roots were presaged in teachings by the Persian prophet Zoroaster and culminated in the great Abrahamic monotheisms.

Regarded as divinely revealed, Zoroaster's teachings argued that good and evil alike were required for creation to exist. A good and an evil god existed, both created by an ultimate deity. Earth was a world of fundamental binaries with sharp boundaries, a battleground between absolute good and absolute evil. Ultimately, divine judgment would punish those who chose evil ways.

In myth male deities had already been pushing aside, sometimes killing, and virtually always subordinating female ones. The Zoroastrian framework accelerated this process. It created stark dualisms, separating male from female, clean from unclean, obedient from disobedient, and sin from sanctity.[7]

Zoroastrianism also demanded women's subservience to men. Women could attain their highest posthumous standing if they "satisfied their husbands and lords, were submissive, respectful, and obedient to them." Transgressions leading to hell were disproportionately sexual and disproportionately applied to women. Adulterous women and women who quarreled with their husbands and lords, did not consent to sex whenever they demanded, or even wore makeup, were condemned to hell.[8] Zoroastrianism established a pattern repeated in the Abrahamic monotheisms to come.

The Chinese Exception

Among major Eurasian civilizations, only Chinese Axial traditions maintained strong positive ties with pre-Axial practices.[9] Confucianism focused on the need for careful attention to maintaining correct relations and ritual lest the world degenerate into chaos, echoing hunter-gatherer spiritualities' value of harmony, but within an intensely hierarchical view of reality absent in them.

Daoism seems to have remained even closer to the preagricultural past. The Tao Te Ching described a former, better time before the degenerate times when, according to Lao-Tsu, morality needed to be taught explicitly.

> When the Tao is lost, there is goodness.
> When goodness is lost, there is morality.
> When morality is lost, there is ritual.
> Ritual is the husk of true faith,
> the beginning of chaos.[10]

From this perspective ethics arises when a way of life integrating decent behavior into skillful practice is superseded by one appearing to reward manipulation and deceit. Behavior once taken for granted no longer could be and even needed to be defended. Daoists often urged those seeking to become sages to live in nature and avoid political involvement, as in the writings attributed to Chuang-tzu.[11] But outside China, at least on the Eurasian mainland, religious goals shifted from maintaining or restoring harmony to seeking salvation or release.

From Monism to Monotheism

As societies traded and warred with one another, the old polytheistic world based on deities of place was challenged by encounters with other peoples' polytheistic systems. Some foreign deities were similar to ones already known; others were very different, and some appeared to combine qualities elsewhere regarded as separate. Thoughtful people wondered whether any kind of unity existed to the varied expressions of gods and goddesses they encountered in the societies around them. From Greece to India, various kinds of monism were postulated as underlying this surface diversity.[12] China also developed a monist perspective, for yin and yang are not dichotomies but interpenetrating aspects of a greater whole.

Monism is the belief that an underlying spiritual unity characterizes existence. All variety is an expression of this unity. No element of the world is truly separate from all other elements. Monism is therefore tolerant of other spiritual perspectives because ultimately *everything* is an expression of the One. In this respect monism differs from monotheism. Transcendental monotheisms like Western Christianity argue that there is only one god and that everything separate from him is derivative and subordinate. Monotheism is intrinsically monopolistic.

In the West monism was supplanted by monotheism. It did not happen through persuasion.

In Egypt Akhenaton (1364–1347 BCE) exalted the sun god Ra into a monotheistic deity who created both himself and all other gods. In time Akhenaton attempted to abolish worship of other Egyptian gods, the first known case of religious repression. His efforts proved too ambitious, his reign too brief for the transformation he sought to put down deep roots. Memories of the old ways had not died. Upon his death the old gods were restored.

Whether Akhenaton influenced Moses is a controversy I doubt will ever be settled, although it seems compelling to me.[13] Regardless, beginning with Moses the notion of God as a single divine entity gained growing influence within Israel. As Michael Ledeen enthusiastically reminded us, Moses succeeded by *exterminating* those who thought differently. More ruthless than Akhenaton, Moses was more successful, although it still took Hebraic monotheism centuries to annihilate its spiritual alternatives.

While the Old Testament prophets could be monarchy's insightful critics, their conception of deity was politically convenient for earthly kings. Conceiving the sacred as a divine hierarchy with a single deity on top helped legitimize secular hierarchies with a king at the top. Kings ruled with Yahweh's approval.

By King David's time, as Karen Armstrong observes, "the covenant that allied Yahweh and the tribes was eclipsed in Judah by the covenant that Yahweh made with King David, promising that his dynasty would last forever."[14] Monopolistic transcendental monotheism was very compatible with societies rooted in domination. They made it possible, and in turn it legitimated them.

In short, the rise of agriculture ultimately strengthened transcendental masculine, feminine-denying religions. Their frequently hierarchical character made it easy to co-opt them to support exploitive political and economic hierarchies.

A NEW SPIRITUAL WATERSHED

Modernity's transformation of human life changed our lives as deeply as had the agricultural revolution. The oppressive and often-lethal environment that supported and lent urgency to messages of individual salvation and liberation no longer dominates our world. Physical life is more secure and materially prosperous than it ever has been. But to what end?

The modern world's spiritual crisis is about whether meaning exists in a world where everything is treated as a means to something else and so is itself valueless. Entertainment and distraction substitute for meaning and value. The expanding and ruthless sociopathy of modern corporations challenges spiritual understanding differently than did the conqueror or king. Ecological collapse could change this picture, but it is not (yet?) a factor in most people's lives.

In the United States today's challenges of meaning and spirit are primarily challenges of the heart. Nearly everything people normally encounter is a commodity, without any other value to its creator. Even human beings are considered "resources" by many of our elites. Meaning survives as personal subjectivity, ultimately as evanescent as a person's life.

In such a world the highest "objective" standard of success is the satisfied consumer. But while we may sometimes envy, we will never respect someone who seeks this ideal. No parents want their children to grow up simply to be satisfied consumers, yet this is the promise modern life strives to fulfill: whatever we possess, the future will give us more for less effort.

From a spiritual perspective, using power and possessions to connect with what we most deeply seek is like relying on empty calories for nutrition. It gives us a momentarily gratifying sense of connection, like a one-night stand, but leaves us empty and craving more of the same, be it money, possessions, pornography, domination, fame, or other kinds of power over something. None connect Thous to Thous, and none can truly fulfill us. Each promises to fulfill the fantasy disappointed by the last. They are the Twinkies of spirit.

Consumerism is probably the most humane response to living in a world without meaning. Certainly the twentieth century has witnessed some hideous alternatives. Consumerism does not merit three cheers, but it merits one or two. In a meaningless world, that is pretty good. But not good enough.

The habits of the past led us to a dead end.

Something Happenin' Here, What It Is Aint Exactly Clear

Religion is said to be a bulwark of morality and stability. The truth is more ambiguous. According to a PEW poll, the Americans who most consistently oppose torture do *not* go to church. Support for torture *increases* with church attendance.[15] Church-going Christians are more supportive of interrogation methods practiced by atheistic totalitarians than are non-Christians. Self-described highly religious people act with less empathy than less religious people or atheists.[16]

Some torture-rejecting Americans are secular liberals, who do not need the threat of divine vengeance to act kindly. Others are exploring alternate spiritual paths or are associated with more liberal Christian congregations that generally reject or ignore threats of damnation for those unlike themselves.

These statistics exist as part of a larger pattern. Nate Silver reports, "Since 2003 . . . the decline in [American] divorce rates has been largely confined to states which have *not* passed a state constitutional ban on gay marriage. These states saw their divorce rates decrease by an average of 8 percent between 2003 and 2008. States which had passed a same-sex marriage ban as of January 1, 2008, however, saw their divorce rates rise by about 1 percent over the same period."[17]

These statistics take on added significance when we reflect on the finding reported in chapter 7 that the most antiabortion states did *least* to help children after they were born or to punish those who caused miscarriages by beating pregnant women. Something profound is happening here.

In political terms, America's cities vote Democratic, and the centers of cultural and economic innovation are the bluest. Many of these were also centers of the sixties counterculture. The San Francisco Bay Area, Seattle, New York, and New England in particular are centers for environmental support and openness to an expanded role of the feminine, even if they are often also centers of corporate power. Blue-state voters are the genuine values voters.

In this time of spiritual crisis, spirit is manifesting new currents in established religious traditions and in new spiritual communities. What they have in common—be they liberal mainstream churches and synagogues, Western Buddhism with its many women teachers, Wicca and other Neo-Pagan religions honoring Goddesses and the Divine Feminine, the more nature-focused neoshamanism, or even secular environmentalists—is a common focus on the importance of sacred immanence and the feminine, often the Divine Feminine.

Hints of Immanence

The role of sacred immanence in American life is not new. Alexis de Tocqueville, in *Democracy in America*, commented: "As conditions become more equal . . . the human mind seeks to embrace a multitude of different objects at once; and it constantly strives to link up a variety of consequences with a single cause." Ultimately, one "seeks to expand and simplify his conception by including God and the Universe in one great whole. . . . Of all the different philosophical systems used to explain the universe, I believe that pantheism is one of those most fitted to seduce the human mind in democratic ages."[18]

In the optimistic democratic culture developing before the Civil War, old messages of world rejection and humanity's fallen state were losing connection with people's experience. Similarly, the vision of God as king lost relevance in societies abandoning traditional attitudes toward hierarchy. When all are equal, it is easier to conceive of the sacred as in all things.

David Abram affirms Tocqueville's insight in his eloquent description of a pantheistic sensibility: "Our greatest hope for the future rests not in the triumph of any single set of beliefs, but in the acknowledgement of a felt mystery that underlies all our doctrines. . . . There are no priests needed in such a faith, no intermediaries or experts necessary to effect our contact with the sacred, since—carnally immersed as we are in the thick of this breathing planet—we each have our own intimate access to the big mystery."[19]

Tocqueville's aristocratic sensibility *opposed* this democratic pantheistic tendency: "Against it, all who abide in their attachment to the true greatness of man should struggle and combine."[20] While many such as Tocqueville were torn, there is a *fundamental* misfit between tradition and modernity. Traditional religious understandings legitimated secular hierarchies as harmonious with divine hierarchies and transcendent patterns. Modernity embraced equality among citizens over social hierarchies and increasingly immanence over transcendence as the most accessible expression of the sacred.

Secular Pantheism

Urban Americans do not have to struggle with nature to wrest a crop from soil and climate. Instead, they often experience nature as a source of peace, perspective, and beauty. A national park or seashore is a place for personal renewal. Nature is not value free at the level of personal experience.

Scientists are confirming Darwin's insight that morality is emergent in nature and does not need to be imposed as divine command or through the dictates of logic and abstract rationality. Neuroscientists have discovered "mirror neurons" whereby we automatically react to experiences of others as if they happened to ourselves. Empathy is hardwired into the human genome as well as that of some other animals.[21] Even before they learn how to reach out, babies are inherently sympathetic to others' suffering and drawn to those who act kindly. They do not need to be taught to disapprove of cruelty.[22]

Research with animals from apes to mice has also shown that they behave in ways indicating concern for the well-being of others.[23] Contests between computer programs have found that cooperative "nice" programs outperform competitive ruthless ones over time.[24] Meaning and care are inherent in the world, a part of the logic that gives it structure.

If ethical value is embedded in logic and emergent in the world, the modern view of life as meaningless is transformed. Value brings meaning. We open to a secular pantheism that is attracting growing numbers of secular moderns.

The very secular E. O. Wilson said of his own experience in the wild, "The effect was strangely calming. Breathing and heartbeat diminished, concentration intensified. It seemed to me that something extraordinary in the forest was very close to where I stood, moving to the surface and to discovery." Wilson named this kind of perception "biophilia."[25] (See "Nature and Health," http://dizerega.com/faultlines/appendices/.)

Geerat Vermeij, a scientist blind since childhood, became extraordinarily tuned to other senses. He wrote about a Panamanian rain forest: "One experiences everything at once. . . . Shapes, sounds, smells, and weather come together to offer the prepared mind an emergent conception of the whole. . . . I am listening to an unrehearsed orchestra of many different instruments playing symphonies and concerti that are at once musically complex and pleasingly transparent."[26]

Wilson, Vermeij, and many others with similar experiences do not identify with any religious tradition. They find deep personal meaning in nature, have a powerful commitment to the well-being of the other-than-human world, consider themselves advocates of a scientific worldview, and are secular in their outlook.[27]

Vermeij writes, "Humans are at one end of a continuum of emergent meaning and control, not on one side of a steep ravine that separates us from the rest of the animate world."[28] With this sensibility secular pantheism and spiritual pantheism blend into each other.

In my terms, direct, open experience of nature often leads toward a naturalistic pantheism that stands in remarkable harmony with forms of spirituality emphasizing sacred immanence. This experience of the world, common to millions if not billions of us, has been belittled and denigrated by both Lockean and Baconian approaches to knowledge and truth, as well as by those who emphasize only transcendental monotheism.

The gap between secular and spiritual pantheists rests on the nature of consciousness. Does it form in some way a greater monistic whole that may or may not also be experienced as transcendent? Very significantly, how one answers this question does not seem to influence the workings of any scientific theory at present. In the final analysis its answer rests on each person's experiences and interpretation of them, which traditional scientific methods are unable to evaluate. (See "Seeing the World as Energy," http://dizerega.com/faultlines/appendices/.)

Sacred Mystery

If the theistic term *God* is the name we apply to the fullest expression of the Divine, it refers to more than humans can grasp. The human cannot comprehend the superhuman. Any belief to the contrary reduces the Ultimate to some conception originating in the human mind.

We cannot grasp the nature of quantum reality or the inseparability of space and time. We need abstract mathematics far removed from our personal experience to work with these concepts. Their world is not our world of juicy peaches, softly falling snow, and the touch of a lover's hand. The great physicist Niels Bohr said of his discoveries, "Anyone who is not shocked by quantum theory has not understood it."[29] So far as we presently know, these principles are the most basic physical foundations underlying our material reality, and they are beyond our normal logical ability to conceptualize.

Perhaps more significantly, Kurt Gödel proved that mathematics could never be described by a complete theory that was also consistent. All mathematical systems rely in part on statements neither provably true nor provably false. The mathematics we use to work with a quantum reality beyond our power to comprehend rests on a mathematics we cannot prove. We are always immersed in mystery.

These examples suggest that we can hardly hope fully to grasp our world through either logocentric or mythological analysis. Each can help and each can mislead. To the extent understanding comes, experience is also required, giving context for a better interpretation of logos and mythos alike.

The great mystics and many others experienced what appeared to be direct personal experiences of the Divine. When they tried to describe them they were thrown back on their language, familiar metaphors, and common experiences shared by their audiences. That is all any of us have to work with when communicating with others. Significantly, even within the Christian tradition's almost-exclusive focus on a male image of deity, many mystics chose *feminine* imagery to communicate their experience. The other alternative is to use negative theology: the Highest is neither this nor that; it is everything, but it is not a thing. From this perspective, any positive description is less than the whole. Yet neither positive nor negative theology is adequate to communicate the ultimate sacred context. Negative theology implies that what cannot be described is good in some ultimate indefinable sense. Positive theology emphasizes the inadequacy of its descriptions, even as it attempts to describe. Any competent description must rely on mythos, because mythos is the language we use for describing the deepest meaning in things, and the sacred is ultimate meaning. And mythos points to what cannot be directly described.

THE DIVINE FEMININE

Immanent divinity sacralizes *both* yin and yang, both feminine and masculine. Truth, goodness, and beauty lie in both and can be best experienced when we see the greater harmony between them, a dance in which no partner leads.

The feminine connects us with the goodness of cycles of change, the great cosmic rhythms of life and death, creation and dissolution. Shining through all things, she shows us that no thing is only a thing. All things are worthy of respect and, when understanding grows enough, of love, as Leonardo saw so clearly, when he wrote, "Love is deep in the same degree as the knowledge is sure."[30]

After religious freedom was established in the United States and other lands long dominated by transcendental monotheism, few people could conceive of spiritual reality in other terms. The historical religions had developed within cultures so deeply rooted in the domination of some by others that they reframed valid spiritual insights in terms of domination and mastery. But this is not the whole story.

Another reason for the persistence of transcendental monotheism is most American religious traditions' reliance on scripture as their source for sacred knowledge. God becomes completely distant, watching us from afar. We read about his desires for us in sacred texts. This scriptural emphasis reinforces the boundary between the sacred and humanity.

People who study the issue have long noted that the media we use influence what we can communicate. From voice to print to video to computers, no medium simply reflects our intentions. In chapter 2 I described how texts strengthen logos at the expense of mythos. More generally, the printed word reinforces masculine metaphors and weakens feminine ones. A masculine God makes more sense when considered purely textually and otherwise remote from experience rather than as manifesting within a world shaped by interacting genders.

In preliterate societies as well as at least some literate but nonalphabetic cultures such as China, qualities are often identified through concrete examples rather than abstract definitions. The meaning of *justice* would be indicated by describing a variety of actions illustrating justice but not defining it. What these illustrations shared in common, something that could not be defined precisely, constituted *justice*. Meaning was grasped nonverbally, intuitively, and people's ability to both act justly and describe other examples of just action indicated competent understanding even though they were unable to define the term precisely.[31]

This way of understanding is primordial, but it is not primitive. Today's common law operates on a similar insight: the law must be discovered on a case-by-case basis, hence the term *case law*. The complexity of contexts in which disputes arise prohibits our ever being able to devise clear and simple legal formulae as an adequate alternative.[32]

Meanings are felt. They reveal a value *most* present in the concrete. For example, abstract efforts to arrive at what it is to be human undermine the perceived value of actual individuals. Anonymous criteria distance us from real individuals, with no way back to them. I think this distancing is the weakness of traditional liberal theories of rights. It obscures what it is about individuals that makes us care that they have rights.

Each of us constructs a world through our experiences, the time we live, the people we meet, the thoughts we have, the memories we treasure, and those we do not. As Yevgeny Yevtushenko put it,

> In any man who dies there dies with him
> His first snow and kiss and fight.
> . . . .
> Not people die but worlds die in them.[33]

This kind of perception disappears when we distance ourselves from the immediacy of encounter and become immersed in abstractions. It takes poetry such as Yevtushenko's to demonstrate most powerfully the value of the concrete. As human beings we possess an unmatched ability to perceive from the very concrete to the very abstract. When we lose sight of the value in both, we cripple our most human capacities.

No wonder abstract logocentric accounts of monotheism lead to power that overrides individuality rather than to love, which cherishes it. (See "Hypnosis of Texts," http://dizerega.com/faultlines/appendices/.)

She Is Always Present

Despite millennia-long efforts by religious authorities to extirpate the Divine Feminine from people's awareness, she repeatedly appears, often in disguised form. The near worship of Mary has long been important for many lay Catholics, although officially Mary was still mortal and passive, more vessel to be filled than actor.[34] The great cathedrals of Europe were frequently named for her. In France, the cathedrals of Paris, Chartres, Reims, and Amiens are all called Notre Dame, "Our Lady." Those devoted to her often asked Mary to intercede with God on their behalf.

Mary's prominence in so much Catholic practice demonstrates the serious spiritual shortcomings of envisioning God as male who is severe, but not merciful unless another acts on behalf of those he will punish. How then can he possibly be considered *perfect*?

The Divine Feminine plays a different role in Eastern Christianity, where she is exalted as Wisdom (the feminine *sophia* in Greek). In Eastern Christianity the most famous church was Hagia Sophia (subsequently converted into a mosque and now a museum). Sophia is "the form in which Yahweh approaches humans. Woman Wisdom mediates between Yahweh and humans, playing before Yahweh as his delight, and playing in the inhabited world and finding her own delight in humans (Prov. 8:30b–31). She has a special role in creation, and she makes statements that, properly speaking, only Yahweh can make: 'Whoever finds me finds life' (Prov. 8:35)."[35]

However, in Orthodoxy this female aspect of God is still subordinated to the male because, writes Bishop Kallistos Ware, "almost always the symbolism used of God by the Bible and the Church's worship has been male symbolism. . . . A Mother Goddess is not the Lord of the Christian Church."[36] She remains safely in her place.

The Abrahamic traditions have been unique in their almost complete rejection of a prominent place for divinity's feminine qualities. Yet even in such hostile environments the Divine Feminine survived in disguised form. As Christianity replaced pagan religions, female saints often took the place of pre-Christian goddesses. Female saints took on the attributes and symbolism of grain goddesses; St. Radegund and St. Macrine served this role in France, as did St. Walpurga in Germany and St. Milburga in England. Probably the most famous of these transformed deities was Ireland's St. Brigit, the Celtic goddess Brigit, largely unchanged except for a Christian label.[37] In Mexico Our Lady of Guadalupe appears to have a close connection with the Nahuan mother-goddess Tonantzin.[38]

This preservation of the Divine Feminine within a Christian context was worldwide. Among the African diasporic traditions, the Yoruba goddess Oya (or Iansa) was equated with St. Theresa and Our Lady of Candelaria in Santeria and St. Barbara in Umbanda. Similar transformations occurred with other African orishas, feminine and masculine alike.[39] These name changes sought to protect devotees from oppression; they were always aware of whom they really honored, and now, with greater toleration, Oya and other female orishas are emerging under their own names.

Among many Peruvian Indian converts to Christianity, Pacahamama, the Earth Mother, is still prayed to. She is more accessible to them than the transcendent Christian God, in whom they also believe. The Peruvian example is different from turning a deity into a saint, for Pachamama is still honored as a divinity.

THE DIVINE FEMININE TODAY

As the sixties unfolded, perceptive religious scholars saw that something unusual was afoot. In 1974 Peter Berger wrote a highly acclaimed essay for *Christian Century* titled "Cakes for the Queen of Heaven: 2500 Years of Religious Ecstasy," which analyzed and criticized the early signs of what I term the resurgence of the Divine Feminine.

He began with the passage from Jeremiah (7:1-20) who claimed that worshipping the Queen of Heaven was an abomination worthy of devastating punishment. Berger's problems with her worship are more interesting. He argued that such worship provided a vastly *inferior* means of approaching the sacred because it focused on the spiritually immanent, not the spiritually transcendent. In addition, her religion's laxity was morally inferior to Yahweh's stern demands. Berger described the Queen of Heaven as "a very old divinity indeed, even then, and she had borne many names. In Mesopotamia she was known as Ishtar, in Syria-Palestine as Ashtoret. She reached Egypt as Ashtartu. . . . All these names . . . have their root in a

Semitic verb that denotes irrigation; everywhere she is associated with the waters that give fertility to the land. There are indications of similar goddesses from other parts of the Mediterranean world and from India. The Greeks called her Astarte and identified her with their own Aphrodite."[40] She appears to have been all but universally known and is the Hebrew goddess Raphael Patai described.[41]

As Berger describes it, her worship emphasized the sacred quality of the "rhythms of nature," which also existed "within human beings, notably in their sexual and agricultural activity." This worship included "the sacramental character of sacred sexuality" as a means for a human being "to establish contact with divine forces and beings that transcend him."

According to Berger, sacred sexuality was emerging in the 1960s counterculture, appearing initially as a "secularized Astartism" and increasingly as "Astartism *de*secularized." In particular, he observed, "Some of the writings of the ecology movement have expressed this second viewpoint eloquently." Had he known about Wicca, I am sure Wiccans would have been included.

While by no means entirely critical (he sees this concern with the sacred as preferable to a purely secular modernity), Berger was deeply worried. The issue "is not sexuality, but *sacred* sexuality, which bothers me in religious terms." There is a "linkage between cult and ethics" he wrote, and in his view a return to sacred Astartism is not up to the demanding ethical challenges of the modern world—the opposite of my argument that transcendental monotheism is not up to today's powerful challenges.

Berger's essay is important for other reasons. He identifies three sides of the culture war: traditional transcendental religion (though he does not distinguish as I do between the mainstream denominations and the religious nihilism of the right), secular modernity in general, and the reappearing response to both that emphasizes sacred immanence. He perceptively saw the connection between sacred immanence and the Divine Feminine and its presence in both ecology and new currents in American spirituality. Most impressively to me, Berger saw this pattern thirty-five years ago.

Old Testament and Pagan Ethics

Berger makes two major points. First, Jeremiah includes treatment of the poor as an important part of his attack on Astarte's devotees. His "assertion that the worship of Yahweh was directly and inevitably linked to the treatment of the lower classes of society" was a striking feature in Jeremiah's charges. Second, Berger argues that this bad treatment of others is connected to Astarte's spiritual immanence, just as Yahweh's ethical demands are intimately connected with his transcendence. The demanding morality required by an utterly transcendent God distinguished worship of Yahweh from worship of the Queen of Heaven. The choice, Berger suggests, is "voluptuous ecstasy or stern demands."

I believe Berger is demonstrably mistaken in both charges, and that the nature of his error helps us understand today's culture wars. At the same time he is profoundly right in arguing there is a "link between cult and ethics."

As Berger observes, worship of Astarte dates to *long before* the time of the prophets. She was associated with agriculture and fertility and with divine cycles and sacred sexuality. Given these characteristics, her roots extend at least to early agricultural life. Much of her symbolism also characterizes nature as experienced by hunting and gathering peoples. Long before agriculture, people could observe how the rain impregnated the earth to bring forth abundance, how everything basic to life itself was characterized by cycles, and how these extended into the normal course of their own lives.

The older her roots, the more she would have been celebrated before the rise of predatory empires and city-states. As Lao-Tsu's observation indicates, during hunting and gathering times, and for some indefinite period thereafter, there was little to no systematic oppression by the rich and powerful, and what we call morality was not argued as an external set of rules but reflected in the experienced flow of life, manifesting as custom. There was continual awareness of being part of an all-embracing community, human and natural alike. Berger is right in arguing that the worship of Astarte did not address powerful social and political failings. *Her roots predated societies in which that was necessary*, and her rituals and practices focused on more basic dimensions of existence.

Berger argued that the prophets taught about a God of justice and a religion that calls us "to combat injustice and to alleviate misery." But those who practiced Astarte's "religion of pleasure" as well as its resurgence in the sixties counterculture supposedly undermine this ethically demanding goal. Berger charges that "in a world of mass murder and mass starvation, of unprecedented terror, odious tyrannies, and the threat of nuclear holocausts—in such a world there is something obscene about an order of priorities that starts off with bigger and better orgasms."

I agree. But this focus on the world's ills as having higher priority than better orgasms has *nothing* to do with sacred sexuality or divine immanence. To argue otherwise is like claiming that the Eucharist celebrates cannibalism.

We do not know anything very specific about the character of Astarte worship. Even the famous sacred prostitutes that so scandalized ancient Christians are described only from a hostile perspective and in no great detail. Astarte's worshippers will never have an opportunity to respond to the charges made against them beyond the revealing reply Jeremiah reproduces. However, the Hebrew women quoted in Jeremiah said nothing about their orgasms and a lot about having enough to eat (44:15–19).

We do have two other relevant sources of information about the sacred feminine as an independent spiritual force. We have the words of some important pagans responding to later Christian attacks, and we have the example of Goddess-oriented religions today, religions that do make sexuality a sacrament. Since Berger paints them all with a similar brush these examples should be good enough.

We do not know how Astarte's followers responded to Jeremiah's words about the poor. What we do know is that the poor have been as much a presence in Hebrew society as in pagan societies. The Romans were well aware of the Jews' religious differences from pagans, but seem never to have noticed greater equality of conditions or concern for the poor, although they certainly did for Christians.[42] Throughout the Old Testament this demand to care for the poor reappears as Israel *continually* failed to live up to it, Astarte or no Astarte. It seems to me that Berger is juxtaposing an absolutist demand never honored for long by Hebrew monotheists to failure to live up to that same demand by Astarte's worshippers.

The only surviving writings by Julian, Rome's last pagan emperor (361–363), are the ones included in Christian rebuttals. The rest were burned. But enough remains for me to begin making my point.

During Julian's time Astarte was still widely venerated outside the Jewish world, her worship not yet suppressed by mob violence and political repression. Julian argued within the Christian world against Christian claims about the moral superiority of their god: "What nation is there by the gods, exclusive of the mandates 'Thou shalt worship no other gods,' and 'Remember the Sabbath,' which does not think it requisite to observe all the other commandments? Hence punishments are established in all nations for those who transgress them."[43]

Julian's words suggest that the ethical difference between pagan and Jewish religion in this regard is one of degree, not of kind.[44] Concern with right behavior was not a central feature in ancient paganism, but it was far from absent. Berger presented a false dichotomy.

Classical societies were so dependent on domination that any sense of social compassion or justice was observed more in word than in deed. Christianity, which claims such moral superiority, had to wait nearly two thousand years for its promise of spiritual equality to matter much. Even then, slavery's Christian opponents referred to the spirit behind the text while its defenders, like their spiritual descendants today, emphasized the letter. But there is more to this issue.

Berger notes that Jeremiah's opposition to Astarte was "violent." Indeed it was. Extreme violence permeates the deeds of Yahweh's followers throughout the Old Testament. Whole peoples were exterminated, infants included. The word *genocide* is appropriate, and if the texts are to be believed it happened repeatedly. Israelites whose behavior was deemed unacceptable to Yahweh were also slaughtered. There is *no* historical record of similar behavior by those who worshipped the Queen of Heaven. (See "Imposing Masculine Monotheism," http://dizerega.com/faultlines/appendices/.)

The Matter of Better Orgasms

Religions focusing on sacred cycles and divine immanence do not focus only on pleasure. They emphasize and honor the *entire* cycle of existence, of which sexuality is a central part. Because Berger sees similarities between worship of the Queen of Heaven and the Neo-Pagan and Goddess-oriented spiritualities that were rapidly growing when he wrote, I will use these latter to instruct us regarding the primordial sexual traditions that left no records.

From a modern Wiccan perspective, not only is sexuality sacred but also birth, growth, old age, and death. *Every* basic aspect of physical existence can be approached in both a mundane fashion and as a sacred dimension of life. What makes sex sacred is not having better orgasms, but having more meaningful ones. Sexuality is the most easily available method for us to move beyond our personal boundaries. It can open fearful and closed hearts to love, just as fearful or angry hearts can pervert it. Sexuality is sacred because of the place it plays in contexts larger than egoic concerns about orgasms. When we erase or blur boundaries within larger-than-human contexts we are entering the realms of sacred immanence. Berger's words about "cheap grace" miss the point as widely as saying "free bread and drink" misses the point of the Eucharist.

Berger concludes his essay by arguing that a purely transcendent view of God is a superior means for honoring the world than is an immanent approach: "It is precisely in the celebration of the world as creation, and *not* in its worship as something divine, that we taste its hauntingly vulnerable sweetness." I wish that two thousand years of Christian action adequately reflected this sensibility! It is one *possible* response from a transcendental point of view, and a wise one, but also a minority one. The governing claim for many, and certainly the loudest, American Christians is to dominate the world, subduing nature or using it up before the Rapture. If the world will soon be destroyed by God, what is the point of conserving it?

On the other hand, the Pagan recognition of cycles points toward honoring the sweetness of the moment because it *is* transitory. It *will* pass. Nothing physical lasts. This moment is the immediate manifestation of the sacred, and while other moments that follow will also be such manifestations, *this* one will have passed. The bloom of youth inexorably moves toward death. Life may repeat this cycle, but *this* life will not.

Day begins with a gradual lightening of the eastern sky, the morning star hanging low, perhaps gentle breezes. Then may come a beautiful dawn, with rosy-tinted clouds, followed by the brilliance of day itself, then the lengthening shadows and warm illuminations of late afternoon, and the quite different display of color and form as the sun sinks behind the horizon. Finally the starry skies of night reign again. With this cycle is intertwined another of the shifting seasons, spring to summer to fall to winter and again to spring.

Taken as a whole, each of these cycles is superior to any moment, *but if the moments have no value, neither does the cycle.* The Pagan truth is that we live in cycles upon cycles intertwining in a kaleidoscope of change. Every moment is one in which the sacred can be seen. As the Wiccan chant goes, "She changes everything She touches, and everything She touches changes." Each part of the cycle is sacred in its own way, and best honored in its own way. To honor is to care, respect, treasure, and love.

Berger writes that the Old Testament prophets were not "Puritans" and accepted sexuality as a good part of physical life, but opposed sacralizing it. There is a curious superficiality to his statement. He focuses on sexuality as a source of pleasure, his "better orgasms." He seems to say that orgasms are just fine, but justice and mercy are better. This focus is that of a single partner carried away by the experience, without any necessary connection to another—a superficial and strongly masculine conception of sexuality.

Sexuality can be a merging of selves far beyond the mutual stimulation of genitals, not in spite of but *because* of and through the wonderful experiences thereby elicited. Better orgasms *can* lead to greater connection with the spiritual. That merging can take place at many levels, from the most superficial to the most transcendent. But it reaches transcendence through immanence. The purely ego-centered "I want you" is not at all bad. But it opens out into the "I take delight in you" and finally "I lose myself in you." And when each is lost in the other?

Once the role of the heart equals that of the groin, sexuality opens deeper possibilities of connection. Through sexuality a duality can briefly become one, enabling us to get a small sense of the nonduality underlying and supporting this world. In the most sacred sexuality, transcendence and immanence are in harmony. This understanding is recognized at least in Tantric Hindu, Buddhist, and Wiccan traditions.[45]

Sexuality is the means through which fertility and creativity enter earthly life. Multicellular existence is made possible by sexuality. The beauty of flowers, birds, and animals is a manifestation of their sexual nature. *All* these other dimensions of sexuality are reflections of its enhancing relationship and connection through beauty and delight.

Humans are one of the most sexual forms of life. Most female animals go into heat periodically; until then sex is not a part of their or their mate's lives. Far from sexuality being animalistic, many animals are only briefly interested. By contrast, human beings are *continually* receptive. There is a message here for those who wish to emphasize the meaning of what is most unique about us.

Some people will reply that sex evolved simply to keep the males around for the long period while human children grow to maturity. Certainly sexuality can serve the purpose of keeping the guy around to support the family, but among bonded pairs, even in the animal world, it need not be necessary. Denigrating sexuality as animalistic is another way to denigrate sacred immanence.

To argue that among human beings sexuality is natural only when used for reproduction slurs the human spirit and the human body and the sacred cycles that pervade this world. A transcendental monotheistic perspective in isolation cannot even begin to do justice to the sacredness of the earth and the sacred cycles within it. Yahweh was a god of demanding and often seemingly arbitrary rules imposed from above, rules to be obeyed—or else he would kill you and curse your lineage for generations (except when he didn't). As a god of pure power he could be as arbitrary as he wished. Even so, inviolable boundaries were set to our behavior, based on promises of future reward and threats of horrendous punishments. No wonder so many preferred Astarte.

Dimensions of Perfection

The aboriginal intuition of a resplendence immanent in matter accords well with a new sense of the sacred now striving to be born.

—David Abram

Rediscovering the Integral

Sacred immanence heals the rift between religion and science. The God of (ever-diminishing) gaps is an artifact created by adherents to transcendental monotheism seeking to keep their faith while respecting reason and knowledge. They wisely rejected Fundamentalist irrationalism, but at the cost of ceding an ever-increasing field to secular science and an ever-diminishing field of divine involvement in the world. As the gaps narrowed, this position led many people to unbelief and others to belief rooted in will alone. But these unfortunate choices arise from an inappropriate conception of the sacred.

From the standpoint of sacred immanence, *there are no gaps*, no place where the sacred is absent. From an immanentist perspective, nothing in the world is meaningless. Every thing, every "it," has a dimension as a Thou, a presence, a context of meaning. We accomplish this kind of integration with our loved ones every day. In principle, and for many of us in practice, we can do this with everything. In doing so we enter the realm best described through mythos and poetry, where the good and the beautiful are dimensions of the true, as the true is a dimension of them.

Recognizing sacred immanence heals our alienation from this world. The Axial faiths generally separated the individual from primary identification with the world and the human community, both of which had become threatening and sources of great suffering. They focused people on their individual relationships to the sacred for salvation, release, or final exit from the wheel of rebirth. A genuinely postmodern spirituality now opens a way to reconnect with our world and with one another from a heightened sense of individuality.

Far from limiting or stifling our individuality, relationships are necessary for us to grow and to flower. When people enlarge their circle of Thous, thereby shrinking their world of Its, greater love and compassion are a natural result achieved not because of divine commandment, to avoid damnation, or from rational self-interest, but as an individual recognition that these qualities are our most appropriate way to relate. As Rabbi Lawrence Kushner writes, "Human beings are joined to one another and to all creation."[1]

The West is unique among civilizations in its respect for the individual as the central moral unit within the world. This insight provided the foundation for liberalism, the rejection of domination, and a transformation in human life.

As Tocqueville grasped, liberalism also leads to appreciating spiritual immanence. But to do so it must be able to transcend its roots in a liberal transcendental monotheism. Western individualism grew from the liberal Christianity of men such as John Locke. At its core lay a belief that individuals were distinct from the world, which could be treated simply as a resource for our needs, wants, and whims. Our only moral obligations were to one another and to a transcendent God.

As science progressed, liberal individualism's base increasingly appeared to be arbitrary distinctions between individuals and the rest of the world. Because our relations with that world were conceived in terms of power, liberalism's moral case weakened. Individuals were reduced to the level of things, to which the rest of the world had already been demoted. Secular modernity lost its moral foundations and lacked the cultural resources to generate new ones.

Recognizing sacred immanence solves this problem. Intrinsic value is *everywhere*. There have never been gaps, not because the sacred does not exist but because there is no place it does not exist. Individuals are foci of value, coming together in individualized gestalts. Each of us is a creator of a world, interlinked with other worlds created by others in a network of breathtaking complexity and beauty. And each of us is an expression of this world and so ultimately an expression of the sacred.

Our subjectivity is not a sign of our disconnection from brute matter; it is the channel through which individuated and unique expressions of the value manifesting in and through matter come into existence. We cannot be separated from our world, for it is through and within it that we are who we are; together we *can* create ever more beauty and manifest ever more love. Far from being antihuman, pantheistic environmentalism enables us to more deeply value the human.

Honoring the Divine Feminine

Just as historically religions of pure transcendence privileged the masculine, so religions of immanence tilt toward the feminine. So far as we know, however, such religions in the past did not denigrate the masculine, certainly not in any degree equivalent to what religions of transcendence did to the feminine. Masculine qualities are *also* essential parts of immanence. Duality manifests as *both* feminine and masculine, and when duality is recognized as sacred, so are they.

Early agricultural ethics preserving an immanental perspective existed within increasingly one-sided relations of masculine domination, so women were increasingly subordinated even as goddesses continued to be honored. Cakes were baked for the Queen of Heaven long after women had become dominated by men. This pattern appears in cultures as different as the classical West, the Middle East, India, and China.

Today this dynamic has reversed. That the sacred feminine is reappearing in a time of increasing focus on sacred immanence and of feminine values is fitting. She offers healing to a culture with the discernment and courage to take advantage of the opportunity.

Acknowledging the Divine Feminine opens us to a wider and deeper range of insights about our lives, our world, and the sacred. As we saw in chapter 4, in secular modernity's most accomplished way of learning, science itself, feminine qualities of knowing are as crucial as masculine ones. Science cannot understand itself nor make the breakthroughs in knowledge for which it is so justly celebrated when committed only to masculine logo-centric styles of thought. A society priding itself only on its masculinity, be it the ideal of the neoconservatives, Fundamentalists, or any others, is *parasitic* on its feminine elements, which it could not survive without but refuses to acknowledge.

By recognizing the feminine as equal to the masculine, we get a clear view of one of humanity's oldest curses: the drive by some to dominate others. Despite liberalism's transformation of social life, this threat remains strong, particularly in the regressive domination by culture warriors and oligarchic corporate militarism. But we have created the means to transcend dominator societies if we have the insight and wisdom.

Recognizing the Divine Feminine and all she represents as equal dimensions of reality and of humanity enriches the lives of real men as much as the lives of real women. No man is composed of purely masculine qualities, just as no woman is purely feminine. Men can embrace and honor their capacity to be open to others and to the world, just as women today are often coming to embrace their personal strength and drive. Thereby both come into greater balance with who they actually are.

As the feminine rises to equality with the masculine in the secular world, so the Divine Feminine becomes recognized as equal to the Divine Masculine. In the process our ways of understanding the sacred are enlarged. As she teaches in the Wiccan tradition, "All acts of love and pleasure are my rituals."[2]

Love of another is recognition of inner beauty, just as seeing beauty elicits love of matter. In all its forms our love of the beautiful lures us into ever-deeper dimensions of love, and with greater love comes a greater recognition of beauty. The two are inseparable. As Leonardo emphasized, they are also one with the true. No spiritual truth is adequate without the beautiful and the good, and for far too long the Western soul has been withered by fear of this fact.

A Polyphonic World

Divine immanence is polyphonic and polyrhythmic, terms I first encountered in music and dance and became further sensitized to after reading Robert Bringhurst on mythos. In polyphonic music more than one tune contributes to a single piece; it is the music of multiplicity. Such music can also be polyrhythmic: more than one rhythm is played, again creating a whole greater than its parts. If we listen to one line of a polyphonic piece, or one rhythm of a polyrhythmic piece, we cannot tell what the others might be.

Polyphony and polyrhythm differ from homophonic music, which develops one melody to the exclusion of others. Homophony bleeds into polyphony when secondary melodies enter and at some point become independent, no longer playing a supporting role. Monorhythm becomes polyrhythm. No rhythm is dominant, and all contribute to the polyphonic whole. Such music can vary from a Bach fugue to a Brazilian samba.

Robert Bringhurst reminds us that the world is polyphonic, and I would add polyrhythmic. "Songbirds sing. That is fact, not metaphor. They sing, and in the forest every morning, when a dozen or a hundred or a thousand individuals of six or ten or twenty different species sing at once, that is polyphonic music. What city dwellers frequently call 'silence' is the ebb and flow of birdsong and the calls of hawks and ravens, marmots, pikas, deer mice, singing voles, the drone of gnats and bees and bee flies, and the sounds of wind and rain and running water. The world is a polyphonic place."[3]

A spirituality honoring sacred immanence honors spiritual polyphony. Each spiritual tradition sings its song, while within any tradition the members sing at different pitches. When freedom exists, traditions have complex harmonies, and all of them together create the beauty of spiritual polyrhythm. Catholics and Protestants, Jews and Muslims, Jains and Hindus, Buddhists and Wiccans, Native Americans and Native Africans, and on and on in as many directions as the human mind and heart have been able to encounter the sacred and to honor and celebrate it.

I want to return to Peter Berger's distinction between the spiritual traditions he symbolized with the names Jerusalem and Benares. For Berger,

Jerusalem refers to a spiritual focus on the transcendental, Benares to one on inner experience. The spirituality Berger denigrated in his essay on the Queen of Heaven as that of "better orgasms" fits into neither. Yet in terms of longevity and numbers of devotees, this tradition, best described as religions of sacred immanence, is as deserving of inclusion as Berger's two favorite Axial cases. It has certainly been around longer.

I argued that the Axial religions Berger encapsulates in his two cities arose with the breakdown of more feminine immanent spiritual traditions originally rooted in preagricultural ways of life. Now that agricultural traditions are losing relevance in the modern world, there is a renewed upwelling of religions honoring sacred immanence and the Divine Feminine. Practitioners of modern forms rooted in these earlier traditions are not only developing their spiritual traditions within a modern context, but inspiring many Christians, Jews, and Buddhists to integrate the sacred feminine in ways preserving their own traditions' values.

There is no single identifying culture or city for religions of the Divine Feminine and sacred immanence. Their origins long preceded cities and existed across many cultures, constituting a universal spiritual inheritance. But perhaps we can do better with their newer manifestations. An ancient classical prophecy said a time would come when the divinities of Egypt would depart as foreigners occupied the country. Asclepius asked Hermes, "Where will the gods go during the dark time? And where will they return?" And Hermes answered, "The gods who rule the earth will (withdraw), and they will be stationed in a city founded at Egypt's farthest distance [border] toward the setting sun, where the whole race of mortals will hasten by land and sea."[4] If we want to pick a city, it is appropriate to honor the sixties and the prophecy and label this tradition "San Francisco."

DIMENSIONS OF PERFECTION

Jerusalem, Benares, San Francisco, the transcendental, the inner, and the immanent paths. Taken as a whole, they describe what I term "dimensions of perfection." This label arises from my claim that there is an ultimate reality that manifests in different ways, each perfect in a way the others are not. *It is not a hierarchy.*

Mathematicians argue there is more than one kind of infinity. Quantum mechanics is filled with paradoxes transcending the power of our minds to visualize. That spiritual perfection takes more than one form is one more liberation from the monotheistic idea that truth is always singular and relations are hierarchical. We should not be surprised.

This insight crystallized after my own powerful nondual experience like those usually associated with the traditions Berger encapsulates as Benares. At the height of this experience, there was no Gus, no awareness of self or of anything but awareness itself. It was wonderful, perfect, complete, and far beyond all these or any other words because each word has a meaning, and each meaning implies something else it does not mean. Of this experience, I can say there was only Awareness. And it was indescribably wonderful.

As awareness of myself as in some way distinct from this experience gradually returned, I remained for a while partially in touch with the reality. It lingered briefly at the periphery of my mind even as I gradually separated myself from it, though hints return at times, usually during meditation.

As I became more aware of the world of duality I was returning to, I realized that *love* requires duality to exist. I could recollect no sense of love in my nondual experience, but that was not a lack. There is no place for love when there is no differentiation. There is no-thing, and love treasures the beauty in what is *different* from itself. Love is a quality of duality.

From a nondual perspective Meister Eckhart agreed, writing, "I put detachment higher than love. . . . Experience must always be an experience of something, but detachment comes so close to zero that nothing but God is rarefied enough to get into it, to enter the detached heart."[5]

I had previously experienced perfect love in the other classical form of mystical experience in which one encounters but is distinct from the One. I have also encountered the same quality in individualized form in encounters with certain divinities. Encountering divinely manifested perfect love elicits love from me in return. In such fulfillment, again there is no search for more, no lack. Here, too, is perfection.

So I suggest there are three kinds of perfection. Or at least as much perfection as this writer has experienced. I think each *requires* the other.

A purely transcendent mystical experience differs from nondual mysticism in that the person having the experience still is aware of being distinct from a maximally transcendent source. There is no loss of self, but rather a perception of its origins. I wrote about my own such experience in *Pagans and Christians*.[6]

With this kind of experience, as John wrote, "God is love" (1 John 4:8). No other quality takes precedence. But because love treasures the concrete, the unique entity, place, and moment, this love is not impersonal. It is a love that encompasses every entity with personal attention, yet is not itself personal in any limited sense. Peter Berger described this mysticism occurring in duality as the "mysticism of personality," while he described the nondual as the "mysticism of infinity."[7]

But there is also an immanent dimension to divine love. A goddess or god exhibits limiting qualities that make relationship possible while continuing to exhibit perfect love.[8] Because we humans have *some* sense of love, we can identify their essence as love, an essence they share with the source. In short, there are degrees of love that exist within sacred immanence, from the human to the divine, and perhaps also in the other direction as well. Many animals seem quite capable of love, and if they differ from us in that capacity it is in the greater concreteness of that care.

To the extent that human beings exhibit love and care, they manifest a dimension of the sacred within the realm of sacred immanence. This dimension makes the mysticism of sacred personality possible. It manifests from encounters with deities to the beauty of the sunrise, a mother holding her child, waves of wind caressing a meadow, and an athlete at the ecstatic peak of performance.

Nondualist religions often claim that the world of duality is illusion. I think this denigration reflects the brutal societies so many people lived in when nondualism first developed as a distinct spiritual path. Hunting-and-gathering cultures did not see or experience the world as an illusion of suffering. As Hugh Brody describes their attitude, their world was "Eden."[9] Jordan Paper suggests that mysticism as a distinct spiritual path may have resulted from the breakdown of the shamanic practices of preagricultural peoples, who certainly knew these kinds of experiences.[10] Certainly the hunter's trance suggests as much.

Along with being the world where love can manifest, the world of duality is also the world of beauty. I would argue that what we often call love is the perception of inner beauty greater than anything we can put into words, just as great natural beauty can call forth our own love, again through an encounter exceeding our words. All great art, natural and human, exemplifies a great truth and points beyond its surface to the meaning it opens to us. Far from being illusion, natural beauty and great art manifest truths available to us in no other way. They are sacred unfoldings of the many wondrous ways that love can manifest. This love extends into the other-than-human that makes human life possible: the forest and savannah, the redwood and the juniper, the salmon and bear, coyote and deer, raven and wren. In Robinson Jeffers's words

> To feel and speak the astonishing beauty of things—earth, stone and water,
> Beast, man and woman, sun, moon and stars.[11]

If the nondual includes all that experiences with all that is experienced, without differentiation—a nothingness that is everything—in another sense everything must still exist in differentiated form. Otherwise how can anything be said to exist in any sense? Even those who point to nonduality always return to duality.

Moreover, as soon as nondual traditions formed, they differentiated. Buddhism is considered the spiritual tradition most focused on the nondual. But the Buddha's teachings soon diversified into many schools and lineages, often jealous of each other, sometimes violently so. Feuding nondual traditions make much ado about nothing.

The nondual includes but does *not* transcend the immanent. Any particular sacred thing, no matter how perfectly loving, is less than the sacred whole. The immanent includes the transcendent as the creative ground of love out of which emerge the particularities that give meaning and fulfill-ment to that love. The nondual, transcendence, and immanence are aspects of a greater spiritual reality, each implied in the others.

If the nondual is a one that is not a fraction of two, and transcendence is a sacred hierarchy, sacred immanence is Indra's web, the divine ecology, ever-changing beauty and creativity and a million forms of love, all linked together, now and forever. The nondual, transcendent, and immanent compose the greatest polyrhythm of all.

BEYOND TOLERATION: CELEBRATING DIVINE MULTIPLICITY

Religious toleration is a hard-won achievement, preceded not by doctri-nal insight but by the exhaustion of endless war. From the standpoint of transcendental monotheism, it is always a second best. Monopoly is better because spiritual truth is a single note played everywhere.

Most Western monotheists today endorse toleration and are aware that its fruits have been sweet for the societies able to practice it. But tolera-tion's doctrinal foundations are lacking. Sooner or later someone again will read their text as giving them divine sanction to extirpate the heathens. Toleration is a secular achievement at odds with the logic of monopolistic transcendental monotheism. And yet the best of monotheists recognize the importance of genuine respect for other paths. As a Muslim cleric wisely observed (his words passed on to me and others by Starhawk), "Religion is like love. You cannot force it, or it is like rape."[12]

Spiritual plurality always grows out of spiritual immanence. The manifes-tations of the sacred are so vast that no single human path can express them all. No path, no tradition, has a claim on ultimate superiority or sole access to spiritual truth. Each offers its followers a unique framework for manifest-ing the true-good-beautiful as it most fittingly appears to them. Spiritual reality is a many-petaled blossom, each petal growing from the sacred center, each petal distinct, and the bloom as a whole of infinite beauty and fragrance, unfolding forever.

This blossom is the spiritual manifestation of the same division of labor and knowledge that has made the modern world so uniquely powerful and wealthy. It is also a spiritual manifestation of the intricate relationships that give us an ecosystem, the beauty of life on earth. We create a whole of greater variety, beauty, and coherence even as individually we play smaller and ever-more-specialized parts within it. Here is a paradox: in these smaller parts we can develop our own individuality far more than we could in a simpler world. Each spiritual path honors the sacred dimension that speaks most strongly to those who follow it, and we can follow the path that speaks to us.

In this postagricultural world, barring catastrophe and maybe even with it, the diversity of spiritual and religious practices will continue to multiply as people discover the sacred speaking to them in their individuality in ever-more meaningful ways. The essence of modernity is a radical expansion of our awareness of alternatives, of choices. Spiritual immanence inevitably elevates personal experience over external dogma because sacred immanence always exceeds dogma, which at best is a tiny part of the whole. The Divine is always with us, calling on us to open our hearts to others. And it does so in infinite ways.

Even in earlier modern times religions that elevated experience over dogma, heart over judgment, and choice over command accomplished immense good for the world. Consider the Quakers, who spearheaded the abolition of slavery in Britain and ultimately the United States, an accomplishment never before achieved in all human history. Spirit spoke to them, and they regarded it as a better guide than scripture read without heart. Christians wedded to scripture alone played no similar role in this achievement. Worse, many quoted scripture in slavery's defense and argued that the Quakers were heretics because they did not allow printed words to suppress their hearts.

Like the Quakers, today's new spiritual developments place an increasing emphasis on experience over dogma. Because no one can credibly claim to speak for all, or for the sacred, this spiritual variety will provide a check on groups that might swing wildly into confusion and error. As John Locke and James Madison learned the principle of political toleration from pragmatic Christian toleration, now principled religious toleration, even the *celebration* of diversity, receives an equivalent gift from their insights. When accompanied by genuine acceptance of other paths, diversity raises *everyone's* level of spiritual awareness, as we come to appreciate the many ways the Divine can be honored among us.

ONE IMMANENT FAMILY

The view I am arguing for shifts attention to passages in Abrahamic scriptures too often ignored. Central parts of the New Testament support immanental perspectives over purely transcendental ones. Consider Matthew 25:35–40: "I was hungry and you gave me food, I was thirsty and you gave me drink, I was a stranger and you welcomed me, I was naked and you clothed me, I was sick and you visited me, I was in prison and you came to me. Truly I tell you, just as you did it to one of the least of these my family, you did it to me."

Jesus explicitly says he is in us all, words in harmony with those of the Wiccan Goddess: "Let my worship be within the heart that rejoiceth; for behold, all acts of love and pleasure are my rituals and therefore let there be beauty and strength, power and compassion, honor and humility, mirth and reverence, within you. And thou who thinkest to seek for me, know thy seeking and yearning shall avail ye not, unless thou knowest the mystery; that if that which thou seekest thou findest not within thee, thou wilt never find it without thee, for behold I have been with thee from the beginning and I am that which is attained at the end of desire."[13]

Hopefully this realization of immanence will empower us to accomplish for humanity and the world the most important task facing us today: reversing the sociopathic political and corporate rape of our world and the desecration of our home. Like a friend, the world is immensely useful, but, again like a friend, we will lose it when we see it as only useful. But the world is much more than a friend. It is humanity's proximate creator and sustainer, and as we diminish it we diminish ourselves. That has been the deepest wound we have suffered from blinding ourselves to sacred immanence.

CHAPTER ELEVEN

To find our own path while respecting those of others, to follow our own way while helping others we encounter along theirs, to tip the balance of our lives in the direction of kindness and compassion, love and beauty, reverence and mirth—that is challenge and reward enough for us two-leggeds.

AFTERWORD

THE ELECTION AND SINCE

The 2012 elections and their aftermath illustrate many of the themes discussed in this book. Mitt Romney's campaign, and the Republican Party in general, exemplified the pathological masculinity and religious and secular nihilism that are such signature qualities of American culture warriors.

During the election, attacks on women's independence and self-determination reached unprecedented intensities. Contraception became a major issue, rape was discounted, and many of its adverse consequences for women denied. Prominent Republicans claimed that women should be forced to take rape-caused pregnancies to term, that "legitimate" rape never caused pregnancies, and that modern science guaranteed women would never die from complications in pregnancy and childbirth. In terms of rational political calculation, these actions are inexplicable.

Romney courted right-wing voters while presenting himself to Americans in general as a moderate interested in bipartisanship. His only constant was opposing tax increases for the wealthiest Americans. Both Romney and his running mate Paul Ryan avoided any details about their proposals, arguing that voters should simply trust them—a strategy for electing a dictator, not the president of a democratic republic. Meanwhile, fraudulent claims of voter fraud filled the media, even as the Republican Party went to unprecedented lengths to deny Democratic-leaning groups access to the polls.

Although the matter rarely received public attention, Romney's neoconservative foreign-policy advisers consistently sought increases in a military budget already equaling that of the rest of the world combined while urging an unprovoked war with Iran.

Republicans frequently invoked religion as a reason to vote for Romney, but it was religion in service to power, not Spirit. Southern Baptist leaders ignored a century of denouncing Mormonism as a cult, and Catholic bishops violated the law in order to get their congregations to vote Republican.

They failed.

Romney's supposed advantages with older white males were constructs of bad reporting. Many polls showed Romney only slightly preferred and sometimes opposed by older white males in almost every state save the neo-Confederate South. There, he was overwhelmingly favored, skewing his numbers for white men as a whole and demonstrating that the South remains America's counterculture.

By contrast, Democrats elected liberal women for higher office, and in Wisconsin openly gay Tammy Baldwin won the Senate, defeating a four-term Republican governor. Twenty-one women now serve in the Senate, a historical record. Gay-marriage initiatives succeeded in Maine, Maryland, and Washington, and an antigay-marriage initiative failed in Minnesota, the first such proposition to fail.

Democrats, which the House is supposed to represent, won a majority of House votes; however, Republican-controlled states gerrymandered enough House districts to prevent this majority from finding fair representation. We are paying a high price for this corruption.

More positively, increasing numbers of Black and Hispanic voters now ensure that no cultural group will have the power to imagine it can impose itself on others in the way the culture warriors have. In this instance, James Madison's emphasis on a plurality of factions to sustain freedom has prevailed over cultural concerns.

As I write this afterword, a new study identifies deep changes in America's religious communities, with old-line conservatives diminishing by generation, replaced by more progressive believers. Nearly 80 percent of religious progressives say religion is mostly about doing the right thing, whereas a majority of religious conservatives say it is primarily about having the right beliefs. This welcome change points to a rebirth of genuine spirituality.

The forces of the past have lost their culture war. They know it.

This knowledge explains the Republican and right-wing response. From petitions advocating secession, to an unprecedented refusal to cooperate with Democrats despite their electoral victories, to insisting that the Republican message was in fact never adequately argued (despite almost every Republican presidential contender being an extreme right winger), we are witnessing something far deeper than a reaction to a lost election. In the Republicans' anger, the basic principle required for all democracies— that the opposition honor the legitimacy of the winners—is being thrown overboard.

Republicans now seek to dominate by making the country ungovernable except on their terms. That our constitution seeks consensus more than majority rule means that large, ruthless minorities can do enormous damage. They have done so by escalating their attack on voting rights, by holding "filibusters" that aim to prevent political appointees from taking office, by blackmail and hostage-taking over budget issues, and by seeking to subvert the Electoral College.

Their strategy seems two pronged: First, to spread chaos nationally, in hopes that Democrats will be blamed enough to achieve a Republican win without attending to genuine issues. Second, to implement the most anti-environmental, anti-woman, and anti-feminine laws possible, knowing that repealing laws is harder than passing them. Should the first strategy succeed, we can expect major efforts to destroy what remains of electoral democracy in the United States, inasmuch as the Republicans now know they cannot win fairly.

Additionally, the electoral defeat of religious and secular right-wing nihilists in no way addressed other serious challenges the country faces. The irresponsible power of the corporate, military, and banking oligarchy continues largely unchecked. The position of America's middle class continues to deteriorate. The dangers of unchecked global warming have been all but completely ignored by both parties.

On these issues the Democratic establishment has proven as bereft of ideas as the Republicans. The country remains in deep, self-generated crisis.

Even so, in 2012 something profound happened. Numerically, intellectually, spiritually, and ethically, American civil society shifted decisively toward values in harmony with those that first found widespread expression in the sixties. Whether this shift will enable the United States to make a successful transition into the new world that it has played such a central role in creating remains to be determined. The answer to that question lies in the future. Only one thing is certain: without such a shift, the country will definitely fail in this challenge.

NOTES

CHAPTER ONE

1. Daniel Bell, *The End of Ideology: On the Exhaustion of Political Ideas in the Fifties*, 2nd ed. (Cambridge, MA: Harvard Univ. Press, 2000).

2. John F. Kennedy, "Acceptance of the Democratic Party Nomination," July 15, 1960, http://millercenter.org/scripps/archive/speeches/detail/3362.

3. Alexis de Tocqueville, *Democracy in America*, vol. 1, trans. John Stuart Mill (New York: Schocken Books, 1961), 365–66.

4. Ed Buckner, "Does the 1796–97 Treaty with Tripoli Matter to Church/State Separation?" http://www.stephenjaygould.org/ctrl/buckner_tripoli.html.

5. Barbara A. McGraw, *Rediscovering America's Sacred Ground: Public Religion and Pursuit of the Good in a Pluralistic America* (Albany: SUNY Press, 2003).

6. Chris Rodda, *Liars for Jesus: The Religious Right's Alternate Version of American History*, vol. 1 (Book Surge Publishing, 2006).

7. Stephen Toulmin, *Cosmopolis: The Hidden Agenda of Modernity* (Chicago: Univ. of Chicago Press, 1990), 101.

8. Peter Gay, *The Enlightenment: The Rise of Modern Paganism* (New York: Norton, 1966), 348.

9. Kevin Phillips, *American Theocracy* (New York: Viking, 2006).

10. McGraw, *America's Sacred Ground*, 41n.

11. "Letter Concerning Toleration," in *Political Writings of John Locke*, ed. David Woollon (London: Mentor, 1993), 417.

12. Jefferson and the Jews, American Jewish Historical Society, http://www.jewishvirtuallibrary.org/jsource/US-Israel/jeffjews.html.

13. George Washington, "Letter to the Hebrew Congregation in Newport, Rhode Island, August 18, 1790," http://www.tncrimlaw.com/civil_bible/hebrew_congregation.htm.

14. "Amendment I: (Religion): Debate in North Carolina Ratifying Convention," http://press-pubs.uchicago.edu/founders/documents/amendI_religions52.html.

15. James Madison, "The Federalist No. 51," *The Federalist Papers,* ed. Clinton Rossiter (New York: Mentor, 1961).

16. "James Madison to Edward Livingston, July 10, 1822," http://www .constitution.org/jm/18220710_livingston.htm.

17. On Hermeticism, see Michael Baigent and Richard Leigh, *The Elixir and the Stone: Unlocking the Ancient Mysteries of the Occult* (New York: Penguin, 1997), 109–231.

18. Toulmin, *Cosmopolis,* 19, 36–42.

19. Stefan Klein, *Leonardo's Legacy* (Cambridge, MA: Da Capo Press, 2010), 202.

20. Toulmin, *Cosmopolis,* 29.

21. Baigent and Leigh, *Elixir and Stone,* 159.

22. Toulmin, *Cosmopolis,* 25

23. Ibid., 77–79.

24. Elaine Pagels, *Beyond Belief: The Secret Gospel of Thomas* (New York: Vintage, 2004), 168–74.

25. Alfred North Whitehead, *Adventures of Ideas* (New York: Macmillan, 1933), 168.

26. Quoted in Brad S. Gregory, *The Unintended Reformation: How a Religious Revolution Secularized Society* (Cambridge, MA: Harvard Univ. Press, 2012), 98.

27. James M. Bryne, *Religion and the Enlightenment: From Descartes to Kant* (Louisville, KY: Westminster John Knox Press, 1996), 13.

28. Toulmin, *Cosmopolis,* 54.

29. Gay, *Enlightenment,* 296.

30. Bryne, *Religion and the Enlightenment,* 29.

31. "Voltaire: Sect," *The Philosophical Dictionary,* http://history.hanover.edu/texts/ voltaire/volsect.html.

32. Toulmin, *Cosmopolis,* 22–44.

33. Ibid., 33. (Unless noted, emphasis in quotations are in originals.)

34. Ibid., 34.

35. Carolyn Merchant, *The Death of Nature: Women, Ecology and the Scientific Revolution* (San Francisco: Harper & Row, 1980), 203.

36. Hans Jonas, *The Phenomenon of Life: Toward a Philosophical Biology* (Chicago: Univ. of Chicago Press, 1966), 72.

37. Pagels, *Beyond Belief,* 155.

38. *The Political Writings of St. Augustine* (Washington, DC: Gateway, 1996), 190–240.

39. Peter Berger, *The Heretical Imperative: Contemporary Possibilities of Religious Affirmation* (New York: Anchor, 1980), 10.

40. Merchant, *Death of Nature*, 1–40. For biblical examples, see Gus diZerega, *Pagans and Christians: The Personal Spiritual Experience* (St. Paul, MN: Llewellyn, 2001), 178–89.

41. Merchant, *Death of Nature*, 10.

42. Fritjof Capra, *The Science of Leonardo: Inside the Mind of the Great Genius of the Renaissance* (New York: Doubleday 2007), 263.

43. Linda Jean Shepherd, *Lifting the Veil: The Feminine Face of Science* (Boston: Shambhala,1993), 68. See also Fritjof Capra, "The Tao of Da Vinci," *Ode*, November 2007, http://odewire.com/58407/the-tao-of-da-vinci.html; Freya Matthews, *For Love of Matter: A Contemporary Panpsychism* (Albany: SUNY Press, 2003), 78–79.

44. Merchant, *Death of Nature*, 109–11, 164–90. See also Matthews, *Love of Matter*, 67–69.

45. Jonas, *Phenomenon of Life*, 189.

46. Merchant, *Death of Nature*, 170.

47. Capra, *Science of Leonardo*, 263.

48. Merchant, *Death of Nature*, 111.

49. Ibid., 192–93.

50. Ibid., 128–29.

51. Stuart A. Kauffman, *Reinventing the Sacred: A New View of Science, Reason and Religion* (New York: Basic Books, 2008), 131.

52. Toulmin, *Cosmopolis*, 70–71; Merchant, *Death of Nature*, 192–93.

53. Charles Hartshorne, *Omnipotence and Other Theological Mistakes* (Albany: SUNY Press, 1984), 6–10; Whitehead, *Adventures of Ideas*, 273–76.

54. Bryne, *Religion and the Enlightenment*, 152; Merchant, *Death of Nature*, 286.

55. Ramon G. Mendoza, *The Acentric Labyrinth: Giordano Bruno's Prelude to Contemporary Cosmology* (Shaftsbury, Dorsey, UK: Element, 1995).

56. Ibid., 194–95; Baigent and Leigh, *Elixir and Stone*, 165–69.

57. Bruce Lipton, *The Biology of Belief* (Santa Rosa, CA: Mountain of Love, 2005).

58. A good introduction to this immense field is Steven Johnson, *Emergence: The Connected Lives of Ants, Brains, Cities, and Software* (New York: Scribner, 2001).

59. Martin Landau, *Political Theory and Political Science* (New York: Macmillan, 1972), 90.

60. Merchant discusses powerful alternative streams of thought during this period, *Death of Nature*, 253–89.

61. Freya Matthews, *The Ecological Self* (Savage, MD: Barnes and Noble, 1991), 22.

62. Steven Shapin, *The Scientific Revolution* (Chicago: Univ. of Chicago Press, 1996), 105.

63. Karl Popper and John C. Eccles, *The Self and Its Brain: An Argument for Interactionism* (London: Routledge, 1984), 97.

64. Bart Ehrman, *God's Problem: How the Bible Fails to Answer Our Most Important Question—Why We Suffer* (New York: HarperCollins, 2008).

CHAPTER TWO

Epigraph. Jeffrey J. Kripal, *Authors of the Impossible: The Paranormal and the Sacred* (Chicago: Univ. of Chicago Press, 2010), 269.

1. Barry Spector, *Madness at the Gates of the City: The Myth of American Innocence* (Oakland, CA: Regent Press, 2010), 37.

2. Karen Armstrong, *The Battle for God* (New York: Ballantine Books, 2000), xv.

3. Richard Tarnas, *Cosmos and Psyche: Intimations of a New World View* (New York: Viking, 2006), 17.

4. Donald Sandner, *Navaho Symbols of Healing: A Jungian Exploration of Ritual, Image, and Medicine* (Rochester, VT: Healing Arts, 1979), 13.

5. Sallustius, *On the Gods and the World*, trans. Thomas Taylor, *Collected Writings of the Gods and the World* (Somerset, UK: Prometheus Trust, 1994).

6. William Irwin Thompson, *The Time Falling Bodies Take to Light* (New York: St. Martin's, 1981), 39.

7. Sallustius, *On the Gods.*

8. Thompson, *Falling Bodies*, 210. See also Charlene Spretnak, *The Resurgence of the Real* (Reading, MA: Addison Wesley, 1997), 183.

9. Patrick Harpur, *The Philosopher's Secret Fire: A History of the Imagination* (Chicago: Ivan R. Dee, 2003), 41.

10. Charlene Spretnak, *States of Grace: The Recovery of Meaning in the Postmodern Age* (San Francisco: HarperSanFrancisco, 1991), 95.

11. William Blake, "A Vision of the Last Judgment," *The Complete Writings of William Blake*, ed. Geoffrey Langdon Keynes (London: Oxford Univ. Press, 1966), 617.

12. Robert Bringhurst, *Everywhere Being is Dancing: Twenty Pieces of Thinking* (Berkeley: Counterpoint, 2008), 15, 16.

13. Ibid., 24.

14. Michael Polanyi, *Personal Knowledge: Towards a Post-Critical Philosophy* (Chicago: Univ. of Chicago, 1974).

15. Robert Bringhurst, *The Tree of Meaning: Language, Mind and Ecology* (Berkeley: Counterpoint, 2008), 309.

16. Evelyn Fox Keller, *Reflections on Gender and Science* (New Haven: Yale Univ. Press, 1985), 164–65.

17. Bringhurst, *Being is Dancing*, 67, 71.

18. David Suzuki and Peter Knudson, *Wisdom of the Elders* (New York: Bantam, 1992).

19. Bringhurst, *Tree of Meaning*, 104, 308. See also David Abram, *Becoming Animal* (New York: Pantheon, 2010), 259–310.

20. Matthews, *Love of Matter*, 80 (see chap. 1, n. 43).

21. George Lakoff and Mark Johnson, *Philosophy in the Flesh: The Embodied Mind and Its Challenge to Western Thought* (New York: Basic Books, 1999).

22. Matthews, *Love of Matter*. 80–81 (see chap. 1, n. 43).

23. Iain McGilchrist, *The Master and His Emissary: The Divided Brain and the Making of the Western World* (New Haven: Yale Univ. Press, 2009), 117.

24. Quoted in McGilchrist, *Emissary*, 117.

25. As in Lawrence Durrell's *Alexandria Quartet* (New York: Penguin, 1991).

26. Spector, *Madness at the Gates*, 130.

27. Abram, *Becoming Animal*, 295, 296.

28. Kripal, *Authors of the Impossible*, 257.

29. Cited in Mary Midgley, *Science as Salvation: A Modern Myth in its Making* (London: Routledge, 1992), 54.

30. Augustine, *Confessions*, trans. R. S. Pine-Coffin (New York: Penguin, 1966), 6.4.6.

31. Sallustius, *On the Gods*.

32. *A Joseph Campbell Reader: Reflections on the Art of Living*, ed. Diane K. Osborn (New York: Harper Collins, 1991), 9.

33. Robert Bringhurst, *A Story as Sharp as a Knife: The Classical Haida Mythtellers and Their World* (Vancouver: Douglas & McIntyre, 1999), 113.

34. Charles Taylor, "Liberal Politics and the Public Sphere," in *New Communitarian Thinking: Persons, Virtues, Institutions, and Communities,* ed. Amitai Etzioni (Charlottesville, VA: Univ. Press of Virginia, 1995), 302n.

35. Kripal, *Authors of the Impossible,* 258.

36. James C. Scott, *Seeing Like a State* (New Haven: Yale Univ. Press, 1998), 331.

37. Jerrold E. Levy, *In the Beginning: The Navajo Genesis* (Berkeley: Univ. of California Press, 1998).

38. Scott, *Seeing Like a State,* 331.

39. Gay, *Enlightenment,* 89–90 (see chap. 1, n. 8).

40. David Abram, *The Spell of the Sensuous* (New York: Pantheon, 1996), 107.

41. Ibid.

42. Joseph Campbell with Bill Moyers, *The Power of Myth* (NY: Random House, 1991), 173–74.

43. Plato, *Phaedrus,* trans. Christopher Rowe (London: Penguin, 2005), 62.

44. Paul Shepard, *Nature and Madness* (San Francisco: Sierra Club Books, 1982), 54.

45. Midgley, *Science as Salvation,* 55.

46. Bryne, *Religion and the Enlightenment,* 174 (see chap. 1, n. 27).

47. Bart D. Ehrman, *Jesus Interrupted: Revealing the Hidden Contradictions in the Bible (and Why We Don't Know about Them)* (New York: HarperOne, 2009).

48. Ehrmann, *God's Problem* (see chap. 1, n. 64).

49. Ehrman, *Jesus Interrupted,* 275.

50. Berger, *Heretical Imperative,* 72, 80 (see chap. 1, n. 39).

51. W. W. Bartley, III, *The Retreat to Commitment* (LaSalle, IL: Open Court, 1984), 47.

52. Berger, *Heretical Imperative,* 72–80 (see chap. 1, n. 39).

CHAPTER THREE

Epigraph. Margaret Fuller, "The Great Lawsuit," in *The Feminist Papers: From Adams to de Beauvoir,* ed. Alice S. Rossi (New York: Columbia Univ. Press, 1973), 179.

NOTES

1. Edward C. Whitmont, *Return of the Goddess* (New York: Crossroads, 1984), 128–29; Robert E. Ornstein, *The Psychology of Consciousness* (New York: Harcourt Brace Jovanovich, 1977), 128. See also Linda Jean Shepherd, *Lifting the Veil: The Feminine Face of Science* (Shambhala: Boston, 1993), 9.

2. Martha Nussbaum, *The Fragility of Goodness* (Cambridge: Cambridge Univ. Press, 2001).

3. Ibid., 20.

4. Keller, *Reflections*, 87 (see chap. 2, n. 16).

5. Ibid., 38.

6. Stephen J. Ducat, *The Wimp Factor: Gender Gaps, Holy Wars, and the Politics of Anxious Masculinity* (Boston: Beacon 2004), 27–28.

7. Daniel Pink, *A Whole New Mind: Why Right-Brainers Will Rule the Future* (New York: Riverhead, 2006), 138.

8. McGilchrist, *Master and Emissary* (see chap. 2, n. 23).

9. Chris Frith, "No One Really Uses Reason," *New Scientist*, July 26–August 8, 2008, 45.

10. Quoted in McGilchrist, *Master and Emissary*, 107 (see chap. 2, n. 23).

11. Nathaniel Comfort emphasizes Barbara McClintock's work as an outstanding instance of both (*The Tangled Field* [Cambridge, MA: Harvard Univ. Press, 2001], 10).

12. Mihaly Csikszentmihalyi, *Creativity: Flow and the Psychology of Discovery and Invention* (Harper Collins, 1996), 71.

13. David Smith, "2050—And Immortality Is within Our Grasp," *The Guardian*, May 21, 2005, http://www.guardian.co.uk/science/2005/may/22/theobserver .technology.

14. George Lakoff and Mark Johnson, *Metaphors We Live By*, 2nd ed. (Chicago: Univ. of Chicago Press, 2003).

15. Antonio Damasio, *Descartes' Error: Emotion, Reason, and the Human Brain* (New York: Avon, 1994).

16. David Hume, *A Treatise on Human Nature*, in *Hume: Moral and Political Philosophy*, ed. Henry B. Aiken (New York: Hafner, 1948), 25.

17. J. Andrew Armour, "Cardiac Neuronal Hierarchy in Health and Disease," *American Journal of Physiology—Regulatory, Integrative and Comparative Physiology* 287, no. 2 (Aug. 2004): R262–71; Walter C. Randall, "Changing Perspectives Concerning Neural Control of the Heart,"

Neurocardiology: Anatomical and Functional Principles, ed. J. Andrew Armour (New York: Oxford Univ. Press, 1994), 3–19.

18. Alva Noë, *Out of Our Heads: Why You Are Not Your Brain, and Other Lessons from the Biology of Consciousness* (New York: Hill and Wang, 2009).

19. Victor Turner, "The Liminal Period in Rites of Passage," in *Betwixt and Between: Patterns of Masculine and Feminine Initiation*, ed. Louis Carus Mahdi, Steven Foster, and Meredith Little (LaSalle, IL: Open Court, 1987), 6.

20. Ducat, *Wimp Factor*, 7.

21. Katrina Woznicki, "Early Retirement May Mean Earlier Death," *Medpage Today*, Oct. 21, 2005, http://www.medpagetoday.com/PrimaryCare/PreventiveCare/1980.

22. Quoted in Nell Noddings, *Caring: A Feminine Approach to Ethics & Moral Education* (Berkeley: Univ. of California Press, 1984), 96.

23. Louann Brizendine, *The Female Brain* (New York: Morgan Road Books, 2006); *The Male Brain* (New York: Three Rivers Press, 2010).

24. Brizendine, *Female Brain*, 13, 18, 25.

25. Ducat, *Wimp Factor*, 179.

26. Brizendine, *Female Brain*, 122, 19.

27. Ibid., 24.

28. Brizendine, *Male Brain*, 24.

29. Brizendine, *Female Brain*, 123.

30. Ibid., 27–28.

31. Abram, *Becoming Animal*, 109 (see chap. 2, n. 19).

32. "Spear-Wielding Chimps Studied," uploaded October 25, 2008, http://www.youtube.com/watch?v=FyGxQq7jSA8&NR=1.

33. Abram, *Becoming Animal*, 110 (see chap. 2, n. 19).

34. Edward O. Wilson, *The Social Conquest of Earth* (New York: W. W. Norton, 2012).

35. For an insightful feminist perspective, see Susan Faludi, *Stiffed: The Betrayal of American Men* (New York: William Morrow, 1999), 600–610.

36. Harvey Mansfield, *Manliness* (New Haven: Yale Univ. Press, 2007).

37. Val Plumwood, *Feminism and the Mastery of Nature* (London: Routledge, 1993), 23.

38. Keller, *Reflections*, 106 (see chap. 2, n. 16).

39. Plumwood, *Feminism*, 42.

40. Ibid., 45–47.

41. In *The Nazi Conscience* (Cambridge, MA: Harvard Univ. Press, 2003), Claudia Koonz explores how the German Nazis saw themselves as a moral movement and how they gradually turned German society against Jews when at one time Germany had a reputation as one of the least anti-Semitic countries in Europe.

42. Sam Keen, *Faces of the Enemy: Reflections of the Hostile Imagination* (New York: Harper and Row, 2004).

43. Malidoma Some, *Ritual: Power, Healing and Community* (New York: Penguin, 1997), 59.

44. Norman Kutcher, "The Fifth Relationship: Dangerous Friendships in the Confucian Context," *American Historical Review* 105, no. 5 (Dec. 2000), http://roosevelt.ucsd.edu/_files/Confucianfriendshipmmw21ecfa12.pdf.

45. Edith A. Howe, *The Essays or Counsels, Civil and Moral of Francis Bacon* (New York: Heath and Company, 1908).

46. Toulmin, *Cosmopolis*, 96 (see chap. 1, n. 7).

47. "Congresswoman Calls Alleged Wiretap 'Abuse of Power,'" CNN, April 21, 2009, http://www.cnn.com/2009/POLITICS/04/21/harman.wiretap/index.html. On Harman's supporting warrantless wiretaps against average Americans, see Ryan Singel, "Harman: It's Not My Fault I Couldn't Figure Out Domestic Wiretapping Was Illegal," *Wired*, March 31, 2008, http://www.wired.com/threatlevel/2008/03/harman-its-not/.

Chapter Four

Epigraph. Ludwig Wittgenstein. *Philosophical Grammar, Part I: The Proposition and Its Sense* (Berkeley: Univ. of California Press, 1974), 370.

1. William Barrett, *The Illusion of Technique* (Garden City, NY: Anchor, 1978), 191–92.

2. Quoted in Jonas, *Phenomenon of Life*, 203 (see chap. 1, n. 36).

3. Quoted in Kauffman, *Reinventing the Sacred*, 10 (see chap. 1, n. 51).

4. Richard Lewontin, "Billions and Billions of Demons," *New York Times Book Review*, January 9, 1997.

5. David Ellerman, "*Translatio versus Concessio*: Retrieving the Debate about Contracts of Alienation with an Application to Today's Employment Contract," *Politics and Society* 33, no. 3 (Sept. 2005), 449–82, http://www.ellerman.org/ Davids-Stuff/Econ&Pol-Econ/Econ%20and%20Pol%20Econ.htm; Malick W. Ghachem, "The Slave's Two Bodies: The Life of an American Legal Fiction," *William and Mary Quarterly* 3rd series, 60, no. 4 (Oct. 2003), 809–42.

6. Kauffman, *Reinventing the Sacred*, 265 (see chap. 1, n. 51); M. Koenigs et al., "Damage to the Prefrontal Cortex Increases Utilitarian Moral Judgments," *Nature*, April 19, 2007, 908–11.

7. The classic Marxist case is made by C. B. MacPherson, *The Political Theory of Possessive Individualism: From Hobbes to Locke* (Oxford: Oxford Univ. Press, 1970). The neoconservative equivalent is Leo Strauss, *Natural Right and History* (Chicago: Univ. of Chicago Press, 1999).

8. *Knowing and Being: Essays by Michael Polanyi*, ed. Marjorie Grene (Chicago: Univ. of Chicago Press, 1969), 49.

9. Thomas Jefferson to Benjamin Rush, Jan. 16,1811, *American History from Revolution to Reconstruction*, http://www.let.rug.nl/usa/presidents/thomas-jefferson/letters-of-thomas-jefferson/jefl208.php.

10. Sir Francis Bacon, *New Atlantis* (Hoboken, NJ: Wiley Blackwell, 1991).

11. Richard Feynman, "What is Science?" address given to National Science Teachers Association, New York, 1966, http://www.fotuva.org/feynman/what_is_science.html.

12. William Graham Sumner, *Earth-Hunger and Other Essays* (New Haven: Yale Univ. Press, 1941), 234.

13. Charles Darwin, *The Descent of Man and Selection in Relation to Sex*, 2nd ed. (London: John Murray,1882), 134, http://darwin-online.org.uk/content/frame set?viewtype=text&itemID=F955&pageseq=157.

14. Wilson, *Social Conquest of Earth* (see chap. 3, n. 34); David Loye, *Darwin's Lost Theory* (Carmel, CA: Benjamin Franklin Press, 2007).

15. Loye, *Darwin's Lost Theory*; Adrian Desmond and James Moore, *Darwin's Sacred Cause* (New York: Houghton Mifflin Harcourt, 2009).

16. Richard Hofstadter, *Social Darwinism in American Thought, 1860–1915* (Philadelphia: Univ. of Pennsylvania Press, 1944).

17. Samuel P. Huntington, *The Soldier and the State: The Theory and Politics of Civil-Military Relations* (Cambridge, MA: Harvard Univ. Press, 1985). 222–24.

18. Hofstadter, *Social Darwinism,* 174.

19. Thomas C. Leonard, "Origins of the Myth of Social Darwinism: The ambiguous legacy of Richard Hofstadter's *Social Darwinism,*" *Journal of Economic Behavior and Organization,* 71 (2009), 42.

20. Friedrich Nietzsche, *The Gay Science,* trans. Walter Kaufmann (New York: Vintage Books, 1974), 181.

21. Friedrich Nietzsche, *The Will to Power,* trans. Walter Kaufmann and J. R. Hollingdale (New York: Vintage Books, 1968), 9.

22. Richard Wolin, *The Seduction of Unreason: The Intellectual Romance with Fascism from Nietzsche to Postmodernism* (Princeton: Princeton Univ. Press, 2004), 52.

23. Ibid., 34.

24. Ibid., 27.

25. *The Portable Nietzsche,* trans. Walter Kaufmann (New York: Viking, 1954), 178.

26. These statistics come from two biographies of Ayn Rand: Anne C. Heller, *Ayn Rand and the World She Made* (New York: Doubleday, 2009); Jennifer Burns, *Goddess of the Market: Ayn Rand and the American Right* (Oxford: Oxford Univ. Press, 2009).

27. *Ayn Rand Answers: The Best of Her Q & A,* ed. Robert Mayhew (NAL Trade, 2005) 103–4. Rand was factually as well as morally wrong. See Charles C. Mann, *1491* (New York: Vintage, 2005), 269–378.

28. Compare Werner J. Dannhauser, "Leo Strauss in His Letters," in *Enlightening Revolutions: Essays in Honor of Ralph Lerner,* ed. Svetozar Minkov and Stéphane Douard (Lanham, MD: Lexington Books, 2007), 360, with Hilail Gildin, "Deja Jew All Over Again: Dannhauser on Leo Strauss and Atheism," *Interpretation: A Journal of Political Philosophy* 25, no. 1 (Fall 1997).

29. John H. Richardson, "Newt Gingrich: The Indispensable Republican," *Esquire,* August 10, 2010, http://www.esquire.com/features/newt-gingrich-0910-8.

30. Leo Strauss, *Natural Right and History* (Chicago: Univ. of Chicago Press, 1999).

31. Russell Kirk, *The Conservative Mind: From Burke to Eliot* (Washington, DC: Regnery, 2001), 469.

Chapter Five

Epigraph. Ron Suskind, "Faith, Certainty and the Presidency of George W. Bush," *New York Times Magazine,* October 17, 2004. See also

Josh Marshall, "The Post-Modern President," *The Washington Monthly*, September 2003.

1. Quoted in Bartley, *Retreat to Commitment*, 23 (see chap. 2, n. 51).

2. "First World War Casualties," *History Learning Site*, http://www .historylearningsite.co.uk/FWWcasualties.htm.

3. Quoted in Chris Hedges, *Death of the Liberal Class* (New York: Nation Books, 2010), 68.

4. Charles Taylor, *A Secular Age* (Cambridge, MA: Harvard Univ. Press, 2007), 407–9.

5. Berger, *Heretical Imperative*, 72–80 (see chap. 1, n. 39).

6. Wolin, *Seduction of Unreason*, 139 (see chap. 4, n. 22).

7. Koonz, *Nazi Conscience*, 223 (see chap. 3, n. 41).

8. Ibid., 166.

9. Wolin, *Seduction of Unreason*, 240 (see chap. 4, n. 22).

10. Ibid., 239.

11. Koonz, *Nazi Conscience*, 100 (see chap. 3, n. 41).

12. Ibid.; Victoria de Grazia, *How Fascism Ruled Women: Italy, 1922–1945* (Berkeley: Univ. of California Press, 1993).

13. Koonz, *Nazi Conscience*, 135 (see chap. 3, n. 41).

14. Ibid., 147.

15. Ibid., 145.

16. Robert O. Paxton, *The Anatomy of Fascism* (New York: Vintage, 2005), 11.

17. E. J. Dionne, *Why Americans Hate Politics* (New York: Simon & Schuster, 1991), especially 147–69.

18. Louis Hartz, *The Liberal Tradition in America* (New York: Harcourt, Brace, & World, 1955).

19. Jane Addams, *Peace and Bread in Time of War* (Champaign, IL: Univ. of Illinois, 2002), 103; http://media.pfeiffer.edu/lridener/dss/Addams/pb9.html.

20. See Gus diZerega, "Spontaneous Order and Liberalism's Complex Relation to Democracy," *Independent Review* 16, no. 2 (Fall 2011), 173–97.

21. Jane Addams, "Americanization," in *The Jane Addams Reader,* ed. Jean Bethke Elshtain (New York: Basic Books, 2002), 244.

22. Herbert Croly, *The Promise of American Life* (Boston: Northeastern Univ. Press, 1989), 276.

23. Ibid., 22.

24. Addams, "Survivals of Militarism in City Government," in *Addams Reader*,161.

25. Croly, *Promise of American Life*, 400.

26. Robert Dahl, *After the Revolution?* (New Haven: Yale Univ. Press 1970), 110.

27. Quoted in Burns, *Goddess of the Marke*, 177 (see chap. 4, n. 26).

28. Quoted in John Ralston Saul, *The Unconscious Civilization* (Concord, Ontario: Anansi, 1995), 84.

29. Walter Lippman, *Public Opinion* (New York: Free Press, 1965), 11.

30. Quoted in Saul, *Unconscious Civilization*, 97, 98.

31. Chris Hedges, *The World as It Is* (NY: Perseus, 2010), 314.

32. Ed Yong, "Lacking Control Drives False Conclusions, Conspiracy Theories and Superstitions," *Not Exactly Rocket Science*, Dec. 27, 2008, http://scienceblogs.com/notrocketscience/2008/12/27/lacking-control-drives-false-conclusions-conspiracy-theories/.

33. George Lakoff, *The Political Mind* (NY: Penguin, 2009).

34. Lawrence Summers, "The Memo," December 12, 1991, http://www.whirledbank.org/ourwords/summers.html.

35. Ibid., "Postscript."

36. "Will Beck Attack Fox News' Gingrich for Citing Mao?" *Media Matters*, http://mediamatters.org/blog/200910160010. See also Joe Klein, *The Natural: The Misunderstood Presidency of Bill Clinton* (Random House, 2002), 103.

37. Quoted in Wolin, *Seduction of Unreason*, 139 (see chap. 4, n. 22).

38. Bringhurst, *Being is Dancing*, 189 (see chap. 2, n. 12). See also Saul, "From Propaganda to Language," in *Unconscious Civilization*, 38–71.

39. Hannah Arendt, *Eichmann in Jerusalem: A Report on the Banality of Evil* (New York: Viking, 1963), 49.

Chapter Six

Epigraph. Tom Robbins, *Jitterbug Perfume* (New York: Bantam,1984), 248.

1. Sarah Pike, *New Age and Neopagan Religions in America* (New York: Columbia Univ. Press, 2004), 52–53.

2. Ibid., 42.

3. Mitch Horowitz, *Occult America: The Secret History of How Mysticism Shaped Our Nation* (New York: Bantam, 2009), 41.

4. Ibid., 3, 58–62.

5. "Abraham Lincoln Speech: The War with Mexico, January 12, 1848," *Animated Atlas*, http://www.animatedatlas.com/mexwar/lincoln2.html.

6. Ralph Waldo Emerson, "Nature," in *The Portable Emerson*, eds. Carl Bode and Malcom Cowley (New York: Penguin, 1981), 43.

7. James William Gibson, *A Reenchanted World* (New York: Henry Holt, 2009), 19–20.

8. Bell, *End of Ideology* (see chap. 1, n. 1).

9. Charlene Spretnak, *Relational Reality: New Discoveries of Interrelatedness That Are Transforming the Modern World* (Topsham, ME: Green Horizon Books, 2011), 189–90.

10. Shepherd, *Lifting the Veil*, 61 (see chap. 1, n 43).

11. Abraham Maslow, *Toward a Psychology of Being* (Princeton: Van Nostrand Reinhold, 1968).

12. Dwight D. Eisenhower, "Eisenhower's Farewell Address to the Nation," *Information Clearing House*, http://www.informationclearinghouse.info/article5407.htm.

13. Hedges, *Death of the Liberal Class*, 42 (see chap. 5, n. 3).

14. Pauline Jelinek, "Iraq Insurgents Hack U.S. Drones For Under $26," *Huffington Post*, Dec. 10, 2009, http://www.huffingtonpost.com/2009/12/17/iraq-insurgents-hack-us-drones_n_395337.html.

15. John Kenneth Galbraith, *The New Industrial State* (New York: Mentor, 1972).

16. William Whyte, *The Organization Man* (Garden City, NY: Doubleday, 1956), 74.

17. Andrew Smith, *Moondust: In Search of the Men Who Fell to Earth* (London: Bloomsbury, 2006).

18. Rebecca Klatch, *A Generation Divided: The New Left, the New Right, and the 1960s* (Berkeley: Univ. of California, 1999).

19. Alan F. Phillips, "20 Mishaps That Might Have Started Accidental Nuclear War," *NuclearFiles*, http://www.nuclearfiles.org/menu/key-issues/nuclear-weapons/issues/accidents/20-mishaps-maybe-caused-nuclear-war.htm.

20. McGraw, *America's Sacred Ground* (see chap. 1, n. 5).

21. "The Kennedy-Nixon Debates," *History*, http://www.history.com/topics/kennedy-nixon-debates.

22. Terry Anderson, *The Sixties*, 3rd ed. (Upper Saddle River, NJ: Pearson, 2007), 158.

23. Jonathan Schell, *The Time of Illusion* (New York: Vintage, 1976), 185.

24. Anderson, *Sixties*, 162.

25. I think the term *counterculture* was first used in this context in Theodore Roszak, *The Making of a Counter Culture* (Garden City, NY: Anchor/Doubleday, 1969).

26. Doug Boyd, *Rolling Thunder* (New York: Dell, 1974).

27. David Kaiser, *How the Hippies Saved Physics* (New York: W. W. Norton, 2011), 275.

28. Philip Slater, *The Pursuit of Loneliness: American Culture at the Breaking Point* (Boston: Beacon, 1970), 100.

29. Spretnak, *Resurgence of the Real*, 178 (see chap. 2, n. 8).

30. Gretchen Lemke-Santangelo, *Daughters of Aquarius: Women of the Sixties Counterculture* (Lawrence: Univ. Press of Kansas, 2009), 158.

31. "Origin of the Name California," *Wikipedia*, http://en.wikipedia.org/wiki/Origin_of_the_name_California.

32. John Markoff, *What the Dormouse Said: How the Sixties Counterculture Shaped the Personal Computer Industry* (New York: Viking, 2006).

33. Kaiser, *Hippies Saved Physics*, 274.

34. William Everson, *Archetype West: The Pacific Coast as a Literary Region* (Santa Cruz: Oyez, 1976), 7.

35. Camille Paglia, "Cults and Cosmic Consciousness: Religious Vision in the American 1960s," *Arion*, 10, no. 3 (Winter 2003), http://www.bu.edu/arion/files/2010/03/paglia_cults-1.pdf. See also Mark Oppenheimer, *Knocking on Heaven's Door: American Religion in the Age of Counterculture* (New Haven: Yale Univ. Press, 1973).

36. Ninian Smart, *The Long Search* (Boston: Little Brown, 1977), 292.

CHAPTER SEVEN

Epigraphs. "Who Is Michael Ledeen," *For Visibility 911.org*, http://www.visibility911.org/who-is-michael-ledeen/; Pat Buchanan, "Why We Can't

Quit the Culture War," *SF Examiner*, Feb.21, 1999, http://www.tysknews.com/ Depts/Our_Culture/why_we_cant_quit_the_culture_war.htm.

1. Aviva Shen, "Arkansas State Rep: 'If Slavery Were So God-Awful, Why Didn't Jesus Or Paul Condemn It?'" *ThinkProgress*, Oct 9, 2012, http://thinkprogress. org/election/2012/10/09/975021/arkansas-state-rep-if-slavery-were-so-god-awful-why-didnt-jesus-or-paul-condemn-it/?mobile=nc.

2. Gordon S. Wood, *The Radicalism of the American Revolution* (New York: Alfred Knopf, 1992).

3. "Mitch McConnell," *Wikipedia*, http://en.wikipedia.org/wiki/ Mitch_McConnell.

4. Patrick J. Buchanan, "The Aggressors in the Culture Wars," March 8, 2004, http://buchanan.org/blog/pjb-the-aggressors-in-the-culture-wars-583.

5. Jonah Goldberg, "Baghdad Delenda Est, Part Two: Get on with it," *National Review Online*, April 23, 2002, http://article.nationalreview.com/?q=YTFhZG Q4Y2IyZmNlY2QyNDkwZTlkZjFkYjZiNWY0YzU.

6. Shadia Drury, *Leo Strauss and the American Right* (New York: St. Martins 1999), 161.

7. William Kristol and Robert Kagan, "Toward a Neo-Reaganite Foreign Policy," *Foreign Affairs* (July/August 1996), http://www.carnegieendowment. org/1996/07/01/toward%2Dneo%2Dreaganite%2Dforeign%2Dpolicy/npc.

8. Corey Robin, "Endgame: Conservatives After the Cold War," *Boston Review*, http://www.bostonreview.net/BR29.1/robin.html.

9. Quoted by John Laughland, "Flirting With Fascism," *The American Conservative*, June 30, 2003, www.amconmag.com/06_30_03/feature.html.

10. Michael Ledeen, "Iraq, What Lies Ahead," *History Commons*, http://www .historycommons.org/context.jsp?item=complete_timeline_of_the_2003_ invasion_of_iraq_3167#complete_timeline_of_the_2003_invasion_of_iraq_3167.

11. Mansfield, *Manliness*, 76 (see chap. 3, n. 36).

12. Alexander Hamilton, "Federalist No. 8." *Federalist Papers* (see chap. 1, n. 15).

13. James Madison to Spencer Roan, September 2, 1819, *The Mind of the Founder: Sources of the Political Thought of James Madison*, ed. Marvin Meyers (Hanover, NH: Univ. Press of New England, 1981), 361–62.

14. Michael Ledeen, *Machiavelli on Modern Leadership: Why Machiavelli's Iron Rules Are as Timely and Important Today as Five Centuries Ago* (New York: St. Martin's, 1999), 90.

15. Harvey Mansfield, "The Case for the Strong Executive: Under Some Circumstances, the Rule of Law Must Yield to the Need for Energy," *The Wall Street Journal*, May 2, 2007.

16. Ledeen, *Machiavelli*, 89–90.

17. Ibid., 187, 173–74. Since Machiavelli sought to defend an Italy of small city-states repeatedly invaded by foreign national monarchies, we would be in an analogous situation if Canada frequently invaded and despoiled us.

18. Mansfield along with William Kristol admires Carnes Lord's *The Modern Prince* (New Haven: Yale 2003), which recommends as models leaders like Pakistani military dictator Pervez Musharraf and Lee Kuan Yew, the authoritarian ruler of Singapore who, happily from Lord's perspective, suppressed American-style liberalism. See Anne Norton, *Leo Strauss and the Politics of the American Empire* (New Haven: Yale, 2004), 130–36.

19. "Jonah Goldberg: Young People Are 'So Frickin Stupid'" (video), *The Daily Caller*, June 12, 2012, http://dailycaller.com/2012/05/12/jonah-goldberg-young-people-are-so-frickin-stupid-video/.

20. Ledeen, *Machiavelli*, 117.

21. I coauthored a book with Phillip Johnson, an evangelical Christian who makes a powerful case for a humane and loving evangelical Christianity: *Beyond the Burning Times* (Cambridge, MA: Lion Hudson, 2008).

22. Buchanan, "Can't Quit the Culture War."

23. Jerry Falwell and Pat Robertson, transcript, the 700 Club, 9/13/01, *Common Dreams*, http://www.commondreams.org/news2001/0917-03.htm

24. Matt Corley, "Hagee Says Hurricane Katrina Struck New Orleans Because It Was 'Planning a Sinful' 'Homosexual Rally,'" *Think Progress*, April 23, 2008, http://thinkprogress.org/politics/2008/04/23/22152/hagee-katrina-mccain/.

25. Rick Joyner with Dutch Sheets, "The True Soldiers of the Cross Are Mobilizing. The Church is About to be Clothed with a Beauty that is Beyond this World!" *The Elijah List*, June 19, 2007, http://www.elijahlist.com/words/display_word/5396.

26. Jeff Sharlet. Sex and Power inside "the C Street House," *Salon*, July 21, 2009, http://www.salon.com/news/feature/2009/07/21/c_street. See also Sharlet, *The Family: The Secret Fundamentalism at the Heart of American Power* (New York: Harper, 2008).

27. Michael Gaddis, *There Is No Crime for Those Who Have Christ: Religious Violence in the Christian Roman Empire* (Berkeley: Univ. of California Press, 2005).

28. Sharlet, "Sex and Power." Pryor denies saying this, but it is in keeping with the Family's sense of mission.

29. C. Peter Wagner, *Dominion! How Kingdom Action Can Change the World* (Grand Rapids, MI: Chosen, 2008).

30. Both quotations are from Forrest Wilder, "Rick Perry's Army of God," *Texas Observer*, August 3, 2011, http://www.texasobserver.org/cover-story/rick-perrys-army-of-god.

31. Katherine Stewart, "How Christian Fundamentalists Plan to Teach Genocide to Schoolchildren," *The Guardian*, May 30, 2012, http://www.guardian.co.uk/commentisfree/2012/may/30/christian-fundamentalists-plan-teach-genocide.

32. Andy Coghlan, "Punitive Acts Linked to Religious Thoughts," *New Scientist*, November 27, 2010, 12. See also Gus diZerega, "Does Religion Decrease Compassion?" *Patheos*, May 10, 2012, http://www.patheos.com/Pagan/Religion-Decrease-Compassion-Gus-diZerega-05-11-2012.html.

33. Greg Palast, "I Don't Have to Be Nice to the Spirit of the Antichrist," *The Guardian*, May 22, 1999, http://www.guardian.co.uk/business/1999/may/23/columnists.observerbusiness1.

34. Glenn Greenwald, "The McCain/Hagee story picks up steam," *Salon*, Feb. 29, 2008, http://www.salon.com/2008/02/29/hagee_2/.

35. Wilder, "Rick Perry's Army of God."

36. Felicia Sonmez, "Santorum says he 'almost threw up' after reading JFK speech on separation of church and state," Feb. 26, 2012, *The Washington Post*, http://www.washingtonpost.com/blogs/election-2012/post/santorum-says-he-almost-threw-up-after-reading-jfk-speech-on-separation-of-church-and-state/2012/02/26/gIQA91hubR_blog.html.

37. George Grant, *The Changing of the Guard: Biblical Principles for Political Action*, Biblical Blueprints Series (Ft. Worth, TX: Dominion Press, 1987). On Christian dominionism, see Chris Hedges, *American Fascists: The Christian Right and the War on America* (New York: Free Press, 2006).

38. Ledeen, *Machiavelli*, 117, 159, 118. I believe this confirms Ronald Bailey's perceptive analysis in "Origin of the Specious," *reason.com*, www.reason.com/news/show/30329.html.

39. Mansfield, *Manliness* (see chap. 3, n. 36). See Martha Nussbaum's review, "Man Overboard," *The New Republic*, June 22, 2006, http://www.powells.com/review/2006_06_22.html; also Gowri Ramachandran, "*Manliness* by Harvey Mansfield," *Yale Journal of Law and Feminism* 19, no. 1 (2007).

40. Mansfield, *Manliness*, 21, 49, 204, 58 (see chap. 3, n. 36). Actually much animal "aggression" does the same, as in establishing hierarchies in a pack.

41. Ibid., 50, 60, 201.

42. Ibid., 70, 71.

43. Ibid., 64, 65, 66.

44. Ibid., 201.

45. Euripides, *Medea*, trans. Eleanor Wilner with Ines Azar, http://www.nytimes.com/books/first/e/euripides1-penn.html.

46. Thomas Jefferson to Roger C, Weightman, June 24, 1826, *The Portable Thomas Jefferson*, ed. Merrill Peterson (New York: Penguin, 1977), 585.

47. Mansfield, *Manliness*, 75, 72, 206, 20, 226 (see chap. 3, n. 36).

48. Ibid., 213.

49. Quoted in Cathy Young, "The Cult of 'Manliness,'" *reason.com*, http://reason.com/archives/2006/07/01/the-cult-of-manliness.

50. Mansfield, *Manliness*, 7–8, 13, 21, 27, 32, 215 (see chap. 3, n 36).

51. Ibid., 234, 70.

52. Ibid., 72.

53. Ibid., 137.

54. Bonnie Erbe, "Kristol's White-Women Problem," *CBS News*, Feb 4, 2008, http://www.cbsnews.com/stories/2008/02/05/usnews/whispers/main3794135.shtml.

55. Mansfield, *Manliness*, 140–41 (see chap. 3, n. 36).

56. Drury, *Strauss and the American Right*, 165–70.

57. Stephanie Coontz, *Marriage, a History: How Love Conquered Marriage* (New York: Penguin, 2006), 292, 299.

58. Garry Wills, "Mousiness," review of *Manliness*, *New York Review of Books* 53, no. 10 (June 6, 2006).

59. Nussbaum, "Man Overboard."

60. Quoted in Bob Allen, "Southern Baptist Scholar Links Spouse Abuse to Wives' Refusal to Submit to Their Husbands," *EthicsDaily*, June 27, 2008,

http://www.ethicsdaily.com/southern-baptist-scholar-links-spouse-abuse-to-wives-refusal-to-submit-to-their-husbands-cms-12832.

61. "Based on the Research, Comprehensive Sex Education is More Effective at Stopping the Spread of HIV Infection, says APA Committee," *American Psychological Association*, Feb. 23, 2005, http://www.apa.org/news/press/releases/2005/02/sex-education.aspx. The "Christian" alternative is also filled with falsehoods (Ceci Connolly, "Some Abstinence Programs Mislead Teens, Report Says," *Washington Post*, Dec. 2, 2004, http://www.washingtonpost.com/wp-dyn/articles/A26623-2004Dec1.html).

62. Cole Petrochko, "Study: Free Contraceptives Slash Abortion rates," *Medpage Today*, Oct. 4, 2012, http://www.medpagetoday.com/OBGYN/Pregnancy/35144.

63. Elisabeth Rosenthal, "Legal or Not, Abortion Rates Compare," *The New York Times*, Oct. 12, 2007, http://www.nytimes.com/2007/10/12/world/12abortion.html?_r=1&oref=slogin.

64. Hilzoy, "The HPV Vaccine and the Christian Right," *Obsidian Wings*, June 9, 2006, http://obsidianwings.blogs.com/obsidian_wings/2006/06/the_hpv_vaccine.html.

65. William Claiborne, "Study Cites Abortion Law, Child Aid Link," *Washington Post*, Oct. 9. 1999, A10, http://www.washingtonpost.com/wp-srv/national/daily/oct99/abortion9.htm. See also Jean Reith Schroedel, *Is the Fetus a Person? A Comparison of Policy Across the Fifty States* (Ithaca: Cornell Univ. Press, 2000).

66. Jim Galloway and Bob Kemper, "Says Zell: Military shortages, Social Security Crisis, and Illegal Immigration All Linked to Abortion," *Atlanta Journal-Constitution*, March 9, 2007.

Chapter Eight

Epigraph. Thompson, *Falling Bodies*, 250 (see chap. 2, n. 6).

1. Coontz, *Marriage*, 229 (see chap. 7, n. 57).

2. Ibid., 250–51.

3. Merchant, *Death of Nature* (see chap. 1, n. 35).

4. On mothers having equal authority over children, see Locke, *Two Treatises of Government*, 2nd ed., ed. Peter Laslett (Cambridge: Cambridge Univ. Press,

1960), 52, 78; on equality between men and women, II, 78; on wife's right to leave, II, 43, 81. See also Melissa Butler, "Early Liberal Roots of Feminism: John Locke and the Attack on Patriarchy," *Feminist Interpretations and Political Theory*, ed. Mary Lyndon Shanley and Carole Pateman (Pennsylvania State Univ. Press, 1991), 83–85.

5. Alan Jay Lerner, "A Hymn to Him," *My Fair Lady*, ST Lyrics, http://www.stlyrics.com/lyrics/myfairlady/ahymntohim.htm.

6. Lemke-Santangelo, *Daughters of Aquarius*, 57–58 (see chap. 6, n. 30).

7. Ibid., 158.

8. Spretnak, *Resurgence of the Real*, 66 (see chap. 2, n. 8).

9. For an insightful study of how ethics can be approached differently from feminine and masculine vantages, see Noddings, *Caring* (see chap. 3, n. 22).

10. Gus diZerega, "Deep Ecology and Liberalism: The Greener Implications of Evolutionary Liberalism," *Review of Politics*, 58, no. 4 (Fall 1996), 699–734.

11. Noddings, *Caring*, 35 (see chap. 3, n. 22).

12. Ibid., 36, 44.

13. Csikszentmihalyi, *Creativity*, 71 (see chap. 3, n. 12).

14. Lemke-Santangelo, *Daughters of Aquarius*, 124 (see chap. 6, n. 30).

15. Marcus Borg, *The God We Never Knew* (San Francisco: Harper San Francisco, 1997), 70.

16. Reza Aslan, *No God but God: The Origins, Evolution, and Future of Islam* (New York: Random House, 2005), 68–71.

17. Rita Gross and Rosemary Ruether, *Religious Feminism and the Future of the Planet: A Buddhist-Christian Conversation* (London: Continuum 2001), 69.

18. Ibid., 40.

19. See, for example, Carol Christ, *The Laughter of Aphrodite: Reflections on a Journey to the Goddess* (San Francisco: Harper and Row 1987), 72.

20. Merlin Stone, introduction to Raphael Patai, *The Hebrew Goddess*, 3rd ed. (New York: KATV, 1967), 17.

21. Rita Gross, *Feminism and Religion: An Introduction* (Boston: Beacon, 1997), 209.

22. Gross and Ruether, *Religious Feminism*, 57.

23. Patai, *Hebrew Goddess*; Elaine Pagels, "What Became of God the Mother?" *Signs* 2, no. 2 (1976), 293–303.

24. Bart Ehrman, *Peter, Paul, and Mary Magdalene: The Followers of Jesus in History and Legend* (New York: Oxford Univ. Press, 2006).

25. Christ, *Laughter of Aphrodite*, 144.

26. Ibid.

27. Rosemary Radford Ruether, *Goddesses and the Divine Feminine: A Western Religious History* (Berkeley: Univ. of California Press, 2005), 131, 220–48.

28. Christ, *Laughter of Aphrodite*, 144.

29. Spretnak, *States of Grace*, 136 (see chap. 2, n. 10).

30. Ruether, *Goddesses*, 307.

31. Rick Fields, *How the Swans Came to the Lake: A Narrative History of Buddhism in America* (Boston: Shambhala, 1981).

32. John Stevens, *Lust for Enlightenment: Buddhism and Sex* (Boston: Shambhala, 1990), 23.

33. Kim Gutschow, *Being a Buddhist Nun: The Struggle for Enlightenment in the Himalayas* (Cambridge, MA: Harvard Univ. Press, 2004).

34. Rita Gross, *Buddhism After Patriarchy* (Albany: SUNY Press, 1993), 38–48.

35. Gross and Ruether, *Religious Feminism*, 99. Stevens's *Lust for Enlightenment* contains much of relevance here.

36. Gross, *Buddhism After Patriarchy*, 25.

37. Gross and Ruether, *Religious Feminism*, 79.

38. Gross, *Buddhism After Patriarchy*, 164, 181.

39. Roger Kamenetz, *The Jew in the Lotus* (San Francisco: Harper Collins, 1994), 210–25; Sandy Boucher, *Turning the Wheel: American Women Creating the New Buddhism* (Boston: Beacon, 1993).

40. Starhawk, *The Spiral Dance: A Rebirth of the Ancient Religion of the Great Goddess* (New York: HarperCollins, 1989), 51.

41. Gross, *Buddhism After Patriarchy*, 284.

42. Tamara Conniff, "The Dalai Lama Proclaims Himself a Feminist: Day Two of Peace and Music in Memphis," *Huffington Post*, Sept. 23, 2009, http://www.huffingtonpost.com/tamara-conniff/the-dalai-lama-proclaims_b_297285.html.

43. Margot Adler, *Drawing Down the Moon* (New York: Penguin, 2006).

44. Lemke-Santangelo, *Daughters of Aquarius*, 166–71 (see chap. 6, n. 30).

45. Barry A. Kosmin, Egon Mayer, and Ariela Keysar, *American Religious Identification Survey*, The Graduate Center of the City Univ. of New York, http://www.gc.cuny.edu/faculty/research_briefs/aris/key_findings.htm.

46. Ruether, *Religious Feminism*, 280–85.

47. Personal communication from Fred Lamond, June 2010.

48. Joseph M. Murphy, *Santeria: An African Religion in America* (Boston: Beacon, 1988), 131.

49. Kosmin, *American Religious Identification Survey*.

50. George Brandon, *Santeria from Africa to the New World: The Dead Sell Memories* (Bloomington: Univ. of Indiana Press, 1997), 104.

51. "'Santeria' in Cuba," *Cuba Facts* 27 (January 2007), http://ctp.iccas.miami.edu/ FACTS_Web/Cuba%20Facts%20Issue%2027%20January2007.htm.

52. Michael Ventura, "Hear That Long Snake Moan: The Voodoo Origins of Rock and Roll, Part 1," *Whole Earth* 54 (Spring 1987), 28–43; "Hear That Long Snake Moan: The Voodoo Origins of Rock and Roll, Part 2," *Whole Earth* 55 (Summer 1987), 82–92.

53. Ruth Landes, *City of Women* (Albuquerque: Univ. of New Mexico Press, 1994).

54. Ibid., 37.

55. Christ, *Laughter of Aphrodite*, 57–58.

CHAPTER NINE

Epigraph. Aldo Leopold, *A Sand County Almanac* (Oxford: Oxford Univ. Press, 1966), 117.

1. Stephen Fox, *The American Conservation Movement: John Muir and His Legacy* (Madison, WI: Univ. of Wisconsin Press, 1985), 341–45.

2. Van Jones, *The Green Collar Economy: How One Solution Can Fix Our Two Biggest Problems* (New York: HarperOne, 2009).

3. Fox, *American Conservation Movement*, 322–26.

4. *Essays and Poems by Ralph Waldo Emerson*, ed. Peter Norberg (New York: Barnes and Noble, 2004), 11.

5. Bron Taylor, *Dark Green Religion: Nature, Spirituality and the Planetary Future* (Berkeley: Univ. of California Press, 2010), 54, 227–47.

6. Henry David Thoreau, *Walden*, Chapter 17 [9], http://thoreau.eserver.org/ walden17.html.

7. Henry David Thoreau, "Walking," http://thoreau.eserver.org/walking2.html.

8. John Muir, *A Thousand Mile Walk to the Gulf*, http://www.sierraclub.org/
john_muir_exhibit/writings/a_thousand_mile_walk_to_the_gulf/chapter_4
.html.

9. John Muir, *The Eight Wilderness Discovery Books* (London and Seattle:
Diadem Books, 1992), 481.

10. Quoted in Roderick Nash, *Wilderness and the American Mind*, 3rd ed. (New
Haven: Yale Univ. Press, 1982), 150, 151, 153.

11. John A. Gable, "Biography of TR," *Theodore Roosevelt Association*, http://www.
theodoreroosevelt.org/life/bullmoose.htm.

12. Leopold, *Sand County Almanac*, 138–39. See also diZerega, "Deep Ecology"
(see chap. 8, n. 10).

13. Capra, *Science of Leonardo*, 263 (see chap. 1, n. 41).

14. Linda Lear, introduction to Rachel Carson, *Silent Spring* (Boston: Houghton
Mifflin, 2002), xvi.

15. This theme is developed in Anodea Judith, *Waking the Global Heart:
Humanity's Rite of Passage from the Love of Power to the Power of Love*
(Fulton, CA: Elite Books, 2006).

16. Gibson, *Reenchanted World*, 94 (see chap. 6, n. 7).

17. Ibid., 95.

18. http://www.noetic.org/.

19. James Lovelock, *Gaia: A New Look at Life on Earth* (Oxford: Oxford Univ.
Press, 1979).

20. "Sulfur Finding May Hold Key to Gaia Theory of Earth as Living
Organism," *Science Daily*, May 15, 2012, http://www.sciencedaily.com/
releases/2012/05/120515203100.htm.

21. Richard Nelson, "Searching for the Lost Arrow: Physical and Spiritual
Ecology in the Hunter's World," in *The Biophilia Hypothesis*, eds. Stephen
R. Kellert and Edward O. Wilson (Washington, DC: Island Press, 1993),
203, 223.

22. Petr Kopecky, *The California Crucible: Literary Harbingers of Deep Ecology*
(Ostrava, Czech Republic: Univ. of Ostrava Press, 2007).

23. Carl von Essen, *Ecomysticism: The Profound Experience of Nature as Spiritual
Guide* (Rochester, VT: Bear and Company, 2010), 35–36. See also Richard
Nelson, *The Island Within* (San Francisco: Northpoint Press, 1989).

24. Gary Snyder, *A Place in Space: Ethics, Aesthetics, and Watersheds* (Washington, DC: Counterpoint, 1995), 76–77.

25. von Essen, *Ecomysticism,* 37, 39. Former Zen abbot Jim Wilson made the same observation to me personally.

26. Terry Tempest Williams, *An Unspoken Hunger* (New York: Vintage, 1994), 84.

27. Abram, *Becoming Animal,* 153 (see chap. 2, n. 19).

28. Lakoff and Johnson, *Philosophy in the Flesh* (see chap. 2, n. 21).

29. McGilchrist, *Master and Emissary,* 117 (see chap. 2, n. 23).

30. Matthews, *Love of Matter,* 80 (see chap. 1, n. 43).

31. "Treaties of Lead," *Gold, Greed and Genocide,* http://www.1849.org/ggg/treaties.html.

32. The Advisory Council on California Indian Policy, *The ACCIP Recognition Report, Equal Justice for California,* September, 1997, https://docs.google.com/viewer?a=v&q=cache:iJDXdc3rFV0J:www.standupca.org/gaming-law/ACCIP%2520Recognition%2520Report.pdf+&hl=en&gl=us&pid=bl&srcid=ADGEEShzGVZltczsvGKm_9Qc1dw1ZcuilG_P93FySZAMqrz0XCGVTyoRnuOHEg6RdX_xRWskhQfc1nWT59mp_0cyGZf68mRmjORnShljApU6Jej2IQ2XFtKYu9Owbn1s3yp7euhNdaQK&sig=AHIEtbREQW_-LXdCOuw2HM_PGPxJz6mlEQ.

33. Marc Bekoff and Jessica Pierce, *Wild Justice: The Moral Lives of Animals* (Chicago: Univ. of Chicago Press, 2009).

34. Merchant, *Death of Nature* (see chap. 1, n. 35).

35. Lakoff and Johnson, *Philosophy in the Flesh* (see chap. 2, n. 21).

36. Peggy Reeves Sanday, *Female Power and Male Dominance: On the Origins of Sexual Inequality* (Cambridge: Cambridge Univ. Press, 1981).

37. Williams, *Unspoken Hunger,* 53.

38. Arne Naess, *Ecology, Community and Lifestyle: Outline of an Ecosophy,* trans. David Rothenberg (Cambridge: Cambridge Univ. Press, 1993).

39. Arne Naess, "Self-Realization: An Ecological Approach to Being in the World," *The Deep Ecology Movement: An Introductory Anthology,* eds. Alan Drengson and Yuichi Inoue (Berkeley: North Atlantic Books, 1995), 14,15. See also Plumwood, *Feminism,* 179 (see chap. 3, n. 37).

40. Quoted in Midgley, *Science as Salvation,* 18 (see chap. 2, n. 29).

41. Richard Dawkins, *A Devil's Chaplain* (New York: Houghton Mifflin, 2003), 15.

42. See for example, Michael Crichton, "Remarks to the Commonwealth Club," September 15, 2003, http://www.sitewave.net/news/s49p1521.htm; Michael S. Coffman, *Environmentalism! The Dawn of Aquarius or the Twilight of a New Dark Age?* (Bangor, ME: Environmental Perspectives,1992).

43. Philip Sherrard, "The Desanctification of Nature," in *Seeing God Everywhere: Essays on Nature and the Sacred*, ed. Barry MacDonald (Bloomington, IN: World Wisdom, 2003), 112.

44. Hans Küng and Karl-Josef Kuschel, eds., *A Global Ethic: The Declaration of the Parliament of the World's Religions* (New York: Continuum, 1993).

45. Edward O. Wilson, "Biophilia and the Conservation Ethic," in *Biophilia Hypothesis*, 32.

46. Jo Barton and Jules Pretty, "What Is the Best Dose of Nature and Green Exercise for Improving Mental Health? A Multi-Study Analysis," *Environmental Science and Technology* 2010, 44 (10), 3947–55, http://pubs.acs.org/doi/abs/10.1021/es903183r.

47. Jules Pretty, "A Walk a Day Keeps the Doctor Away," *Univ. of Essex*, May 2, 2010, http://www.essex.ac.uk/news/event.aspx?e_id=1588.

48. David Dobbs, "The Green Space Cure: The Psychological Value of Biodiversity," *Scientific American*, Nov.13, 2007, http://www.scientificamerican.com/blog/60-second-science/post.cfm?id=the-green-space-cure-the-psychologi.

49. von Essen, *Ecomysticism*, 120.

50. von Essen, *Ecomysticism*, 1.

Chapter Ten

Epigraphs. Albert Gelpi, ed., *The Wild God of the World: An Anthology of Robinson Jeffers* (Palo Alto, CA: Stanford Univ. Press, 2003), 189; Arundhati Roy, "Confronting Empire," ZNET, January 28, 2003, http://www.zcommunications.org/confronting-empire-by-arundhati-roy.

1. Carlo A. Corsini and Pier Paolo Viazz, eds., *The Decline of Infant and Child Mortality: The European Experience: 1750–1990* (The Hague: Martinus Nijhoff Publishers, 1997).

2. Karen Armstrong, *The Great Transformation* (New York: Anchor, 2007).

3. Thomas McEvilley, *The Shape of Ancient Thought* (New York: Allworth Press, 2002).

4. Berger, *Heretical Imperative*, 143–72 (see chap. 1, n. 39).

5. Alan Watts emphasizes this two-sided nature of maya in *Beyond Theology: The Art of Godmanship* (New York: World, 1967), 17, 144. A similar contrast can be seen with Buddhism and nature: see William R. LaFleur, "Saigyo and the Buddhist value of Nature," *Nature in Asian Traditions of Thought*, ed. J. Baird Callicott and Roger Ames (Albany: SUNY Press, 1989), 183–209.

6. McEvilley, *Shape of Ancient Thought*, 588–90.

7. Hugh Brody, *The Other Side of Eden: Hunters, Farmers, and the Shaping of the World* (New York: North Point, 2000), 235; Plumwood, *Feminism* (see chap. 3, n. 41).

8. I. P. Couliano, *Out of This World: Otherworldly Journeys from Gilgamesh to Albert Einstein* (Boston: Shambhala, 1991), 111–13.

9. Armstrong, *Great Transformation,* 80–91.

10. Lao-Tzu, *Tao Te Ching,* chapter 38, trans. S. Mitchell, http://academic.brooklyn.cuny.edu/core9/phalsall/texts/taote-v3.html.

11. *Chuang-tzu: Basic Writings*, trans. Burton Watson (New York: Columbia Univ. Press, 1996).

12. McEvilley, *Shape of Ancient Thought*, 300.

13. Jan Assman, *Moses the Egyptian: The Memory of Egypt in Western Monotheism* (Cambridge, MA: Harvard Univ. Press, 1998).

14. Armstrong, *Great Transformation*, 55.

15. "The Religious Dimensions of the Torture Debate," *The PEW Forum on Religion and Public Life*, May 7, 2009, http://pewforum.org/Politics-and-Elections/The-Religious-Dimensions-of-the-Torture-Debate.aspx.

16. "Highly Religious People Are Less Motivated by Compassion Than Are Non-Believers," *Science Daily*, April 30, 2012, http://www.sciencedaily.com/releases/2012/04/120430140035.htm.

17. Nate Silver, "Divorce Rates Higher in States With Gay Marriage Bans," *FiveThirtyEight Politics Done Right*, Jan 12, 2010. http://www.fivethirtyeight.com/2010/01/divorce-rates-appear-higher-in-states.html.

18. Alexis deTocqueville, *Democracy in America*, vol. 2, trans. George Lawrence (Garden City, NY: Anchor Books, 1969), 451–52.

19. Abram, *Becoming Animal*, 278 (see chap. 2, n. 19).

20. Tocqueville, *Democracy in America*, vol. 2, 35 (see chap. 1, n. 3).

21. "Do Mirror Neurons Give Us Empathy? Interview with V. S. Ramachandran," *Greater Good: The Science of a Meaningful Life*, March 29, 2012, http://greatergood.berkeley.edu/article/item/do_mirror_neurons_give_empathy.

22. Paul Bloom, "That Warm Fuzzy Feeling," *New Scientist*, October 16, 2010. 44–45; Stephanie Pappas, "Even Babies Think Crime Deserves Punishment," *Live Science*, November 28, 2011, http://www.livescience.com/17204-babies-prefer-punishment.html.

23. Bekoff and Pierce, *Wild Justice* (see chap. 9, n. 33).

24. Robert Axelrod, *The Evolution of Cooperation* (New York: Basic Books, 2006).

25. E. O. Wilson, *Biophilia: The Human Bond With Other Species* (Cambridge, MA: Harvard Univ. Press, 1984), 7. See also Kellert and Wilson, *Biophilia Hypothesis* (see chap. 9, n. 21).

26. Geerat Vermeij, *The Evolutionary World: How Adaptation Explains Everything From Seashells to Civilization* (New York: St. Martin's, 2010), 167–68.

27. Taylor, *Dark Green Religion* (see chap. 9, n. 5); Sharman Apt Russell, *Standing in the Light: My Life as a Pantheist* (New York: Basic Books, 2008).

28. Vermeij, *Evolutionary World*, 127.

29. Quoted in Margaret J. Wheatley, *Leadership and the New Science: Discovering Order in a Chaotic World* (San Francisco: Berrett-Koehler, 1999), 32.

30. Quoted in Shepherd, *Lifting the Veil*, 68 (see chap. 1, n. 43).

31. Abram, *Spell of the Sensuous*, chapters 4–7 (see chap. 2, n. 40).

32. Ibid.; Bruno Leoni, *Freedom and the Law* (Princeton, NJ: Van Nostrand, 1961).

33. Yevgeny Yevtushenko, "People," *Selected Poems* (NY: Penguin, 1967), 85.

34. Charlene Spretnak, *Missing Mary: The Queen of Heaven and Her Re-Emergence in the Modern Church* (New York: Palgrave Macmillan, 2004).

35. Leo D. Lefebure, "The Wisdom of God: Sophia and Christian Theology," *The Christian Century* 111, no. 29 (October 19, 1994), http://www.questia.com/library/1G1-15861175/the-wisdom-of-god-sophia-and-christian-theology.

36. Bishop Kallistos Ware, *The Orthodox Way* (Crestwood, NY: St. Vladimir's Seminary Press, 1979), 34.

37. Pamela Berger, *The Goddess Obscured* (Boston: Beacon, 1985) 49–76, 85–87.

38. D. A. Brading, *Mexican Phoenix: Our Lady of Guadalupe: Image and Tradition across Five Centuries* (Cambridge: Cambridge Univ. Press, 2001), 2.

39. Migene Gonzalez-Wippler, *Santeria: The Religion: A Legacy of Faith, Rites, and Magic* (New York: Harmony Books, 1989), 74.

40. Quotations in this and the two following sections, unless otherwise noted, are from Peter Berger "Cakes for the Queen of Heaven: 2,500 Years of Religious Ecstasy," *Christian Century*, December 25, 1974, 1217–23, http://www.religion-online.org/showarticle.asp?title=1577.

41. Patai, *Hebrew Goddess*, 4, n. 9 (see chap. 8, n. 20).

42. Robin Lane Fox, *Pagans and Christians* (San Francisco: Harper and Row, 1986).

43. *The Arguments of the Emperor Julian Against the Christians* (Chicago: Hermetic Pub. Co., 1809), 46.

44. See my discussion of moral issues in diZerega, *Pagans and Christians* (see chap. 1, n. 40).

45. Stevens, *Lust for Enlightenment* (see chap. 8, n. 32).

CHAPTER ELEVEN

Epigraph. Abram, *Becoming Animal*, 299 (see chap. 2, n. 19).

1. Lawrence Kushner, *The River of Light* (Woodstock, VT: Jewish Lights, 1990), quoted in Russell Targ, *Limitless Mind* (New World: Novato, 2004), 18.

2. Janet Farrar and Stewart Farrar, *The Witches' Way: Principles, Rituals and Beliefs of Modern Witchcraft* (London: Robert Hale, 1984), 298.

3. Bringhurst, *Being is Dancing*, 37 (see chap. 2, n.12).

4. Walter Scott, ed. and trans., *Hermetica: Introduction, Texts and Translation* (Boulder CO: Hermes House, 1982), 341–61; G. R. S. Mead, trans., *Thrice Greatest Hermes* (York Beach, ME: Samuel Weiser, 1992), 221–26; Brian P. Copenhaver, trans. and ed., *Hermetica* (Cambridge: Cambridge Univ. Press, 1992), 81–83; Garth Fowden, *The Egyptian Hermes* (Princeton: Princeton Univ. Press, 1993), 38–40. My gratitude to Don Frew, who clarified Christian translations, changing into pagan terms, as originally intended.

5. Quoted in Richard Smoley, *Forbidden Faith: The Gnostic Legacy from the Gospels to the Da Vinci Code* (San Francisco: HarperSanFrancisco, 2006), 208.

6. diZerega, *Pagans and Christians* (see chap. 1, n. 40).

7. Berger, *Heretical Imperative*, 156 (see chap. 1, n. 39).

8. Gus diZerega and Philip Johnson, *Beyond the Burning Times* (Cambridge, MA: Lion Hudson, 2008).

9. Brody, *Other Side of Eden* (see chap. 10, n. 7).

10. Jordan Paper, *The Mystic Experience: A Descriptive and Comparative Analysis* (Albany: SUNY Press, 2004), 141–43. Paper has not only experienced and written about the nondual, he has also experienced and written about the world of polytheistic immanence. See *The Deities Are Many: A Polytheistic Theology* (Albany: SUNY Press, 2005).

11. "The Beauty of Things," *The Selected Poetry of Robinson Jeffers*, ed. Tim Hunt (Stanford: Stanford Univ. Press, 2001), 652.

12. Starhawk, spoken at Pantheacon, San Jose, CA, February 16, 2009.

13. Farrar and Farrar, *Witches' Way*, 298.

BIBLIOGRAPHY

Abram, David. *Becoming Animal*. New York: Pantheon, 2010.

_____. *The Spell of the Sensuous*. New York: Pantheon, 1996.

Addams, Jane. "Americanization." In *The Jane Addams Reader*. Edited by Jean Bethke Elshtain. New York: Basic Books, 2002.

_____. *Peace and Bread in Time of War*. Champaign, IL: Univ. of Illinois, 2002. http://media.pfeiffer.edu/lridener/dss/Addams/pb9.html.

Adler, Margot. *Drawing Down the Moon*. New York: Penguin, 2006.

Anderson, Terry. *The Sixties*. 3rd ed. Upper Saddle River, NJ: Pearson, 2007.

Arendt, Hannah. *Eichmann in Jerusalem: A Report on the Banality of Evil*. New York: Viking, 1963.

Armstrong, Karen. *The Battle for God*. New York: Ballantine Books, 2000.

_____. *The Great Transformation*. New York: Anchor, 2007.

Aslan, Reza. *No God but God: The Origins, Evolution, and Future of Islam*. New York: Random House, 2005.

Assman, Jan. *Moses the Egyptian: The Memory of Egypt in Western Monotheism*. Cambridge, MA: Harvard Univ. Press, 1998.

Axelrod, Robert. *The Evolution of Cooperation*. New York: Basic Books, 2006.

Baigent, Michael, and Richard Leigh. *The Elixir and the Stone: Unlocking the Ancient Mysteries of the Occult*. New York: Penguin, 1997.

Bartley, W. W., III. *The Retreat to Commitment*. LaSalle, IL: Open Court, 1984.

Barton, Jo, and Jules Pretty. "What is the Best Dose of Nature and Green Exercise for Improving Mental Health? A Multi-Study Analysis." *Environmental Science and Technology* 2010, 44 (10): 3947–3955. http://pubs.acs.org/doi/abs/10.1021/es903183r.

Bekoff, Marc, and Jessica Pierce. *Wild Justice: The Moral Lives of Animals*. Chicago: Univ. of Chicago Press, 2009.

Bell, Daniel. *The End of Ideology: On the Exhaustion of Political Ideas in the Fifties*. 2nd ed. Cambridge, MA: Harvard Univ. Press, 2000.

Berger, Pamela. *The Goddess Obscured*, Boston: Beacon, 1985.

Berger, Peter. "Cakes for the Queen of Heaven: 2500 Years of Religious Ecstasy." *Christian Century*, December 25, 1974, 1217–23. http://www.religion-online. org/showarticle.asp?title=1577.

_____. *The Heretical Imperative: Contemporary Possibilities of Religious Affirmation.* New York: Anchor, 1980.

Boucher, Sandy. *Turning the Wheel: American Women Creating the New Buddhism.* Boston: Beacon, 1993.

Boyd, Doug. *Rolling Thunder.* New York: Dell, 1974.

Brandon, George. *Santeria from Africa to the New World: The Dead Sell Memories.* Bloomington: Univ. of Indiana Press, 1997.

Bringhurst, Robert. *Everywhere Being is Dancing: Twenty Pieces of Thinking.* Berkeley: Counterpoint, 2008.

_____. *A Story as Sharp as a Knife: The Classical Haida Mythtellers and Their World.* Vancouver: Douglas & McIntyre, 1999.

_____. *The Tree of Meaning: Language, Mind and Ecology.* Berkeley: Counterpoint, 2008.

Brizendine, Louanne. *The Female Brain.* New York: Broadway Books, 2006.

_____. *The Male Brain.* New York: Three Rivers Press, 2010.

Brody, Hugh. *The Other Side of Eden: Hunters, Farmers, and the Shaping of the World.* New York: North Point, 2000.

Bryne, James M. *Religion and the Enlightenment: From Descartes to Kant.* Louisville, KY: Westminister John Knox Press, 1996.

Burns, Jennifer. *Goddess of the Market: Ayn Rand and the American Right.* Oxford: Oxford Univ. Press, 2009.

Butler, Melissa. "Early Liberal Roots of Feminism: John Locke and the Attack on Patriarchy." In *Feminist Interpretations and Political Theory.* Edited by Mary Lyndon Shanley and Carole Pateman. Pennsylvania State Univ. Press, 1991.

Callicott, J. Baird, and Roger Ames, eds. *Nature in Asian Traditions of Thought.* Albany: SUNY Press Press, 1989.

Campbell, Joseph, with Bill Moyers. *The Power of Myth.* New York: Random House, 1991.

Campbell, Joseph. *A Joseph Campbell Reader: Reflections on the Art of Living.* Edited by Diane K. Osborn. New York: Harper Collins, 1991.

Capra, Fritjof. *The Science of Leonardo: Inside the Mind of the Great Genius of the Renaissance*. New York: Doubleday 2007.

Carson, Rachel. *Silent Spring*. New York: Houghton Mifflin, 2002.

Childr, Doc, and Howard Martin. *The Heartmath Solution*. San Francisco: Harper, 1999.

Christ, Carol. *The Laughter of Aphrodite: Reflections on a Journey to the Goddess*. San Francisco: Harper and Row, 1987.

Chuang-tzu. *Chuang-tzu: Basic Writings*. Translated by Burton Watson. New York: Columbia Univ. Press, 1996.

Coontz, Stephanie. *Marriage, a History: How Love Conquered Marriage*. New York: Penguin, 2006.

Copenhaver, Brian P., trans. and ed. *Hermetica*. Cambridge: Cambridge Univ. Press, 1992.

Couliano, I. P. *Out of This World: Otherworldly Journeys from Gilgamesh to Albert Einstein*. Boston: Shambhala, 1991.

Croly, Herbert. *The Promise of American Life*. Boston: Northeastern Univ. Press, 1989.

Csikszentmihalyi, Mihalyi. *Creativity: Flow and the Psychology of Discovery and Invention*. New York: Harper Collins, 1996.

Dahl, Robert. *After the Revolution?* New Haven: Yale Univ. Press, 1970.

Dalai Lama, *Beyond Religion: Ethics for a Whole World*. Boston: Houghton Mifflin, 2011.

Damasio, Antonio. *Descartes' Error: Emotion, Reason, and the Human Brain*. New York: Avon, 1994.

Dawkins, Richard. *The Devil's Chaplain*. New York: Houghton Mifflin, 2003.

Desmond, Adrian, and James Moore. *Darwin's Sacred Cause*. New York: Houghton Mifflin Harcourt, 2009.

Dionne, E. J. *Why Americans Hate Politics*. New York: Simon and Schuster, 1991.

diZerega, Gus. *Pagans and Christians: The Personal Spiritual Experience*. Woodbury, MN: Lewellyn, 2001.

_____. "Deep Ecology and Liberalism: The Greener Implications of Evolutionary Liberalism," *Review of Politics*. Fall 1996.

_____. "Spontaneous Order and Liberalism's Complex Relation to Democracy." *Independent Review*. Fall 2011: 173-97.

diZerega, Gus, and Philip Johnson. *Beyond the Burning Times*. Cambridge, MA: Lion Hudson, 2008.

Dobbs, David. "The Green Space Cure: The Psychological Value of Biodiversity." Nov.13, 2007. http://www.scientificamerican.com/blog/60-second-science/post.cfm?id=the-green-space-cure-the-psychologi.

Drengson, Alan, and Yuichi Inoue, eds. *The Deep Ecology Movement: An Introductory Anthology*. Berkeley: North Atlantic Books, 1995.

Drury, Shadia. *Leo Strauss and the American Right*. New York: St. Martin's, 1999.

Ducat, Stephen. *The Wimp Factor: Gender Gaps, Holy Wars, and the Politics of Anxious Masculinity*. Boston: Beacon, 2004.

Ehrman, Bart. *God's Problem: How the Bible Fails to Answer Our Most Important Question—Why We Suffer*. New York: HarperCollins, 2008.

_____. *Jesus Interrupted: Revealing the Hidden Contradictions in the Bible (and Why We Don't Know About Them)*. New York: HarperOne, 2009.

_____. *Peter, Paul, and Mary Magdalene: The Followers of Jesus in History and Legend*. New York: Oxford Univ. Press, 2006.

Etzioni, Amitai, ed. *New Communitarian Thinking: Persons, Virtues, Institutions, and Communities*. Charlottesville, VA: Univ. Press of Virginia, 1995.

Everson, William. *Archetype West: The Pacific Coast as a Literary Region*. Santa Cruz: Oyez, 1976.

Faludi, Susan. *Stiffed: The Betrayal of American Men*. New York: William Morrow, 1999.

Farrar, Janet, and Stewart Farrar. *The Witches' Way: Principles, Rituals and Beliefs of Modern Witchcraft*. London: Robert Hale, 1984.

Fields, Rick. *How the Swans Came to the Lake, A Narrative History of Buddhism in America*. Boston: Shambhala, 1981.

Fowden, Garth. *The Egyptian Hermes*. Revised ed. Princeton: Princeton Univ. Press, 1993.

Fox, Robin Lane, *Pagans and Christians*. San Francisco: Harper and Row, 1986.

Fox, Stephen. *The American Conservation Movement: John Muir and His Legacy*. Madison, WI: Univ. of Wisconsin Press, 1985.

Gaddis, Michael. *There Is No Crime for Those Who Have Christ: Religious Violence in the Christian Roman Empire*. Berkeley: Univ. of California, 2005.

Galbraith, John Kenneth. *The New Industrial State*. New York: Mentor, 1972.

Gay, Peter. *The Enlightenment: The Rise of Modern Paganism.* New York: W. W. Norton, 1966.

Ghachem, Malick W. "The Slave's Two Bodies: The Life of an American Legal Fiction." *William and Mary Quarterly.* 3rd series, LX:4 (Oct. 2003): 809–42.

Gibson, James William. *A Reenchanted World.* New York: Henry Holt, 2009.

Gonzalez-Wippler, Migene. *Santeria: The Religion: A Legacy of Faith, Rites, and Magic.* New York: Harmony Books, 1989.

Gregory, Brad S. *The Unintended Reformation: How A Religious Revolution Secularized Society.* Cambridge, MA: Harvard Univ. Press, 2012.

Gross, Rita. *Buddhism After Patriarchy.* Albany: SUNY Press, 1993.

_____. *Feminism and Religion: An Introduction.* Boston: Beacon, 1997.

Gross, Rita, and Rosemary Ruether. *Religious Feminism and the Future of the Planet: A Buddhist-Christian Conversation.* London: Continuum, 2001.

Gutschow, Kim. *Being a Buddhist Nun: The Struggle for Enlightenment in the Himalayas.* Cambridge, MA: Harvard Univ. Press, 2004.

Harpur, Patrick. *The Philosopher's Secret Fire: A History of the Imagination.* Chicago: Ivan R. Dee, 2003.

Hartshorne, Charles. *Omnipotence and Other Theological Mistakes.* Albany: SUNY Press, 1984.

Hartz, Louis. *The Liberal Tradition in America.* New York: Harcourt, Brace, & World, 1965.

Hedges, Chris. *American Fascists: The Christian Right and the War on America.* New York: Free Press, 2006.

_____. *Death of the Liberal Class.* New York: Nation Books, 2010.

_____. *The World as It Is.* New York: Perseus, 2010.

Heller, Anne C. *Ayn Rand and the World She Made.* New York: Doubleday, 2009.

Herro, Alana. "Biodiversity Can Provide Mental Health Benefits." *Worldwatch Institute.* May 30, 2007. http://www.worldwatch.org/node/5096.

Hilzoy. "The HPV Vaccine and the Christian Right." *Obsidian Wings.* June 9, 2006. http://obsidianwings.blogs.com/obsidian_wings/2006/06/the_hpv_vaccine.html.

Hofstdater, Richard. *Social Darwinism in American Thought.* Boston: Beacon, 1992.

Holmes, Stephen. *The Anatomy of Antiliberalism.* Cambridge, MA: Harvard Univ. Press, 1993.

Horowitz, Mitch. *Occult America: The Secret History of How Mysticism Shaped Our Nation.* New York: Bantam, 2009.

Hume, David. *A Treatise on Human Nature.* In *Hume: Moral and Political Philosophy.* Edited by Henry B. Aiken. New York: Hafner, 1948.

Huntington, Samuel P. *The Soldier and the State: The Theory and Politics of Civil-Military Relations.* Cambridge, MA: Harvard Univ. Press, 1985.

Jeffers, Robinson. Letter to Sister Mary James Power, 1 October 1934. In *The Wild God of the World: An Anthology of Robinson Jeffers.* Edited by Albert Gelpi. Stanford: Stanford Univ. Press, 2003.

_____. *The Selected Poetry of Robinson Jeffers.* Edited by Tim Hunt. Stanford: Stanford Univ. Press, 2001.

Jefferson, Thomas. *The Portable Thomas Jefferson.* Edited by Merrill Peterson. New York: Penguin, 1977.

Johnson, Steven. *Emergence: The Connected Lives of Ants, Brains, Cities, and Software.* New York: Scribner, 2001.

Jonas, Hans. *The Phenomenon of Life.* Chicago: Univ. of Chicago Press, 1966.

Jones, Van. *The Green Collar Economy: How One Solution Can Fix Our Two Biggest Problems.* New York: Harper One, 2009.

Judith, Anodea. *Waking the Global Heart: Humanity's Rite of Passage from the Love of Power to the Power of Love.* Fulton, CA: Elite Books, 2006.

Julian. *The Arguments of the Emperor Julian against the Christians.* Chicago: Hermetic Pub. Co., 1809.

Kaiser, David. *How the Hippies Saved Physics.* New York: W. W. Norton, 2011.

Kamenetz, Roger. *The Jew in the Lotus,* San Francisco: Harper Collins 1994.

Kauffman, Stuart A. *Reinventing the Sacred: A New View of Science, Reason and Religion.* New York: Basic Books, 2008.

Keen, Sam. *Faces of the Enemy: Reflections of the Hostile Imagination.* New York: Harper and Row, 2004.

Keller, Evelyn Fox. *Reflections on Gender and Science.* New Haven: Yale Univ. Press, 1985.

Kellert, Stephen R., and Edward O. Wilson, eds. *The Biophilian Hypothesis.* Covelo, CA: Island Press, 1993.

Kirk, Russell. *The Conservative Mind: From Burke to Eliot.* Washington, DC: Regnery, 2001.

Klatch, Rebecca. *A Generation Divided: The New Left, the New Right, and the 1960s*. Berkeley: Univ. of California, 1999.

Klein, Stefan. *Leonardo's Legacy*. Cambridge, MA: Da Capo Press, 2010.

Koonz, Claudia. *The Nazi Conscience*. Cambridge, MA: Harvard Univ. Press, 2003.

Kopecky, Petr. *The California Crucible: Literary Harbingers of Deep Ecology*. Ostrava: Univ. of Ostrava Press, 2007.

Kripal, Jeffrey J. *Authors of the Impossible: The Paranormal and the Sacred*. Chicago: Univ. of Chicago Press, 2010.

Küng, Hans, and Karl-Josef Kuschel, eds. *A Global Ethic: The Declaration of the Parliament of the World's Religions*. New York: Continuum, 1993.

Kushner, Lawrence. *The River of Light*. Woodstock, VT: Jewish Lights, 1981.

Kutcher, Norman. "The Fifth Relationship: Dangerous Friendships in the Confucian Context." *American Historical Review* 105.5. 2000: 12 September, 2007. http://www.historycooperative.org/cgi-bin/cite.cgi?f=ahr/105.5//ah001615.html.

Lakoff, George. *The Political Mind*. New York: Penguin, 2009.

Lakoff, George, and Mark Johnson. *Metaphors We Live By*. 2nd ed. Chicago: Univ. of Chicago Press, 2003.

_____. *Philosophy in the Flesh: The Embodied Mind and Its Challenge to Western Thought*. New York: Basic Books, 1999.

Landau, Martin. *Political Theory and Political Science*. New York: Macmillan, 1972.

Landes, Ruth. *City of Women*. Albuquerque: Univ. of New Mexico Press, 1994.

Ledeen, Michael. *Machiavelli on Modern Leadership: Why Machiavelli's Iron Rules Are as Timely and Important Today as Five Centuries Ago*. St. Martin's, 1999.

Leopold, Aldo. *A Sand County Almanac*. Oxford: Oxford Univ. Press, 1966.

Lemke-Santangelo, Gretchen. *Daughters of Aquarius: Women of the Sixties Countercuture*. Lawrence: Univ. Press of Kansas, 2009.

Lippman, Walter. *Public Opinion*. New York: Free Press, 1965.

Lipton, Bruce. *The Biology of Belief*. Santa Rosa, CA: Mountain of Love, 2005.

Locke, John. *Political Writings of John Locke*. Edited by David Woollon. London: Mentor, 1993.

_____. *Two Treatises of Government II*. Edited by Peter Laslett. Cambridge: Cambridge Univ. Press, 1960.

Louv, Richard. *Last Child in the Woods: Saving Our Children from Nature Deficit Disorder*. Chapel Hill, NC: Algonquin Books of Chapel Hill, 2008.

Lovelock, James. *Gaia: A New Look at Life on Earth*. Oxford: Oxford Univ. Press, 1979.

Loye, David. *Darwin's Lost Theory*. Carmel, CA: Benjamin Franklin Press, 2007.

MacPherson, C. B. *The Political Theory of Possessive Individualism: From Hobbes to Locke*. Oxford: Oxford Univ. Press, 1970.

Madison, James. *The Mind of the Founder: Sources of the Political Thought of James Madison*. Edited by Marvin Meyers. Hanover, NH: Univ. Press of New England, 1981.

Madison, James, Alexander Hamilton, and John Jay. *The Federalist Papers*. Edited by Clinton Rossiter. New York: Mentor, 1961.

Mann, Charles C. *1491*. New York: Vintage, 2005.

Mansfield, Harvey. *Manliness*. New Haven: Yale Univ. Press, 2007.

Markoff, John. *What the Dormouse Said: How the Sixties Counterculture Shaped the Personal Computer Industry*. New York: Penguin, 2006.

Maslow, Abraham. *Towards a Psychology of Being*. Princeton: Van Nostrand Reinhold, 1968.

Matthews, Freya. *The Ecological Self*. Savage, MD: Barnes and Noble, 1991.

_____. *For Love of Matter: A Contemporary Panpsychism*. Albany: SUNY Press 2003.

McEvilley, Thomas. *The Shape of Ancient Thought*. New York: Allworth Press, 2002.

McGilchrist, Iain. *The Master and His Emissary: The Divided Brain and the Making of the Western World*. New Haven: Yale Univ. Press, 2009.

McGraw, Barbara A. *Rediscovering America's Sacred Ground: Public Religion and Pursuit of the Good in a Pluralistic America*. Albany: SUNY Press, 2003.

Meine, Curt. *Aldo Leopold: His Life and Work*. Madison: Univ. of Wisconsin Press, 1988.

Mendoza, Ramon G. *The Acentric Labyrinth: Giordano Bruno's Prelude to Contemporary Cosmology*. Shaftsbury, Dorsey, UK: Element, 1995.

Merchant, Carolyn. *Death of Nature, Women, Ecology and the Scientific Revolution*. San Francisco: Harper and Row, 1980.

Midgley, Mary. *Science as Salvation: A Modern Myth in its Making*. London: Routledge, 1992.

Muir, John. *Our National Parks,* http://www.sierraclub.org/john_muir_exhibit/
writings/our_national_parks/.

———. *A Thousand Mile Walk to the Gulf.* http://www.sierraclub.org/john_muir_
exhibit/writings/a_thousand_mile_walk_to_the_gulf/chapter_4.html.

Murphy, Joseph M. *Santeria: An African Religion in America.* Boston: Beacon 1988.

———. *Working the Spirit: Ceremonies of the African Diaspora.* Boston, Beacon,
1994.

Nabhan, Gary Paul, and Paul Trimble. *The Geography of Childhood: Why Children
Need Wild Places.* Boston: Beacon, 1994.

Naess, Arne. *Ecology, Community and Lifestyle: Outline of an Ecosophy.* Translated
by David Rothenberg. Cambridge: Cambridge Univ. Press, 1993.

Nash, Roderick. *Wilderness and the American Mind.* 3rd ed. New Haven: Yale
University Press, 1982.

Nelson, Richard. *The Island Within.* San Francisco: Northpoint Press, 1989.

Nichols, John, ed. *Against the Beast: A Documentary History of American Opposition
to Empire.* New York: Nation Books, 2004.

Nietzsche, Friedrich. *The Gay Science.* Translated by Walter Kaufmann. New York:
Vintage, 1974.

———. *The Portable Nietzsche.* Translated by Walter Kaufmann. New York:
Penguin, 1954.

———. *The Will to Power.* Translated by Walter Kaufmann and J, R. Hillingdale.
New York: Vintage, 1968.

Noddings, Nell. *Caring: A Feminine Approach to Ethics & Moral Education.* Berkeley:
Univ. of California Press, 1984.

Noë, Alva. *Out of Our Heads: Why You Are Not Your Brain, and Other Lessons
from the Biology of Consciousness.* New York: Hill and Wang, 2009.

Norton, Anne. *Leo Strauss and the Politics of the American Empire.* New Haven:
Yale Univ. Press, 2004.

Nussbaum, Martha. *The Fragility of Goodness.* Cambridge: Cambridge Univ. Press,
2001.

Oppenheimer, Mark. *Knocking on Heaven's Door: American Religion in the Age of
Counterculture.* New Haven: Yale Univ. Press, 1973.

Ornstein, Robert E. *The Psychology of Consciousness.* New York: Harcourt, Brace
Jovanovich, 1977.

Pagels, Elaine. *Beyond Belief: The Secret Gospel of Thomas.* New York: Vintage, 2004.

Paper, Jordan. *The Deities Are Many: A Polytheistic Theology*. Albany: SUNY Press Press, 2005.

_____. *The Mystic Experience: A Descriptive and Comparative Analysis*. Albany: SUNY Press, 2004.

Pappas, Stephanie. "Even Babies Think Crime Deserves Punishment." *Live Science*. November 28, 2011. http://www.livescience.com/17204-babies-prefer-punishment.html.

Patai, Raphael. *The Hebrew Goddess*. New York: KATV, 1967.

Paxton, Robert O. *The Anatomy of Fascism*. New York: Vintage, 2005.

Phillips, Kevin. *American Theocracy*. New York: Viking, 2006.

Pike, Sarah. *New Age and Neopagan Religions in America*. New York: Columbia Univ. Press, 2004.

Pink, Daniel. *A Whole New Mind: Why Right-Brainers Will Rule the Future*. New York: Riverhead, 2006.

Plumwood, Val. *Feminism and the Mastery of Nature*. London: Routledge, 1993.

Polanyi, Michael. *Knowing and Being: Essays by Michael Polanyi*. Edited by Marjorie Grene. Chicago: Univ. of Chicago Press, 1969.

_____. *Personal Knowledge: Towards a Post-Critical Philosophy*. Chicago: Univ. of Chicago Press, 1974.

Popper, Karl, and John Eccles. *The Self and its Brain: An Argument for Interactionism*. London: Routledge, 1984.

Pretty, Jules. "A Walk a Day Keeps the Doctor Away." Univ. of Essex, Colchester Campus. May 2, 2010. http://www.essex.ac.uk/news/event.aspx?e_id=1588.

Rawls, John. *A Theory of Justice*. Cambridge, MA: Harvard Univ. Press, 2005.

Robbins, Tom. *Jitterbug Perfume*. New York: Bantam, 1984.

Rodda, Chris. *Liars for Jesus: The Religious Right's Alternate Version of American History*. Vol. I. Book Surge Publishing, 2006.

Roszak, Theodore. *The Making of a Counter Culture*. Garden City, NY: Anchor/Doubleday, 1969.

Ruether, Rosemary Radford. *Goddesses and the Divine Feminine: A Western Religious History*. Berkeley: Univ. of California Press, 2005.

Russell, Sharman Apt. *Standing in the Light: My Life as a Pantheist*. New York: Basic Books, 2008.

Sallustius. *On the Gods and the World*. Translated by Thomas Taylor. *Collected Writings of the Gods and the World*. Somerset, UK: Prometheus Trust, 1994.

Sanday, Peggy Reeves. *Female Power and Male Dominance: On the Origins of Sexual Inequality*. Cambridge: Cambridge Univ. Press, 1981.

Sanford, Peter. "How to Change Your Life in Five Minutes a Day: Go Outside." *The Independent*. May 9, 2010. http://www.independent.co.uk/opinion/commentators/peter-stanford-how-to-change-your-life-in-five-minutes-a-day-go-outside-1969209.html.

Saul, John Ralston. *The Unconscious Civilization*. Concord, Ontario: Anansi, 1995.

Schell, Jonathan. *Time of Illusion*. New York: Vintage, 1976.

Scott, James C. *Seeing Like a State*. New Haven: Yale Univ. Press, 1998.

Sessions, George, ed. *Deep Ecology for the 21st Century*. Boston: Shambhala, 1995.

Shapin, Steven. *The Scientific Revolution*. Chicago: Univ. of Chicago Press, 1996.

Sharlet, Jeff. *The Family: The Secret Fundamentalism at the Heart of American Power*. New York: Harper, 2008.

Shepard, Paul. *Nature and Madness*. San Francisco: Sierra Club Books, 1982.

Shepherd, Linda Jean. *Lifting the Veil: The Feminine Face of Science*. Boston: Shambhala,1993.

Slater, Philip. *The Pursuit of Loneliness: American Culture at the Breaking Point*. Boston: Beacon, 1970.

Smart, Ninian. *The Long Search*. Boston: Little Brown, 1977.

Smith, Andrew. *Moondust: In Search of the Men Who Fell to Earth*. London: Bloomsbury, 2006.

Smoley, Richard. *Forbidden Faith: The Gnostic Legacy From the Gospels to the Da Vinci Code*. San Francisco: HarperSanFrancisco, 2006.

Snyder, Gary. *A Place in Space: Ethics, Aesthetics, and Watersheds*. Washington, DC: Counterpoint, 1995.

Some, Malidoma. *Ritual: Power, Healing and Community*. New York: Penguin, 1997.

Spretnak, Charlene. *Missing Mary: The Queen of Heaven and Her Re-Emergence in the Modern Church*. New York: Palgrave Macmillan, 2004.

_____. *Relational Reality: New Discoveries of Interrelatedness That Are Transforming the Modern World*. Topsham, ME: Green Horizon Books, 2011.

_____. *The Resurgence of the Real*. Reading, MA: Addison Wesley, 1997.

_____. *States of Grace: The Recovery of Meaning in the Postmodern Age*. San Francisco: HarperSanFrancisco, 1991.

Starhawk. *The Spiral Dance: A Rebirth of the Ancient Religion of the Great Goddess*. New York: Harper Collins, 1979.

Stevens, John. *Lust for Enlightenment: Buddhism and Sex*. Boston: Shambhala, 1990.

Strauss, Leo. *Natural Right and History*. Chicago: Univ. of Chicago Press, 1999.

Sumner, William Graham. *The Conquest of the United States by Spain and Other Essays*. Edited by Murray Polner. Chicago: Henry Regnery, 1965.

Suzuki, David, and Peter Knudson. *Wisdom of the Elders*. New York: Bantam, 1992.

Targ, Russell. *Limitless Mind*. Novato, CA: New World, 2004.

Tarnas, Richard. *Cosmos and Psyche: Intimations of a New World View*. New York: Penguin, 2006.

Taylor, Bron. *Dark Green Religion: Nature, Spirituality and the Planetary Future*. Berkeley: Univ. of California Press, 2010.

Taylor, Charles. *A Secular Age*. Cambridge, MA: Harvard Univ. Press, 2007.

Thompson, William Irwin. *The Time Falling Bodies Take to Light*. New York: St. Martin's, 1981.

Tocqueville, Alexis de. *Democracy in America*. Translated by John Stuart Mill. New York: Schocken, 1961.

Toulmin, Stephen. *Cosmopolis: The Hidden Agenda of Modernity*. Chicago: Univ. of Chicago, 1990.

Vermeij, Geerat. *The Evolutionary World: How Adaptation Explains Everything from Seashells to Civilization*. New York: St. Martins, 2010.

von Essen, Carl. *Ecomysticism: The Profound Experience of Nature as Spiritual Guide*. Rochester, VT: Bear and Company, 2010.

Ware, Bishop Kallistos. *The Orthodox Way*. Rev. ed. Crestwood, NY: St. Vladimir's Seminary Press, 1979.

Washington, George. "Letter to the Hebrew Congregation in Newport, Rhode Island." August 18, 1790. http://www.tncrimlaw.com/civil_bible/hebrew_congregation.htm.

Watts, Alan. *Beyond Theology: The Art of Godmanship*. New York: World, 1967.

Whitmont, Edward C. *Return of the Goddess.* New York: Crossroads, 1982.

Whyte, William. *The Organization Man.* Garden City, NY: Doubleday, 1956.

Williams, Terry Tempest. *An Unspoken Hunger.* New York: Vintage, 1994.

Wilson, Edward O. *The Social Conquest of Earth.* New York: W. W. Norton, 2012.

Wolin, Richard. *The Seduction of Unreason: The Intellectual Romance with Fascism from Nietzsche to Postmodernism.* Princeton: Princeton Univ. Press, 2004.

Wood, Gordon S. *The Radicalism of the American Revolution.* New York: Alfred Knopf, 1992.

Yevtushenko, Yevgeny. "People." *Selected Poems.* New York: Penguin, 1967.

INDEX

A

abortion, 150–51

Abrahamic traditions, 165–66, 200, 212

Abram, David

 on body and sentience, 60

 on connection to earth, 189, 192, 206, 222

 on literal truth, 36

 on written form of Greek myths, 39–40

Adams, Ansel, 195

Adams, John, 6

Adams, John Quincy, 111, 134

Addams, Jane, 96, 98, 99

Afghanistan, 114

African Americans, 190

African diasporic traditions, 39, 172–75, 213

aggression, 59, 143–44

Agnew, Spiro, 122

agricultural societies

 arising from hunter-gatherers, 198–99

 divine feminine traditions and, 215, 224, 227

 transcendental religions and, 202–3

Agrippa, 13

Akhenaton, 202

alienation, healing, 222–23

Amalekites, 141

American Dream, 31

American Indians, 32, 189

"Americanization" (Addams), 98

American people, as warlike, 135

Anabaptists, 8

anthropomorphism, 34–35

antiabortion laws, 151

antistatism, 100

antiwar movement, 111, 177

Aphrodite, 30–31, 214

Arendt, Hannah, 108

Ares, 30–31

Armour, Andrew, 55

Armstrong, Karen, 202

art, meaning in, 33

artists, 53

Artyukhin, Yuri, 185–86

Asclepius, 227

ashe (life force), 172

Related Quest Titles

Beyond Religion, by David N. Elkins

*The Boundless Circle: Caring for Creatures
and Creation*, by Michael W. Fox

Freedom: Alchemy for a Voluntary Society,
by Stephan A. Hoeller

The Fundamentalist Mind, by Stephen Larsen

The Goddess Re-Awakening, by Shirley J. Nicholson

Sophia: Goddess of Wisdom, by Caitlin Matthews

*Thriving in the Crosscurrent: Clarity and Hope in a Time
of Cultural Sea Change*, by Jim Kenney

More Praise for Gus diZerega's
FAULT LINES

"With admirable historical research and considerable erudition, Gus di Zerega shows just how the cultural schizophrenia of the modern world arose, continues to be perpetuated, and imperils our lives and the very world itself. The dualities now called Materialism versus Creationism, Logos versus Mythos, are built on a more ancient dichotomy, not just male/female, but the Masculine and the Feminine as approaches to life. The once flourishing religion of the Great Mother has yielded to patriarchal models, but at our own peril—both environmentally and spiritually. diZerega's unflinching analysis is nonetheless interwoven with a basically humanistic emphasis that leaves the reader feeling optimistic and somehow wiser at the end. A must read for people both alarmed and hopeful about the current condition of the world."

> —**Stephen Larsen**, PhD, Professor Emeritus, SUNY, and author of
> *The Shaman's Doorway, A Fire in the Mind*, and
> *The Fundamentalist Mind*

"Gus diZerega persuades us that the return of the Goddess in all her exuberant forms heralds a new and possibly renewed post-Axial age, now coming alive again through the creative and compassionate sensibilities of the Divine Feminine."

> —**Dr. John Berthrong**, Associate Professor of Comparative Theology,
> Boston University School of Theology

"With his academic background in political science and environmentalism and his lived experience of a vibrant Pagan spirituality, Gus diZerega is uniquely suited to address the deep, ongoing changes in our culture and society that are forcing us to re-think the connections between science, culture, and religion. Gus is one of the best and most profound Pagan writers of the modern age, and his work can be of the great benefit to all."

> —**Donald H. Frew**, founder and director of the Lost and
> Endangered Religions Project